Blender 2.5 Materials and Textures Cookbook

Over 80 great recipes to create life-like Blender objects

Colin Litster

BIRMINGHAM - MUMBAI

Blender 2.5 Materials and Textures Cookbook

First published: January 2011

Production Reference: 1200111

Published by Packt Publishing Ltd.
32 Lincoln Road
Olton
Birmingham, B27 6PA, UK.

ISBN 978-1-849512-88-6

www.packtpub.com

Cover Image by Colin Litster (www.cogfilms.com)

Credits

Author
Colin Litster

Reviewers
Darrin Lile
Sanu V.M
Willem Verwey

Acquisition Editor
Sarah Cullington

Development Editor
Meeta Rajani

Technical Editors
Pallavi Kachare
Ajay Shanker

Indexer
Tejal Daruwale

Editorial Team Leader
Aanchal Kumar

Project Team Leader
Lata Basantani

Project Coordinator
Rebecca Sawant

Proofreader
Ting Baker

Production Coordinator
Melwyn D'Sa
Aparna Bhagat

Cover Work
Melwyn D'Sa

About the Author

Colin Litster started his passion for animation, and things 3D, after studying for an Art degree with 3D in its title. At that time computer animation had not even happened, but working as a special effects cameraman in the British film industry convinced Colin that there must be better ways of generating film effects other than directly in the camera, or by post processing in the labs. After studying further he discovered the microprocessor and became hooked on using this new computer technology to further those ideas.

Colin moved into higher education, eventually to the position of Head of IT and Media Services in the south east of England. In 2002, Colin discovered the relatively unknown Open Source 3D suite called Blender. After working with all of the commercial 3D applications up until that point, Colin thought that this young upstart of an application must be inferior. However, after just one week of use Colin realized that Blender was not only capable of most things 3D, it was also incredibly easy to use. At this point, Colin realized that an ambition to produce a full-length 3D feature was possible to achieve with this package. Embracing the Open Source ethos, Colin wanted to give something back to the community so he decided to document and create tutorials for others to see its potential. Some of Colin's ocean, smoke, and special effect tutorials have become a driving force in how to stretch the use of this superb 3D tool.

Colin was a contributor to the Blender Summer of Code documentation project with the Blender Foundation in 2006. Since then he has been a contributing author to the *Essential Blender* book edited by Roland Hess, and Ton Roosendaal. Colin has also been a presenter at the Blender Conference showing others how he approaches material and texture creation to create the impossible using the Blender 3D suite.

I would like to thank Sarah Cullington, my commissioning editor, and all the wonderful people at Packt Publishing who have gently guided and encouraged my development of this book. I would also like to thank Tony Mullen who has been urging me to put together my material experiments since 2006. I also cannot forget Ton Roosendaal and all the wonderful developer community of Blender. But mostly, I must thank my lovely wife Eveline as without her complete encouragement and support this book could not have been written. I love you very much.

About the Reviewers

Darrin Lile received Bachelor of Arts and Master of Arts degrees in Film and Media Studies from the University of Kansas. He has worked as a producer and director of educational videos, a sound editor for film and television, a control systems programmer, and a network security analyst. Check out his latest media project at www.darrinlile.com.

Sanu Vamanchery Mana is a 3D artist from India with over 11 years of experience in the field of animation, gaming and special effects and Lecturer of Interactive Media Design/Animation and Game Design at Raffles Design Institute, Singapore. As a lecturer, he has given many workshops, trainings, and presentations in many countries of Europe, Asia, and Latin America. Currently, he is reviewing two Blender 3D books for Packt Publishing.

He has worked for gaming projects like Golden Eye 007 (Electronic Arts), Neopet (Sony Entertainment), and World Series of Poker (Sony Entertainment). He was also involved in the short movie *JackFrost*, which was nominated for a BAFTA.

In 1992, **Willem Verwey** started working in 3D Studio back in the days when we used DOS. He later moved to 3D Studio Max 1.2!

He founded the 3D Animation Network in 2007 and developed the ANIM8 program introducing school children and young people to the world of animation.

Since 2007 Willem has been focusing on Blender, developing the ANIM8 program and freelancing. You can contact him at willem@3danim8.net.

Willem is a member of the Blender Foundation Certification Review Board.

"I believe there is a great future for Blender to professionals since it is a great package to use.

In my opinion Blender does have a place in the market and we will see a great increase in professionals using Blender in the world!"

www.PacktPub.com

Support files, eBooks, discount offers, and more

You might want to visit www.PacktPub.com for support files and downloads related to your book.

Did you know that Packt offers eBook versions of every book published, with PDF and ePub files available? You can upgrade to the eBook version at www.PacktPub.com and as a print book customer, you are entitled to a discount on the eBook copy. Get in touch with us at service@packtpub.com for more details.

At www.PacktPub.com, you can also read a collection of free technical articles, sign up for a range of free newsletters and receive exclusive discounts and offers on Packt books and eBooks.

http://PacktLib.PacktPub.com

Do you need instant solutions to your IT questions? PacktLib is Packt's online digital book library. Here, you can access, read and search across Packt's entire library of books.

Why Subscribe?

- Fully searchable across every book published by Packt
- Copy and paste, print and bookmark content
- On demand and accessible via web browser

Free Access for Packt account holders

If you have an account with Packt at www.PacktPub.com, you can use this to access PacktLib today and view nine entirely free books. Simply use your login credentials for immediate access.

Table of Contents

Preface

The Blender 3D suite is probably one of the most used 3D creation and animation tools currently in existence. The reason for that popularity is both its tool set and the extraordinary fact that it can be downloaded free of charge. Blender has been around since 1998 but it was not until it entered the GNU General Public License, open source market in 2002 that it grew in popularity to its current position.

Over the last year Blender has been going though a major update to its user interface, which has been named Blender 2.5. This radical restructure of the 3D suit has introduced not only a more up-to-date interface but also some advanced features that make Blender a capable 3D tool for professional productions. Indeed the Blender Foundation has been keen to develop these capabilities by applying Blender to create open source productions. 2010 saw the premiere of Sintel, a 15-minute cinema quality fantasy, which had over one million views on YouTube in less than four days.

Blender 2.5 is therefore an ideal tool for the aspiring 3D animator, and seasoned professional, to turn their ideas into professional quality renders and productions. Of course, producing a great model and animating it is only part of the process necessary to bring a production to life. We need to add color and texture to our models to make them appear real or give that extra artistic flare to change a computer 3D model into a stunning-looking creation. We do this by adding materials and textures to our 3D models and Blender 2.5 offers some unique and easy to use tools that are covered in this book. By studying the recipes described here you will learn how to use and manage many of the Blender 2.5 material and texture techniques to transform your 3D objects into spectacular creations.

What this book covers

Chapter 1, Creating Natural Materials in Blender shows how to apply materials to create a range of stone-like substances that demonstrate the use of both procedural textures and photo images to aid the simulation of random surface properties found in these natural substances. You will experience standard material creation as well as Node textures and materials.

Chapter 2, Creating Man-made Materials shows how to simulate manufactured materials such as metals and pattern-repeated materials like slate roofs and cobbled paths. You will learn how Blender 2.5 offers unique abilities to help mask seams and repeats to turn your man-made material simulations into convincing material creations.

Chapter 3, Creating Animated Materials shows how to manipulate materials and textures over time. Thus, adding animated effects to a surface using superb Blender 2.5 material and texture animation techniques.

Chapter 4, Managing Blender Materials deals with ways to make your use of Blender 2.5 materials and textures more structured. You will learn how to organize and name materials as well as how to set up the interface to better suit your material needs.

Chapter 5, Creating More Difficult Man-made Materials shows how to create convincing reflective surfaces that not only look good but are quick and easy to produce. You will also learn various techniques employed in Blender 2.5 to simulate grime and other surface irregularities to bring difficult man-made materials to life.

Chapter 6, Creating More Difficult Natural Materials shows how to create spectacular natural surfaces such as entire oceans with complex waves and wake. The new recipes described here are entirely produced using the new material features found in Blender 2.5 but without the overheads usually associated with such large-scale simulations. You will also learn how material transparency can be used to model quite complex objects using a very simple material technique.

Chapter 7, UV Mapping and Sub Surface Scattering shows how to create a natural-looking human face using Blender 2.5 UV mapping and Sub Surface Scattering. You will be shown how to create, and manipulate, high-quality photo images for use in this usually difficult 3D material simulation.

Chapter 8, Painting and Modifying Image Textures in Blender shows how to use some of the quick material and post processing techniques found in Blender 2.5 to transform a surface appearance simply and quickly. You will learn ways to alter a surface appearance, such as adding grime or age to a surface, as well as how to radically alter a pre-rendered animation to give extra atmosphere or post process a surface appearance after it is rendered.

Chapter 9, Special Effects Materials shows how to create some of the spectacular and new Blender 2.5 effects materials such as smoke, explosion, and flames. You will discover different methods to ease the creation of these intensive material effects as well as ways to produce stock effects that can be easily and quickly implemented into your own productions.

What you need for this book

All of the recipes in this book were created in Blender 2.56a, which at the time of writing was the latest official version available. Blender 2.56a can be freely downloaded from the Blender Foundation site in various computer system varieties. Currently it is available both in 32-bit and 64-bit versions for Linux, MAC, and Windows Operating Systems.

```
http://www.blender.org/development/release-logs/blender-256-beta/
```

Blender is being developed constantly but this version is feature complete and was used to produce all the recipes found in this book. As Blender moves towards its next milestone, Blender 2.6, its material and texture capabilities will improve but the settings described in the recipes should produce similar if not identical appearances to the images displayed.

Several recipes make use of images that are either created or modified in a paint package. You can use whatever paint package you are used to but if you haven't got one available I would suggest downloading GIMP, which is also free under a GNU General Public License.

```
http://www.gimp.org/
```

Who this book is for

This book is aimed at the semi-proficient modeler who wishes to improve their work in Blender 2.5 by employing better and more efficient material and texture techniques.

Although not an introduction to Blender 2.5, or all of its new UI facilities, the methods used in this latest version are relatively straightforward and therefore the novice will be able to use many of the recipes while learning a great deal about the Material and Node systems of the latest Blender 3D suite.

Conventions

In this book, you will find a number of styles of text that distinguish between different kinds of information. Here are some examples of these styles, and an explanation of their meaning.

Code words in text are shown as follows: "Save your blendfile as `slate-roof-01.blend`."

New terms and important words are shown in bold. Words that you see on the screen, in menus or dialog boxes for example, appear in the text like this: "Ensure you have a **Node Editor** window displayed".

Warnings or important notes appear in a box like this.

 Tips and tricks appear like this.

Reader feedback

Feedback from our readers is always welcome. Let us know what you think about this book—what you liked or may have disliked. Reader feedback is important for us to develop titles that you really get the most out of.

To send us general feedback, simply send an e-mail to feedback@packtpub.com, and mention the book title via the subject of your message.

If there is a book that you need and would like to see us publish, please send us a note in the **SUGGEST A TITLE** form on www.packtpub.com or e-mail suggest@packtpub.com.

If there is a topic that you have expertise in and you are interested in either writing or contributing to a book, see our author guide on www.packtpub.com/authors.

Customer support

Now that you are the proud owner of a Packt book, we have a number of things to help you to get the most from your purchase.

 Downloading the example code for this book

You can download the example code files for all Packt books you have purchased from your account at http://www.PacktPub.com. If you purchased this book elsewhere, you can visit http://www.PacktPub.com/support and register to have the files e-mailed directly to you.

Errata

Although we have taken every care to ensure the accuracy of our content, mistakes do happen. If you find a mistake in one of our books—maybe a mistake in the text or the code—we would be grateful if you would report this to us. By doing so, you can save other readers from frustration and help us improve subsequent versions of this book. If you find any errata, please report them by visiting http://www.packtpub.com/support, selecting your book, clicking on the **errata submission form** link, and entering the details of your errata. Once your errata are verified, your submission will be accepted and the errata will be uploaded on our website, or added to any list of existing errata, under the Errata section of that title. Any existing errata can be viewed by selecting your title from http://www.packtpub.com/support.

Piracy

Piracy of copyright material on the Internet is an ongoing problem across all media. At Packt, we take the protection of our copyright and licenses very seriously. If you come across any illegal copies of our works, in any form, on the Internet, please provide us with the location address or website name immediately so that we can pursue a remedy.

Please contact us at copyright@packtpub.com with a link to the suspected pirated material.

We appreciate your help in protecting our authors, and our ability to bring you valuable content.

Questions

You can contact us at questions@packtpub.com if you are having a problem with any aspect of the book, and we will do our best to address it.

1
Creating Natural Materials in Blender

In this chapter, we will cover:

- ▶ Creating a realistic pebble material using procedural textures and node materials
- ▶ Creating a gray limestone pebble
- ▶ Creating the quartz pebble material
- ▶ Creating an opalescent quartz material
- ▶ Creating a mask to represent the quartz veins
- ▶ Combining two materials, to make a third, using nodes
- ▶ Creating a large rock material using procedural, and node textures
- ▶ Creating a texture node to simulate seaweed at the base of a rock
- ▶ Creating a large rock face using photo reference

Introduction

The surface of a natural material may seem one of the easiest to reproduce in a 3D suite such as Blender. However, natural surfaces can be quite complex in their appearance. Color, specularity, and reflection can organically change across a surface as a result of location, climate interaction, and variations in the natural substance. In many ways simulating natural objects in Blender will require more complex materials and textures than man-made objects to make them look convincing. Fortunately, learning how to create believable natural surface materials will help you in the development of many other material types. After all, most manufactured objects are created from, or based on, natural materials.

Blender offers a vast array of material and texture tools to aid you in the creation of natural-looking surfaces. Because of this there are many ways to produce similar, and equally pleasing, results. However, there are approaches that will speed material creation and make the process easier, adaptable, and more enjoyable.

Although there are no prerequisites to using the recipes for this first chapter it would be useful for you to know how Blender materials are organized and the various methods of mapping them to mesh objects. If these concepts are unfamiliar, or new to you, visit the free support documentation at the BlenderWiki: `http://wiki.blender.org/index.php/Main_Page`

At the time of writing most of this documentation is based on prior versions of Blender. However, I can recommend the *Blender Summer of Documentation* section on Materials and Procedural Textures written by me in 2006.

`http://wiki.blender.org/index.php/Doc:Tutorials/Materials/BSoD`

Although utilizing images from the 2.49 series of Blender it still covers many of the basic principles of material creation.

This book, however, will take you beyond the basics and into the new Blender v2.5 materials and textures interface.

Good observation will be your greatest asset

When trying to simulate any surface, your eyes will be your greatest asset. Carefully observing either the real material, or good reference photos, will make the task of simulation in Blender much easier. This is particularly important with natural materials, which have complex structures giving fine variation in surface color, specularity, and texture. Understanding what these details are will make any material simulation easier and give the viewer the correct visual clues so that they know what they are meant to be looking at. Even if you intend to represent a surface in a non-photo-realistic manner it is important to provide the viewer with some essential surface properties that will give them the visual essence of a surface.

The good thing is that natural materials are usually easy to study because we can pick them up around us. If the natural object you are trying to create isn't at hand, then use the Internet to look for photo references.

`http://images.google.co.uk`

`http://uk.images.search.yahoo.com`

`http://www.flickr.com/photos/`

Alternatively, try to take your own photo reference shots by carrying a digital camera around with you. Even a mobile phone camera can be good enough to take reference photos.

Another useful tool is a magnifying lens. Being able to closely study the real surface that you are trying to simulate, can aid your perception of the detailed color variations and surface texture of a natural object. Just using your eyes should give you enough information about a natural surface to enable you to simulate it in Blender.

It is also a good idea to set up the default scene in Blender to provide better lighting for material and texture creation. You will need to regularly render the objects you are creating textures for, just to see a more accurate example of a materials effect. Improving the lighting, from that given in the factory settings, will aid you in that process.

You will find a recipe in Chapter 4, *Setting a default scene for materials creation*, that provides a better materials setup.

Creating a realistic pebble material using procedural textures

For this first recipe we will create a realistic-looking pebble based on one that could found on many beaches across the world.

The previous screenshot shows three pebbles, one that mostly comprises hard gray sandstone, another consisting of quartz, and a third that has both types of rock fused in layers. The pen is shown to provide a sense of scale for these pebbles.

Although all three recipes are designed to simulate a surface when dry, it can be useful to know what it looks like when wet. For instance, the gray sandstone will look much darker when wet because light will be spread less across its surface. In contrast, quartzrock will hardly alter at all when wet because its surface is much more reflective anyway. Knowing these surface properties will aid you in your simulation.

Getting ready

To start off this exercise we are going to create a simple pebble-like mesh on a white plane background and then apply a pebble material, based on our observations of the reference photo, to the pebble mesh. We are not going to create the exact pebble as shown in the reference photo, but the essence of such a surface that could be applied to any shaped pebble mesh.

The easiest way to create a simple pebble shape is to use the default cube and:

- ▸ subdivide, in edit mode by three to four subdivisions, to give you a few more vertices to play with
- ▸ make the mesh smooth from the tool shelf
- ▸ add a Subdivision Surface modifier at about level 3
- ▸ then move vertices around in proportional edit mode until you get a reasonable pebble like shape. I scaled my cube by about 150 percent during this process

You could also use the **Multiresolution** modifier, and the **Sculpt** tool to achieve a similar effect.

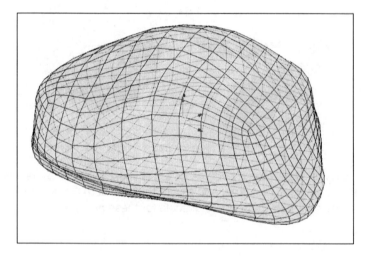

Also create a simple plane below the pebble mesh and scale this until it is larger than the camera view. This will give a surface on which to display our pebble.

Save your work as `pebble-00.blend`.

Creating a gray limestone pebble

One of the simplest materials to create is a gray sandstone pebble using just procedural textures. We will apply this material again in other recipes that follow so the naming of each material will become clearer as you work your way through each recipe. If you start any of the recipes out of order you can still complete them by downloading the named blendfiles of any of the uncompleted preceding recipes.

Getting ready

You will need to have created the base mesh as described above. However, you can also download a starting blendfile from the Packt Publishing website.

How to do it...

We will take the base blendfile and create a new material that will simulate gray sandstone. So, open up the saved `pebble-00.blend` file, or one downloaded earlier.

1. With the pebble mesh selected, select the **Materials** button from the **Properties** tab.

2. On the **Materials** properties editor panel click the **+** button to create a new material. Name this `Surface-Color`.

3. Change the **Diffuse** color to a lighter gray. If you click on the color box, a color selector appears where you can change the **R**(ed), **G**(reen), and **B**(lue) values to specific settings. Use `0.750` for **R**, **G**, and **B**.

4. You can also change the **color** value by **H**(ue), **S**(aturation), and **V**(alue) as well as **Hex** values. You can, of course, judge the color, saturation, and lightness by directly manipulating the color wheel marker and lightness slider with the mouse. Change the **Specular** settings to type **Wardiso**, **Intensity** value to `0.411`, and **Slope** to `0.400`.

The Wardiso specular setting allows finer control over the specular light across a surface. It suits the spread of specular light found on dry pebble surfaces. You will find that all the specular and diffuse shading methods have different characteristics that may be suited to specific surface types. Experiment to find out their benefits as well as drawbacks.

All that we have done here is create the basic surface properties of color and specularity. To make the material more believable it is necessary to add textures to give variety to the surface color, bumpiness, and specularity. Save your work at this stage, naming the file `pebble-01.blend`.

1. Select the **Texture** panel.

2. Add a new **Texture** (the **+** button) of type **Clouds**, and name the texture **Clouds**.

3. Under the **Clouds** settings make sure that **Grayscale** and **Soft** are selected and alter the **Size** to `0.05` and **Depth** to `5`.

4. Under **Influence/diffuse** settings select **Color** and set to `0.686`.

5. Select **Intensity** under **Specular** and set its value to `-1.000`.

6. Also select **Normal** under **Geometry** and set its value to `0.500`.

7. In the **Blend** settings change the blend type to **Mix** and in the **color** selector create a darker gray than the base color by changing each of the **RGB** sliders to `0.46`. Alter the **DVar** value to `0.484`.

8. Finally, check the **Old Bump Mapping** checkbox to make sure we are using the original Blender **Normal** method.

 Blender 2.5 comes with an improved **Normal** method but you can still employ the older method if that suits the material. Basically, the newer method provides a more detailed bump from a grayscale texture. However, the Blender old, or original, method, is more subtle and ideal for this recipe. We will meet the newer method later in this chapter.

We have produced a varied gray stone-like surface with a few bumps and a slight specular reflection across the surface, indicating that the pebble has reflective crystals embedded in its surface. Now let's add some surface wear to indicate damage as the sea water bashes the pebble about. Once again, save the blendfile, incrementing the filename, to `pebble-02.blend`.

9. Create a new texture of **Type Distorted Noise**. Name it `DistNoise`.

10. In the **Distorted Noise** settings tab set **Distortion** to `1.00` and **Size** to `0.25`.

11. Under **Influence/Geometry** select **Warp** and set to `0.040`. This should be the only setting selected under **Diffuse, Shading, Specular,** or **Geometry.**

12. Ensure that **RGB to Intensity, Negative,** and **Stencil** are selected.

The stencil setting will not visibly change the surface but it will affect the texture that follows.

13. Create a new texture of **Type Musgrave**, and name it **Musgrave**.

14. Under the **Musgrave** tab set **Dimension** to 0.441, **Lacunarity** to 2.00, **Octaves** to 6.358, and **Intensity** to 1.660. Also set the **Size** to 0.64.

15. In the **Colors** tab **Adjust** the **Brightness** to 0.411 and the **Contrast** to 2.469.

16. In the **Influence** tab select **Color** and set to 0.191. Then under **Geometry** select the **Normal** setting it to -1.00.

17. Set the **Blend** type to **Mix** and from the **color** selector create a darker gray with values **RGB** of 0.14. Check the **Old Bump Mapping** checkbox as we will be using the original Blender **Normal** method for this texture.

Save your work as `pebble-03.blend` before rendering an image of your gray sandstone pebble. Regularly saving as you progress through any project will mean you can at least recover back to the last save.

What you have produced is a good approximation of a gray sandstone pebble surface.

How it works

In the Blender Material panel you are apparently only offered three color settings; Diffuse, Specular, and Mirror. These set the overall color for each surface property. However, the parameters of each type of shader, **Diffuse**, **Specular**, and **Mirror** can radically alter the way the shader reacts to light and displays the surface. In our case we have set a gray color for the diffuse setting, and a simple white color for specularity. However, we have altered the specular shader to Wardiso, which offers a wider degree of light spread via its **Slope** setting. In fact, we have set it to 0.400, which will give the widest specular spread using **Wardiso**. The color settings for specular and mirror can be altered to any color. However, in the majority of cases they can be left at the default white setting as in the pebble example.

To add variety to the diffuse color we need a texture mixed in some way to simulate the surface color variations. Blender allows a large number of textures to be added to a material. The total number seems to increase each year. However, I have never needed to use any more than 16 textures in any material that I have ever produced. Learning how to economically apply textures is a skill that can only improve with practice but try to keep it down to a more manageable number. Your material solution will be much clearer when you view it, maybe several months later.

When you add a texture to a material try to name it immediately. The defaults Tex.001, Tex.002, etc will become confusing, especially if you have to create your material over several days.

In our case we added a texture of type **Clouds**. There are many other texture types available, ranging from procedural, mathematically produced random types, through to images, such as photographs or drawn images. All Blender textures have settings to alter their properties, such as color and scale, as well as how the texture will be mapped to a material, and what influence it will have.

Procedural textures are mostly grayscale but can be applied via **Mix**, **Add**, **Multiply**, **Screen**, etc to alter the underlying material colors. These blend types work in a similar way to those found in paint packages, such as **Gimp**. In this pebble recipe we have used relatively simple mix methods to simulate a complex surface. Later recipes will show the effect of the other blend types available.

In this recipe we have used a number of textures to vary the color across the surface, as well as altering both the bumpiness (the normal) and specularity. Employing textures to add these variations is the way complex surfaces can be synthesized in Blender. We have used a variety of procedural textures to affect color, specularity, and normal. In fact, the first texture, **Clouds**, affects all three of these settings. Blender allows you to use any texture to change these and other settings with values that are controllable for each influence you wish to use. Here we used the Clouds texture to alter the color, specularity, and bump of the pebble material. However, the second texture, **DistNoise**, does not affect any of the influence settings of the material; its only task is to warp the texture that follows it. Using a texture to do this is a great way of changing the appearance of a procedural texture. The variation avoids repetition in the surface, which can be a problem if you employ procedural textures many times in a scene. Here it is used in a subtle way with a low **Warp** setting of 0.040. Another important setting here is the **RGB to Intensity** from the **Influence** tab. This will ignore the color values of the texture, which are not needed when applied to several of the influence types. In our case the **Distorted Noise** texture is grayscale anyway, but getting into the habit of checking this setting will avoid problems when using a color texture for such influence examples.

We also set **Stencil** in the **Influence** tab. This fascinating setting uses the texture to mask following textures. We can use it to allow the following textures to affect the surface (any white areas of the texture), partially affect the surface (any gray areas of the texture), or obscure following textures surface influences (any black areas of the texture). We can reverse that effect by selecting the **Negative** setting above it. Masking is one of the fundamental techniques to create a good texture. The stencil setting is extremely effective at giving that facility. However, it will only work with grayscale textures or with the RGB to Intensity set.

The third texture, **Musgrave**, adds further levels of color and bump variation. In the **Musgrave** tab we have altered the settings to produce distinct bump maps to create the kind of dents found when pebbles crash in the surf. Having several textures affecting the normal of a surface means we can simulate complex bump structures using simple procedural textures. By varying the contrast of a texture, we can limit and increase the edge detail of a bump quite simply. Here we did not set the RGB to **Intensity** under the **Influence** tab as the texture is already grayscale. If you want, set that now and render again and see if there is any difference.

Exploring the settings for any texture can be one of the most creative and stimulating exercises in 3D design. Finding the right settings will become easier as you explore Blender but experimenting as the accidental breakthrough may be the answer to your next material simulation.

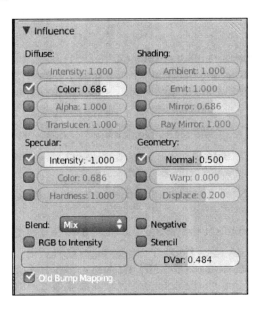

Creating the quartz pebble material

Quartz is an extremely common type of stone that is usually layered inbetween other rock types. However, pebbles on beaches where this type of rock is common often break off from the layers and are tossed in the sea to form pebbles. The second pebble we will create is based on such a variety of rock.

Getting ready

If you have completed the previous recipe load up the saved `pebble-03.blend` file.

Alternatively, you can download a pre-created file from the following location the Packt Publishing website.

How to do it

Let's create a new material to represent the quartz pebble. To do so we need to have the pebble object selected and temporarily unlink the `Surface-Color` material, giving a clean surface upon which to design our quartz material. However, once you unlink a material from an object it will only be available for reuse during your current working session. As soon as you close that Blendfile, even if you have saved it, the material will be lost. Blender normally only saves materials assigned to objects. However, we can fix a material or texture by clicking the **F** button to the right of the material or texture name.

With the pebble object selected click the **F** button, next to the material name in the Material properties panel, to fix the material into the blendfile. Then click the **X** button to unlink it from the **Materials** panel.

If you hover over **X** it will display **unlink datablock**. You will notice that if you *Shift-click* the **X** you will permanently remove the material the next time you save. So be careful as we only want to temporarily remove the link to our `Surface-Color` material, while we create the quartz material.

1. Click the **New** tab to create a new blank material and name it `Quartz`.

2. We can keep all the default material properties set apart from the **Diffuse** color. So change this to pure white or **RGB** `1.00`.

3. Switch to the **Textures** panel and add a new texture of **Type Clouds** and name it `QuartzClouds`.

4. Under the **Clouds** tab set **Grayscale** and **Soft**, **Size** to `0.36`, and **Depth** to 2.0.

5. Under **Influence** only have **Normal** selected and set to `-1.00` and under **Blend** type **Screen**. Select **RGB to Intensity**, **Negative**, and **Stencil**. Also check **Old Bump mapping**. Finally, change the color selector to **R, G, B** `0.700`.

That has created a slight bump map to the texture and a stencil, of which only some of the following textures will appear through.

6. In the **Texture properties** select the next free texture slot and create a new texture of type **Musgrave**, and name it QuartzMusgrave.

7. Under the **Musgrave** tab set the type to **Multifractal**, and **Basis Voronoi F1** with **Size** 0.05.

8. Under the **Colors** tab set **Adjust/ Brightness** to 0.467 and **Contrast** to 5.000.

9. Under **Influence** select **Diffuse Color** set to 1.00 and **Geometry Normal** to 10.00. Set the **Blend** type to **Screen** and adjust the color picker to **R** and **G** to 0.84 and **B** to 0.68. Also select **Old Bump Mapping.**

This will give a weathered and slightly dirty appearance to our quartz material. The quartz in the pebble example is contaminated with other rock fragments. Something that only becomes apparent when you look through a magnifying lens at the real material. If you were to render at this point, then you have a texture that could be used as a pebble material as it is. But we can take it further by varying the worn surface across the pebble.

10. Select an empty texture slot below the QuartzMusgrave texture. However, rather than creating a new texture we will load up the same QuartzMusgrave texture into the new slot but make some modifications to how it is used in our material.

Select the checkered icon that precedes the texture name shown in the following screenshot:

From the displayed list select QuartzMusgrave. The number **2** should appear just past the texture name to show that this texture is used twice.

11. Under **Influence** and **Geometry** change the **Normal** value to 5.00, the **Blend** value to **Screen**, and change the **color** selector to black (**RGB** values to 0.00).

Save your work so far, incrementing the filename to pebble-04.blend, and perform a test render.

We have produced a surf-damaged pebble showing the effect of being crashed across other pebbles as the tide ebbs and flows.

How it works

The second material that we created was to simulate the quartz veins in the pebble. Each of the textures used in this material produce a surface, in much the same way as the first. Procedural textures vary in the surface color and normals (bump) to produce the desired effect. However, there are several special techniques used that are worth highlighting as they can add a little bit of magic to a surface simulation task.

The first texture is named `QuartzClouds` and this has only been used to influence the normal of the material. However, you will notice that under the **Influence/Blend** setting **Negative**, **RGB to Intensity**, and **Stencil** have all been checked.

  ▸ **Negative** will reverse the effect of the texture. This is an overall setting and any of the set influences will be affected. In our case only normal is set.

  ▸ **RGB to Intensity** will internally convert the image to grayscale, so that only those intensity values affect any of the other influence settings. If the color intensity had been set the default magenta color would have been mixed with the material color based on the proportions of gray in the texture. We can therefore even add color with a black and white texture. In our case color influence is not used so we can ignore this effect. However, although the default color is magenta we can alter this color using the color picker within the **Influence** tab.

  ▸ **Stencil** creates a mask, or stencil, to filter all following textures in the material.

However, **Stencil** will only work if **RGB to Intensity** is set, even if it's just a grayscale texture, such as cloud.

Creating an opalescent quartz material

Quartz is a crystal and as a result tends to spread any light falling on it, producing a kind of opalescence that almost makes the surface glow. We can add additional textures, to our previously created quartz material, to recreate this opalescence thus producing a third pebble material.

Getting ready

If you have created the previous recipe, reload the `pebble-04.blend` blendfile. You can also download a pre-created file from the Packt Publishing website.

How to do it

With the `pebble-04.blend` open reselect the pebble mesh object and move to the **Texture** panel. Rather than creating an entirely new material from scratch we will amend the quartz material created in the last recipe. However, you will see later that you will still have access to that other pebble material for use in any Blender project.

1. Select the second of the `QuartzMusgrave` textures and in the **Influence** tab, select **Stencil.**

2. Select the next empty texture slot and choose **New** and name the texture `Opalescence`. Make it **Type Clouds**. Set **Hard, Size** 0.03, **Depth** 6.

3.   Under **Influence** select **Color** and set to `1.00`, and select **Emit** and set to `1.00`. Set the **Blend** type to **Mix** with the color selector set to **R** `1.000`, **G** `0.730`, and **B** `0.160`.

Ensure that you save the blendfile, incrementing the filename to `pebble-05.blend`.

These three simple steps modify the material to produce quite a difference in the quartz simulation.

How it works

When we added the stencil setting to the `QuartzMusgrave`, we had two stencil textures, now limiting the effect of the last texture slot that we named `Opalescence`.

Stencil is one of the most underrated of the Blender material tools, providing a means of controlling where textures are applied to a surface. It will be used many times in the recipes of this book.

There is one disadvantage to this method of stenciling one texture after another. Once a stencil has been set all following textures will be affected within the material. You cannot turn it off in later textures, so that it no longer has an effect. That means you will have to think carefully about where within a material you set any stencil. There are techniques using Node materials that can be applied to circumvent this problem.

The last texture in the quartz material we called is `Opalescence` and if you examine its Influence settings you will observe that not only **Color** has been set but also **Emit**.

- ▸ **Emit** is an unusual setting in that it controls how the texture will cause the surface to self illuminate. That does not mean it behaves like a light. It will not illuminate anything else. It just partially makes the surface shadeless, varied by the texture that controls it.

 Blender 2.5 introduces a new texture influence called indirect lighting. It also employs the **Emit** influence. However, objects and textures can directly illuminate the surrounding scene. Although that type of physical simulation is beyond the scope of this book, it does provide increased methods of simulating illuminated surfaces.

Why use **Emit** here? Well, some materials are quite difficult to simulate because of the way light spreads through the surface. Quartz has a generally white but translucent surface that spreads through the material. This is often called Sub Surface Scattering. Blender has very good sub-surface scattering controls but these can be render-intensive to use for all materials. This **Emit** trick can be used with very little overhead on render time and therefore is worth using in our example. However, use it with caution if your object is meant to be seen in different light levels, especially an animated change in illumination, as the surface may give the impression of glowing under certain low light conditions.

 We will meet the Blender Sub Surface Scattering controls in later recipes.

Creating a mask to represent the quartz veins

The layered quartz is quite common in gray sandstone and can be found in many pebbles scattered across a beach. The layers of quartz were laid down over the millennia, sometimes in thick layers, and sometimes thin. Earthquake movement altered the angles of the rock layers as these quartz deposits were being laid. As a result the quartz layers are occasionally at varying angles to each other. The quartz layers also have flecks of broken rock, some containing iron or sulphur deposits, which give a slightly yellow color variation.

The quartz part of these pebbles is worn more because its density is lower than the gray sandstone in which it is encased. Because the pebble has been tossed and polished by the sea, the quartz veins run right through the pebble, sometimes at strange angles.

We have produced a gray sandstone, and quartz material in previous recipes. We can combine them then using a mask to represent the veins as might be seen in real pebbles of this type. So this recipe provides a way of producing a mask ready for combination in the final material of this section.

Getting ready

Reload the `pebble-05.blend` saved at the end of the last recipe. If you haven't completed that recipe you can download a pre-created one from the Packt Publishing website.

How to do it

As in previous recipes we will have to temporarily clear the material last created so we have a clean slate to create this new mask material. However, we also need to fix that last material, so that we don't lose it if we need to split this exercise into several days.

1. With the pebble object selected click the **F** button, next to the material name `Quartz` in the **Material** panel. Then click the **X** button to **unlink datablock**. As in previous recipes, we only want to temporarily unlink the material so that we can create a new one.

2. In the **Materials** panel create a new material and name it `QuartzMask`.

3. Set the **Diffuse** color to black **RGB** `0.00`, and under **Shading** set **Shadeless**.

You now have a purely black material, so let's add some purely white veins to complete the mask.

4. From the **Texture** properties panel create a new texture of **Type Marble**, and name it `QuartzThick`.

5. Under **Marble**, set **Sharper** and **Tri**, and **Noise** to **Soft**. Set **Size** to `0.91`, **Turbulence** to `7.04`, and **Depth** to `2`.

6. Under **Colors/Adjust** set **Brightness** to `0.556` and **Contrast** to `5.000`.

7. Under **Mapping** set **Size X** to `1.30`, **Y** to `-0.77`.

8. Under **Influence** set **Color** to `1.00`, and **Blend** to **Screen**. Change the color selector to **R G B** `0.000`, black.

If you perform a quick test render at this point you will see that thick veins have been produced. This will act as the start of our quartz veins to which we will add some thinner veins as seen in the reference photo.

9. Select the next free texture slot in the **Textures** properties panel and create a new **Marble** texture with the name `Quartzthin1`.

10. In the **Marble** tab select **Sharper** and **Tri**, and under **Noise** select **Soft**. Set **Size** `1.18`, **Turbulence** `2.53`, and **Depth** `6`.

11. Under the **Colors** tab set **Adjust/Brightness** `1.711`, and **Contrast** `2.773`.

12. Under the **Mapping** tab, set **Size Y** `-2.09` (**X** and **Z** remain the default `1.00`).

13. Under the **Influence** tab, set **Color** to `1.00` and **Blend** to **Screen**. Alter the color selector to **R**, **G**, **B** `0.000`, black.

You could once again test render after you have saved, but we shall move on to add a final thin vein on our mask material.

14. Select a free texture slot and create a new texture of type **Marble** and name it `Quartzthin2`.

15. Under **Marble** tab select **Sharper** and **Tri**, and **Noise Soft**. From the **Basis** menu select **Improved Perlin**. Set **Size** to `0.88`, **Turbulence** to `1.93`, and **Depth** to `4`.

16. Under the **Colors** tab set **Adjust/ Brightness** to `2.000` and **Contrast** to `5.00`.

17. Under the **Mapping** tab set **Size Y** to `-1.48` and **Z** to `0.86`.

18. Finally, under the **Influence** tab set **Diffuse/Color** to `1.00`, and **Blend** to **Screen**.

Save the blendfile, incrementing the file name to `pebble-06.blend`, and render the `QuartzMask` material.

This material is not designed to be used as a direct pebble-like texture. Its purpose is to act as a mask when we mix the other pebble type created in earlier recipes.

How it works

The third material created is a mask to use within a material node setup. The idea being that it will combine the two material types by the amount of black, controlling the gray surface material, or white, controlling the quartz material. Since this material has no surface features, other than color, it's a lot easier to create.

Under the **Material** panel the **Shading/Shadeless** setting has been checked and the **Diffuse** color is set to completely black. This ensures that its light level will not be affected by shadows or scene lighting. In other words, the mask will work across the entire objects surface.

Three textures have been used to create the vein-like strata through the pebble shape. These are all based on the **Marble** procedural texture type but with varied settings. Apart from the **Marble** type settings there are two areas that are vital to the way each texture is applied and positioned onto our pebble.

Colors

This setting under **Colors/Adjust/Brightness** and **Contrast** has been employed to alter the thickness and sharpness of the simulated quartz veins. In most cases, the **Contrast** has been set quite high, while the **Brightness** has been varied to give different results.

Size

Under **Mapping/Size** the **X**, **Y**, **Z** values have been changed for each of the three vein textures. This scaling can be used to both alter the rotation of where the marble texture veins will appear, as well as alter the space between the veins. Obviously, if you reduce the scale too much, the texture will appear to become just streaks across the surface and therefore rather unnatural. Because procedural textures are mathematically generated they appear to occupy the whole 3D space. Therefore, because they are mapped to our pebble mesh they look as though they travel right through the surface.

This technique of using scale to rotate a procedural texture is useful in other circumstances and will therefore be used in future recipes. There are also other techniques that can be used to scale and rotate textures without the inherent distortion that this scaling can sometimes give. These will also be explored in future recipes.

You may wonder why we have created this third material when it could have been created with **Node** textures directly within the node tree. When creating any texture, it's a good idea to see exactly how it will map to the mesh surface. Creating within its own material means we can just see where the veins will be and how they mix with each other. It can be very difficult to conceptualize a surface material without constant test renders. It is faster to render a single material than a complex node setup when you are at the development stage. It is a bit like getting your ingredients correct before baking your perfect cake.

Combining two materials, to make a third, using Nodes

We will create a node material made up from the three materials created in the previous recipes. One representing the base gray sandstone texture, another representing the quartz layers, and a third that will act as a mask to mix the final result.

Getting ready

To help manage material node creation, it is a good idea to rearrange the interface as shown below. This gives a large Node editing window with the **Material** and **Texture** properties conveniently on the right of the screen. It provides a camera view and an **Image** editor with the render result. If you don't feel confident about setting this up yourself refer to Chapter 4, *Managing Blender Materials*, which includes a simple recipe for creating such a view.

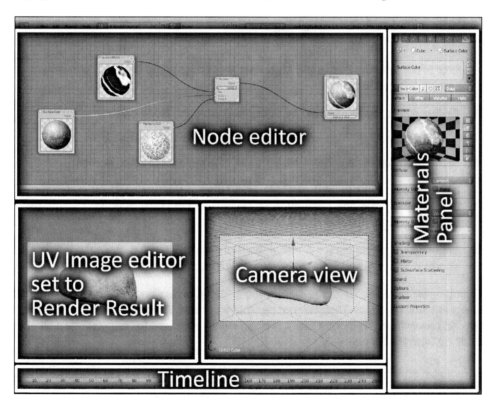

How to do it....

Load up the `pebble-06.blend` saved at the end of the last recipe. Should you have not completed that recipe you can download it from the Packt Publishing website.

To create a node material we should have the object selected and ideally start with the main material selected. In our case, it is the `Surface-Color` material created at the beginning of the first recipe in this section.

1. With the pebble object selected change the **Node** type to **Material** in the **Node** editor.

2. Now select the **Surface Color** material using the **Browse ID data button** from the **Materials** panel in the header. That's the little material icon next to the material name.

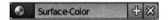

This selector is the same as that in the **Materials** properties panel but more convenient when we are working with nodes.

3. Finally, select the **UseNodes** check-box to enable the **Node** editor.

    A blank **Material** node linked to an **Output** node should be displayed.

4. In the **Material** node choose the SurfaceColor material created earlier.

    If you render at this point the pebble would display the SurfaceColor material because that's the only node material being fed to the **Output** node. It's time to add our `Quartz` material to the node tree.

5. Ensure your mouse cursor is within the **Node** editor view and press the keyboard shortcut *Shift+A*, and from the displayed list add another **Material** node.

Depending on what node is selected, before you added this new node, Blender will attempt to make a link automatically. This may not be what you need. To remove an incorrect link, just drag the link away from the input it may have incorrectly attached to. You can learn all about node editing from the BlenderWiki.

`http://wiki.blender.org/index.php/Doc:Manual/Materials/Nodes/Usage`

6. In this **Material** node, choose the `Quartz` material created earlier.

7. Press *SHIFT+A* and add a **Mix** node from the Color menu. Link the **Color** output socket from the SurfaceColor material node to **Color1** input, and the **Color** output socket from the Quartz material node to **Color2** input. Change the mix type to **Screen**.

8. Add a new **Input/Material** node, and select material QuartzMask. Connect its **Color** output to the **Mix/Fac** input node.

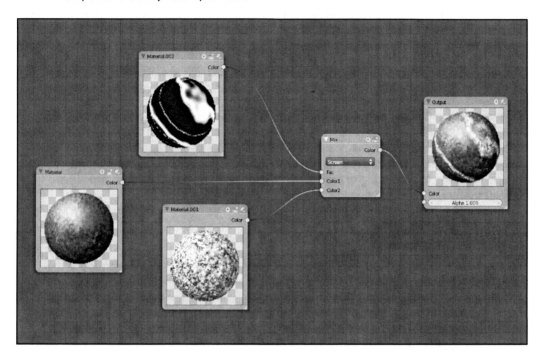

Save your work as pebble-07.blend and render to view your simulated quartz-veined pebble material.

How it works...

Blender Node editor is incredibly useful in combining materials in all kinds of new ways. It allows multiple materials to be combined on single objects. We have employed a simple mask here to accurately combine totally different materials onto our pebble simulation. In a sense we have created a new form of stencil to mix different textures controlled by a mask material. The difference with a node material is that the mask is much more flexible than the texture example we used in the individual materials.

Of course, that is not the only thing that material nodes can achieve. However, it is a very useful technique simply achieved using three materials and an uncomplicated mixing method.

Material nodes in Blender are one of the unique features that make it such a versatile 3D suite. Nodes can be used to create really detailed and interesting materials, something that is not possible with materials alone. We have used it here to mix two separate materials, using a third to filter the mix result. Later, we will examine more complex examples of node tree set ups. However, it's important to realize that a good node material does not have to be complex to work.

There's more...

You may have noticed that your renders are not quite the same as those illustrated in this book. That is because I have set up some variations in the lighting and rendering options to produce a better quality render. This is not necessary while you are developing a material solution as it will increase the render times for all test renders. However, if you would like to know how to duplicate the look of the renders in this chapter there is a recipe included in Chapter 4, *Managing Blender Materials*.

See also

Chapter 5, *Creating rust on iron-based metals*

Chapter 5, *Varying environment map reflections to simulate corrosion or wear*

Creating a large rock material using procedural, and node textures

Larger rock materials, for boulders, stone statues, or Stone Age circles, follow many of the principles learned in the previous pebble recipe. The main difference is one of scale and learning to obtain the correct scale for any object is an important step to producing good textures.

Although procedural textures can be used to create any scale rock occasionally, we will require photo reference to aid the organic structure that defines many rocks. We might not have ready access to larger rock formations for either direct observation or taking photo reference. While there are references available on the Internet, their resolution can be too low to use within a material. We will, therefore, also discuss other methods of creating images for larger rock formations. The approach with these recipes is not to create a finished image but rather explore approaches that can be applied to any larger rock surface.

Getting ready

Preparation for this recipe involves creating a simple scene comprising several box-like shapes subdivided a few times and tweaked in mesh edit to vary their shape. A simple plane is created to represent the ground and the two default lights adjusted to cast interesting shadows across the rock surface. Increase or decrease their intensity to obtain the best contrast in your render. You should be setting the lights up to aid your material creation at this stage rather than for a final render. You can also move the camera for a better angle if you like. The mesh needn't be complex; the one I created is just a few simple cubes subdivided with some added edge loops (*Ctrl+R* in mesh edit mode). Set your mesh to smooth shading and add a sub-surface modifier. To aid the process of shaping the mesh, ensure the **Apply modifier to editing cage during Editmode** button is selected.

To give the scene a pleasant and more seaside/desert/planet surface-like quality, you might want to change the world background and add a plane from which the rocks appear to project. A simple sky blend background, from a yellowish white at the horizon to a light blue in the sky, will silhouette the darker rocks against the light background.

It is a good idea to apply any scaling to the object using the *Ctrl+A* keyboard shortcut. This will ensure that the scaling will apply to the mesh, making the mapping of the material and textures consistent.

Save this as a blendfile, naming it `rock-default.blend`. This default scene, with no materials created, can then be used with each of the following rock recipes.

Should you wish to use the same mesh as I have used you can download it from the Packt Publishing website.

How it works...

This is a simple scene with no materials created. However, you will see that Blender will still render the scene, making surfaces visible with specularity together with shadows giving some idea as to the shape of our created mesh. Blender has a default material that is light gray in color with a small specular setting that makes the surface look like plastic. When creating an animation it can be useful to test render complex scenes without textures applied to speed the process of animation blocking. Once happy with the movement you can go on to create spectacular materials to bring the scene alive. We will use this Blender scene in each of the following recipes creating those spectacular materials.

Creating a sea rock material

Rocks on the sea edge are always fascinating. They are pounded at least twice a day through tides and storms. Life clings to them where it can and, apart from the natural elements that shape its surface, they are textured by birds and other transitory creatures that leave their mark on its surface.

Getting ready

You will need to load the `rock-default.blend` blendfile created earlier. Or if you have not been able to complete the previous recipe you can download the file from the Packt Publishing website.

Because we will be using this same blendfile for other recipes in this section you are advised to save it immediately after loading, and rename it `Sea-Rock-00.blend`.

How to do it...

Let's add an initial material to our rock mesh. To do so make sure the object is selected.

1. Click the **+** button in the **materials** panel to create a new material and name it `Sea-Rock`.
2. Set **Diffuse** color to **R** to `0.237`, **G** to `0.234`, and **B** to `0.205`.
3. Set the **Specular** type to **Wardiso**, with **Intensity** set to `0.014` and **Slope** to `0.400`.
4. All other settings in the **materials** panel can stay at their default values.

Now, let's create some textures to define our sea rock surface.

5. Switch to the **Texture** panel and create a new texture of **Type Clouds** and name it cloud.
6. In the **Clouds** settings, ensure that **Grayscale** and **Soft** are selected as well as **Basis** of type **Improved Perlin**, **Size** of `0.60`, and **Depth** of `5`.
7. Under **Colors** set **Adjust/Brightness** to `1.000`, and **Contrast** to `3.500`.
8. Under **Mapping** set **Size X** to `1.00`, **Y** to `2.00`, and **Z** to `0.30`.

For the moment we will not use this texture to add any color, bump, or specular changes to our material. We will, however, use it to modify the shape of our rocks via the **Modifiers** panel. To use this ensure that your mesh has been set to **Smooth** shading and that you have a **Subdivision Surface** modifier already in the stack. The settings for this can be quite small at **2 Subdivision** levels for **View** or **Render**.

9. Switch to the **Modifiers** panel and add a new modifier of type **Displace**.
10. Under **Texture**, click the checker icon and you should see your cloud texture as a selection. Select it and under **Strength** set the value to `0.100`.

You should immediately see the mesh distort slightly. If it's too much, reduce the **Strength** value a little more.

11. Switch back to the **Texture** panel and deselect the `cloud` texture just created. The tick mark should be off. We will not be using this texture for any other purpose just yet.

We could actually delete it here because that would only disconnect the texture from our material. It still exists because it's now being used by the Distort modifier. In fact, you may have noticed that a number has since appeared to the right of the texture name `cloud`. This shows that this texture is being used that number of times. It should be 2, because it's in the modifier and in the Material, even if it's not turned on at the moment. It sounds quite confusing but you don't need to worry about it at this stage.

12. Select the next clear texture slot and click the **new** button. Select the **Clouds** texture type and name the texture `rock-cracks`.

13. In the **Clouds** tab select **Grayscale** and **Hard** and set **Depth** to 6, and **Size** to 0.250.

    Under the **Mapping** tab change the **Size Z** value to 0.20.

14. In the **Influence** tab change the **Influence/Diffuse Color** to 0.500. In the **Geometry** select **Normal** and set to -2.000.

15. Under **Blend**, select type **Multiply** and check the **Stencil** checkbox. Finally, change the default color to **R** 0.05, **G** 0.04, and **B** 0.03.

Time to save your work to ensure you don't lose anything should the unforeseen happen. Name your file `Sea-Rock-01.blend`.

A quick render produces a quite nice rock. Remember, the only thing adding those deep and complex cracks and the green growth streaks is a simple cloud texture.

How it works...

Textures can be applied to an object in Blender other than via the materials settings. Here we used a texture that we temporarily loaded into a material texture slot and then applied it as a modifier to distort the mesh to give some variety to the surface. To use a texture for such purposes it must exist in the data structure of the blendfile. The easiest way to do this is to load it into a spare texture slot of a material, name it so it can be recognized, then use it with the modifier. Once that has been done you can 'unlink the datablock', from the material if you want. Alternatively, just leave the texture in the material but turn off its influence.

Employing a simple clouds texture to add vertical elongated cracks to our rocky surface is a really easy way to create larger rocks. Here we employed a scaled cloud texture to add both color and a bump to the surface. Procedural textures like cloud are ideal for this purpose as they are randomly generated just like the natural surface of rocks can be. However, cracks in large rocks tend to be in a certain direction and by rescaling in the Z axis we give the impression that the cracks are vertical striations. We had to reduce the Z scale to achieve this. Scaling below 1 will actually increase the stretch of a procedural texture. Scaling above 1 will squash the texture in the scaled axis.

Water can also play an important part in the surface properties, adding extra specularity and reflection at certain times of the day. We shall be dealing with water in later chapters, so for these recipes we will assume that the tide is out. We will combine future water exercises with some of these chapter rock recipes later.

See also

Chapter 6, *Creating realistic large-scale water in Blender 2.5*

Creating a texture node to simulate seaweed at the base of a rock

In this recipe we will create a simulation of seaweed, or other living crustacean, that can be found on the sea washed base of rocks on the edge of a beach. We will explore texture nodes in this recipe, using some comprehensive texture node modifiers.

Getting ready

You will need to load the blendfile saved at the end of the last recipe. If you have not completed that recipe you can download a pre-created blendfile from the Packt Publishing website.

How to do it

We can add more to bed our rock into the life rich environment of the seashore.

1. Select a free texture slot, below the last one created, and create a new **node** texture. Name it `NT-Blend-mask` and delete the **Checker** input.

2. Add a **Blend** texture with *SHIFT+A* (that is the 5th selection down on the **Add** menu, and the 2nd in the **Textures** sub menu). In future, you should know how to add a texture node using this key combination.

In its settings select type **Easing** and ensure it is a **Horizontal** blend. Now connect it to the **Output** node.

Blends are very useful to help mask parts of a texture. However, we can modify the blend to do much more than just go from black to white.

3. Create an **Add/Color/RGB Curves** node between the texture and output. Use your mouse to modify the curve to look something like in the following screenshot:

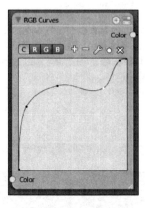

Change the default name of the **Output** node to `Vegetation-stencil`.

Back in the **Texture** panel let's set the way this texture will be applied to our material.

4. Below the texture name in the panel you will see that there is a new selector called **Output:** if you click on this a list of available outputs for that node texture will be shown. Select `Vegetation-stencil`.

It is possible to set up multiple named outputs that can individually be selected in the **Texture** panel. Each named output can have multiple nodes to control that output thus making a truly versatile texture tool.

5. Under **Influence** select **Color** and set to 0.420. Under **Blend** select **Overlay**, and **Stencil**, and finally select **RGB to Intensity** and set the color to **R** 0.16, **G** 0.10, **B** 0.09.

6. Select a free texture slot below the NT-Blend-mask texture previously created. This time, rather than creating a new texture select from the list, click on the checker icon by the name and select NT-Blend-mask. Yes, it's the same texture but we are going to add a new output after further modifying the **Blend**.

7. Copy the **RGB Curves** node (select and *Shift+D*) and move it below. You could have just created a new node but sometimes it's quicker to copy one already in the node tree. Modify the curve so that it looks like the following screenshot.

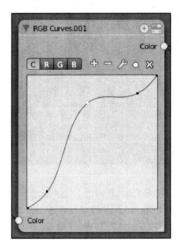

8. Connect the **Blend Color** output socket to this new RGB Curves node input socket.

9. You can create a **Viewer** node and connect the **Blend** output socket to the **Viewer** node. This will enable you to see its output at this stage of the node tree.

10. Create a new **Add/Textures/Clouds** node and set to **Grayscale Soft**, **Depth** 2, and **Size** 0.250.

11. Create a **Add/Color/Mix** node and connect the second **RGB Curves** node to **Color1** and the **Clouds** Texture node to **Color2**, and the **Mix** type to **Overlay**. You can feed its output socket to the **Viewer** node to see what it looks like.

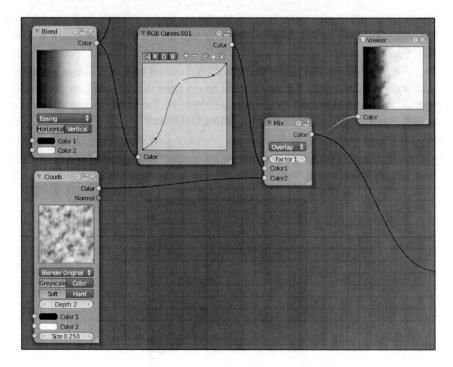

12. Create, or copy, another **RGB Curves** node and connect it from the **output** socket of the **Mix** node. Modify the curve so that it looks like the following screenshot. You will see that the **Viewer** node has been moved to after the **Mix** node.

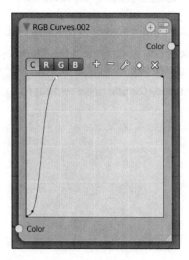

13. Feed its output socket to the **Viewer** node to see how that has altered the **Blend**.

You have three more jobs to do to complete this new output. Firstly, we will scale it slightly and then invert it, and finally create a new named output that we can use in the material.

14. Create an **Add/Distort/Scale** node connected from the last **RGB Curves** node. Set its scale as **X** to 0.70, **Y** to 0.70, and **Z** to 1.00.

15. Create an **Add/Color/Invert** node from the **Scale** node.

16. Create a new **Add/output** node and name it Water-stencil.

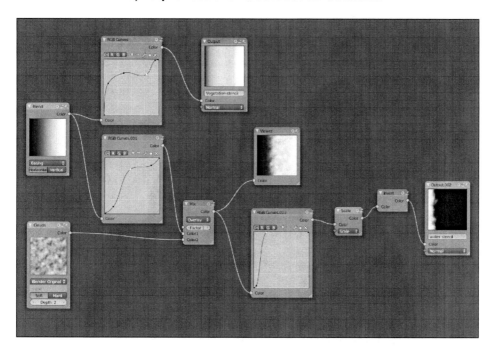

Switch back to the **Texture** panel, so that we can set the influence of this new modified texture node output.

17. Select the Water-stencil **Output** and in the **Influence** tab select **RGB to Intensity** and **Stencil**.

As you can see, it has no visual impact on the material as yet. This node texture output has become an irregular mask for a texture we will create to simulate crustaceans, or seaweed growth on the base of the rocks.

18. Select the next free texture slot and create a new texture of type **Clouds** and name it Limpets.

Please note that it is not designed to represent limpets per se. It's just a nice shorter name that gives the gist of what we are trying to simulate.

19. Under **Influence/Diffuse** select **Color** and set to 0.345. Under **Influence/Geometry** select **Normal** and set to -2.000. Set **Blend** type to **Mix**, and **RGB to Intensity** and the **color** values to **R** 0.00, **G** 0.09, **B** 0.01.

20. Finally, under **Clouds** set **GrayscaleGrayGrayscale**, **Noise Soft**, **Basis** as **Improved Perlin**, **Size** 0.03, **Depth** 2.

Save your completed blendfile, incrementing the filename. It's time for a final render.

How it works...

This recipe has used the Texture node system to demonstrate the extraordinary capabilities now offered in the Blender 3D suite. Node textures enable any procedural or image texture to be filtered and modified in many exciting ways. Here we used it to create some quite complex stencils or masks. These were then used to mix and combine textures in quite subtle ways. However, there are only three textures used to produce this effect.

A texture node was created with two outputs, both acting as masks or stencils for the last texture. Although it is possible to create almost any texture variation with a node texture, we have actually covered those areas that are most frequently used. These include mixing methods, levels adjustment, and distortions.

A node texture can be used in both node and standalone materials. Here we used a standalone material but later we will take this same material and integrate it into a node material, adding extra details to simulate the progress of creatures on its surface.

Procedural textures are superb at simulating natural organic surfaces such as stone. However, you can also use real rock face photos to modify a surface. Used in combination with procedurals you can produce some stunning results.

There's more...

When creating node textures one must be careful not to produce a loop in the node structure. It is currently possible to link an output back into itself. However, the connector will turn red, showing that you are creating a loop.

It is also possible to add the same named node texture back into itself via the **Add/Input/ Texture**. In such a case the small view will turn bright red, as will the output. But the texture will still render, sometimes producing weird results. As Blender is in a constant state of development these easily avoided annoyances will be tidied up. You can keep up to date with all the developments by checking the Bug Tracker or joining one of the support forums.

Here are some really useful websites to help you get the best out of a constantly developing 3D graphics suite.

- Graphical Org is the place to download the latest builds of Blender `http://www.graphicall.org/builds/index.php`.

- CIA.vc is the open source version control informant for Blender `http://cia.vc/stats/project/Blender`.

- The Blender Bug Tracker (you will need to register to submit a bug) `https:// projects.blender.org/tracker/?atid=498&group_id=9&func=browse`.

- The Blender release logs for all versions of Blender `http://www.blender.org/ development/release-logs/`.

Creating a large rock face using photo reference

Rock faces are extremely dramatic structures shaped by tremendous forces, such as earthquakes, volcanic eruptions, and glacial erosion over millions of years. Trying to simulate that kind of surface history can be daunting. So far we have explored procedural textures for most of the rocks created. It's time to show how images can be employed to create variety over the standard procedurals available.

In my part of the world we have some very beautiful rocks called bluestone. They have a structure that the ancients believed were a direct map of the stars. Their blue surface, with lighter blue highlights, was so different from other rock types that they collected them into stone henges, transporting them many hundreds of miles across these islands at a time when there were no cranes or heavy transport vehicles. Outcrops of these natural rocks can be found on many of the hills surrounding me. In fact, the mesh we created earlier looks very much like these stones. So why not try to recreate a surface material of their beauty?

Carn Edward with view to Cerrig Lladron for SN0536 © Copyright ceridwen and licensed for reuse under a Creative Commons License.

Getting ready

Open the `rock-default.blend` blendfile you created in the *Creating a large rock material using procedural, and node textures* recipe earlier in this chapter. Or if you have not completed that exercise download a pre-created version from the Packt Publishing website.

Rename and save it as `large-rock-blue-stone-01.blend`. This will ensure that we can start working on this recipe without overwriting the default rock scene created earlier. You will learn in Chapter 5 how important it is to manage your files to help ensure you do not accidentally destroy, or radically alter, a previously created blendfile, material, or texture masterpiece.

You will also need to download an image `PEMBROKESHIRE-CLIFF-ROCKS.png` for use in this recipe from the Packt Publishing website.

Save it to the textures sub-directory below where you saved the blendfile.

How to do it...

1. With the rock mesh object selected create a new material in the **Materials** panel. Name it `Blue-Stone`.

2. Set the **Diffuse color** to **R** `0.173`, **G** `0.194`, and **B** `0.240`. A nice gray/blue color.

3. Under **Specular** set the specular type to **Wardiso**, with **Intensity** set to `0.083` and **Slope** to `0.400`.

4. Switch to the **Textures** panel and create a new texture of type **Clouds** in the first slot calling it `large-cloud`.

5. In the **Clouds** settings select **Grayscale** and **Noise/Soft**. Set **Basis** to **Blender Original**, **Size** to `0.40`, and **Depth** to `3`.

6. Under **Colors** set **Adjust/Brightness** to `1.100`, and **Contrast** to `1.300`.

7. Under **Mapping** set the **Size X** to `0.20`.

8. Under **Influence** select **Diffuse/Color** and set to `1.00`, **Geometry/Normal** to `3.142`, and the **Blend** color to **RGB** `0.05`.

Save your work and do a test render.

You will notice that the clouds texture has added a little normal and color variety to the surface. You might also notice that there is a little too much surface specularity in this render. We will create textures to tone that down a little in a moment. But if you turn specularity totally off it will look very flat and uninteresting. Even substances like black velvet, that absorb light very evenly, will show some specularity when they are creased.

It's time to add a photographic image that will add some natural looking stratification to this bluestone rock surface.

9. Select the next free texture slot and create a new texture and make it an Image or Movie node texture. Name it `Pembs-Cliff-Image`.

10. In the **Image** tab **Open** the `PEMBROKESHIRE-CLIFF-ROCKS.png` image from your textures directory.

11. Under the **Image Sampling** tab reduce the **Filter Size** to its minimum of 0.10.

The picture is quite large at 3,472 x 2,314 pixels. This means we can utilize all of its detail without worrying about aliasing and therefore reduce the filter size to its minimum. The image itself has been modified to even out the levels and also converted to grayscale.

12. In the Image **Mapping** tab change the **Crop Mininum X** and **Y** values to 0.350. Also change the **Crop Maximum** X and Y values to 0.650. This has enlarged and cropped the image to remove the sky in the top left of the original image. We could have done this in a paint program but it's quite possible directly in Blender.

13. Under the **Influence** tab select **Geometry/Normal** and set to -2.500. Finally, select **RGB to Intensity**. Ensure all other influences are unselected.

If you render now you will see an extremely worn rock surface. Although this might be OK for certain simulations we can map the image a bit more creatively.

14. In the 3D view set the cursor to the center, *Shift+S,* **Cursor to Center**, and create an **Empty**. Name it rock-rotate and set its rotation as follows, **X** 47.051, **Y** -19.503, and **Z** 31.622. You can do this by pressing the *N* key while your cursor is in the 3D view. This will bring up the **Transform** pallet where you can enter the rotation amounts directly. While in this view alter the **Location X** value to -1.250. This will move the **Empty** to the left slightly.

15. Select the rock mesh object again and in the **Texture** panel under **Mapping/Coordinates** select **Object**, and from the **Object** list select the rock-rotate empty you just created.

Render once more and you should see some better stratification across the rock surface. Now we will add the lighter blue strata in this bluestone simulation.

16. Select a free texture slot below the `Pembs-Cliff-Image` and add a new texture of type **Image or Movie** and name it `Blue-stone-MASK`.

17. Under the **Image** tab click the image icon next to the **New** and **Open** button. This will display a list of images currently in Blender. Select the same image as before, `PEMBROKESHIRE-CLIFF-ROCKS.png`. Although we are using the same image we will make some changes to the way it is used.

18. In the **Colors** tab **Adjust** the **Brightness** to `1.100` and the **Contrast** to its maximum of `5.000`.

You should see in the preview that we have increased the contrast of our image, which we shall use to mask, or stencil, another material.

19. Under **mapping** select **Coordinates/Object** and select `rock-rotate`, the empty we created earlier.

20. In the **Image Mapping** change the **Crop Minimum X** and **Y** to `0.350` and the **Crop Maximum X** and **Y** to `0.650`. This is the same cropping as the previous texture.

21. Under **Influence** set **RGB to Intensity** and **Stencil**. Ensure no other settings are selected as this texture is only being used as a stencil. It will not contribute any color or bump to the material.

22. Select the next free texture slot and create a new texture of type **Musgrave** and name it `Small-Musgrave`.

23. Under the **Musgrave** settings select **Type/Multifractal** with **Dimension** `0.100`, **Lacunarity** `6.000`, and **Octaves** `8.000`.

24. Under **Influence/Diffuse** select **Intensity** with a setting of `1.00`, and **Color** `0.161`. Under **Geometry** set **Normal** to `1.195`. Set the **Blend** type to **Screen** as well as **RGB to Intensity**, and a **color** of **R** `1.00`, **G** `0.92`, **B** `0.93`.

Do a final render to view our bluestone material simulation.

How it works...

Images can be used in all kinds of ways within Blender. In this recipe we have taken a black and white image and mapped it to our surface, not worrying about repeats or seams in the image. We have used procedural textures to enhance and cover-up any inconsistencies that are certainly there. We have filtered the same image in the texture panel controls using cropping, contrast, and other object mapping to create a rescaled and improved contrast mask without having to resort to a paint program or load yet another memory-intensive image into Blender.

Blender's versatility, in what can be achieved using images, is almost unrivaled. You will see in future recipes how seams and repeats can be avoided and how to use paint programs to create better images for use in materials later.

See also

Chapter 7, *Applying UVs to create an accurate skin material*

In that recipe, you will discover how to wrap images around a mesh using UV mapping. This is the preferred way when mapping to a mesh that must move and distort in an animation. Fortunately, our rock recipes do not bend or twist as a cartoon character might.

2
Creating Man-made Materials

In this chapter, we will cover:

- ▸ Creating a slate roof node material that repeats but with ultimate variety
- ▸ Using a tileable texture to add complexity to a surface
- ▸ Warping a texture to disguise seams in a repeated texture
- ▸ Adding weathering by copying and reusing textures
- ▸ Combining materials using nodes
- ▸ Creating metals
- ▸ Creating a realistic copper material
- ▸ Using image maps to suggest man-made metal materials
- ▸ Using specular maps to add age and variety to man-made surface materials
- ▸ Adding oxidization weathering to our copper material
- ▸ Adding grime and artistic interest to our copper material
- ▸ Creating a road or path material that never repeats
- ▸ Repeating a tiled texture to duplicated objects
- ▸ Deforming materials and textures in Blender

Introduction

Man-made materials and textures are probably the most used and applied in any 3D environment. The need to simulate created and manufactured objects is therefore an important skill to learn and apply within Blender. Fortunately, the techniques necessary to simulate man-made surfaces are no more difficult than creating natural surfaces.

Blender offers many tools to aid the process of creating man-made materials. Its material system makes it easy to manipulate textures and apply them to a surface, reproducing properties such as:

- Color changes, due to oxidization, or other environment-specific interaction
- Scratches, due to wear and tear, specifically on those areas of an object that are more frequently handled or interact with other objects
- Dirt and grime that collect on man-made surfaces like rust, dust in any gullies, or vegetation that will grow on man-made materials if exposed to air and moisture for any length of time.

All these things will place our object in the context of its man-made origins. Identifying these attributes and reproducing them within a Blender material will sell your material solution as being man made.

So, even though a man-made material may be fashioned out of natural substances, its surface, as well as its shape, will provide the clues as to its man-made origins.

The things that differentiate such surfaces from natural counterparts often describe the process of manufacture and the way we interact with them. So, a man-made surface will have been:

- **Moulded** – beaten, pressed, folded, and cut, each of which will have an effect on the surface.
- **Cast** – clay and metals are often cast to produce new shapes. These castings will produce new surface bumps specific to the casting method. Cast iron can have a lovely granulated surface because sand is used as the casting mould.
- **Coated** – many man-made materials have to be coated to protect them from the elements. Paint, anodizing, and other coating methods may change the appearance of the surface but the underlying substance can affect the bump and sometimes the coverage of the coating. So, rust and other oxidization on metals can eventually wear through the coating.
- **Polished** – man-made objects are often polished in some way, either by coating with varnishes and polishes, or by their designed interaction with other items. So, a cast metal cylinder may be rough on the outside, but cut accurately in its center, to allow a piston to move, with the actions of the piston continually polishing the bore of the cylinder.

▸ **Marked** – Human handling, or the environment-specific location, will lead to handling marks or task-specific grime. So, man-made materials will have different specularity levels across its surface, particularly where human hands have been in contact. Also, exposed edges of man-made materials often wear more because of their vulnerability to human interaction.

All these things should set a man-made surface into context. Recognizing these surface attributes and finding ways to simulate them within Blender will improve your chances of convincing the viewer that what they see is actually meant to represent a manufactured object.

That doesn't mean you have to create absolute reality in your man-made material designs. Sometimes, you can fake a material by giving just enough surface information to fool the eye. This is valuable because we may not be able to use enormous image maps, with their inherent memory-hogging disadvantages, with every man-made material simulation. So, keeping things simple will help you as a designer, as well as improve render times, the size of your blendfiles, and the complexity of models. This is particularly important when you consider how complex you wish to make the mesh representing the man-made object.

A good material can add detail to a simple mesh with little of the memory overheads associated with millions of vertices. In fact, a cube made from 8 vertices will look exactly the same as one with 87,848. However, the first will render in 4.69 sec, on my computer, while the second will take 10.05 sec. That's twice as long and with the other disadvantages of a large memory overhead that will slow your computer to a crawl. Therefore, consider adding just structural detail via the Blender material rather than trying to model all the dents, curves, indentations, and other complexities of the real surface.

As a 3D designer, you will also be expected to create visually interesting surfaces. Sometimes, it will be better to emphasize surface attributes to make the render more exciting. Just as with natural material simulation, our task is to provide the viewer with the essence of the surface we are trying to duplicate but also add that magic flare that will transform our man-made material simulation to the next level.

Several of the recipes in this chapter require the use of a paint package. You will struggle if you do not have access to one. I can recommend GIMP, which is another free open source package like Blender. It is available for any of the major computer platforms from:
`http://www.gimp.org/downloads/`

Creating a slate roof node material that repeats but with ultimate variety

We discovered early in the first chapter that man-made materials will often closely resemble their natural surface attributes. Slate is a natural material that is used in many building projects. Its tendency to shear into natural slices makes it an ideal candidate for roofing. However, in its man-made form it is much more regularly shaped and graded to give a nice repeating pattern on a roof surface. That doesn't mean that there is no irregularity in either the edges or surface of manufactured slate tiles. In fact, architects often use this irregularity to add character and drama to a roof.

Repeat patterns in a 3D suite like Blender can be extremely difficult to control. If repeats become too obvious, particularly when surface and edges are supposed to be random, it can ruin the illusion. Fortunately, we will be employing Blender controls to add randomness to a repeated image representing the tiled pattern of the roof.

Of course, slates like any building material need to be fixed to a roof. This is usually achieved with nails. After time, these metal joiners will age and either rust or channel water to add streaks and rust lines across the slate, often emphasizing the slope of the roof. All these secondary events will add character and dimension to a material simulation. However, such a material need not be complex to achieve a believable and stimulating result.

Getting ready

The preparation for this recipe could not be simpler. The modeling required to produce the mesh roof is no more than a simple plane created at the origin and rotated in its Y axis to 30°. The plane can be at the default size of one blender unit and should have no more than four vertices. That's just about the simplest model you can have in a 3D graphics program.

Position the camera so that you have a reasonably close-up view as shown in the following image:

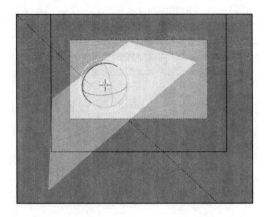

The default lights, as suggested in Chapter 4, *Setting a default scene for materials creation*, will be fine for this simulation. But, you are welcome to place lights as you wish. Please bear in mind that a slate roof tends to be quite a dark material. So, if test renders appear too dark, raise the light energy until a reasonable render can be produced. You can also turn off **Raytrace** render and **Ambient Occlusion**, if it has been previously set, as they are not required for this material. This will save considerable time in rendering test images.

Save your blendfile as `slate-roof-01.blend`.

You will also need to either create or download a small tileable image to represent the pattern of the slate roof. Instructions are given on how to create it within the recipe but a downloadable version is available from the Packtpub website.

How to do it...

We need to create an image of the smallest repeatable pattern of our slates. This can act both as a bump map and also to mask and apply color variation to the material.

The image is very simple and is based on the shape and dimension of a standard rectangular slate. You will see later how the shape can be changed to represent other slate patterns.

This was created in GIMP, although any reasonable paint package could be used. Here are the steps to aid you in creating one yourself:

1. Create a new image with size `260 x 420` pixels. I will show later how you can scale an image to give better proportions for more efficient use within Blender.

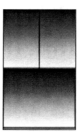

2. Either place guides or create a grid to sub-divide the rectangle into four sections.
3. In the top half of the rectangle, create a blend fill from black at the top to white at the middle. Do the same for the bottom half of the rectangle.
4. Create a new layer and draw a black line, of three pixels' width, from the middle of the top rectangle section to divide the top rectangle into two.

5. Draw black lines of the same thickness on each side of the whole rectangle. If you used a grid, you should find that one of these verticals is two pixels' width and the other one. Obviously, when this image is tiled, the black lines will all appear as equal in thickness.

6. Finally, create another blend fill from the bottom of each rectangle from black to white upwards about ten pixels.

7. Save your completed image as `slate-tile.png` to your Blender textures directory.

If you want to skip these steps you can download a pre-created one from the Packtpub website.

How it works...

The image that you want to tile must be carefully designed to hide any seams that might appear when repeated. Most of the major paint packages, such as Photoshop and GIMP, have tools to aid you in that process. However, manual drawing, or editing of an image, will almost always be necessary to create accurate tileable images. Even tiny variations between seams will show up if repeated enough times across a surface. Fortunately, there are techniques available in Blender that will help mask these repeat image shortcomings.

See also

Later in this chapter:

▶ *Repeating a tiled texture to duplicated objects*

Using a tileable texture to add complexity to a surface

We will use the tileable texture created in the previous recipe and apply it to a slate roof material in Blender.

1. Reload the `slate-roof-01.blend` file saved earlier and select the roof mesh object.

2. From the **Materials** panel, create a new material and name it `slate-roof`. In the **Diffuse** tab, set the color selector to **R** `0.250`, **G** `0.260`, and **B** `0.300`.

3. Under **Specular** tab, change the specular type to **Wardiso**, with **Intensity** to `0.400` and **Slope** to `0.300`. The color should stay at the default white.

That's set the general color and specularity for the first material that we will use to start a node material solution for our slate roof shader.

1. Ensure you have a **Node Editor** window displayed.

> Chapter 4 shows you how to set up a really useful range of Blender windows to make material creation much easier.

2. In the **Node Editor**, select the material node button and check the **Use Nodes** checkbox.

3. A blank material node should be displayed connected to an output node.
4. From the **Browse ID Data** button, on the **Material node**, select the material previously created named `slate-roof`.
5. To confirm that the material is loaded into the node, re-select that node by left clicking it.

> This is a bug and may be resolved by the time you read this book.

Of course, at the moment, the material is no more than a single color with a soft specular shine. To start turning it into a proper representation of a slate roof, we have to add our tileable texture and set up some bump and color settings to make our simple plane look a little more like a slate roof with many tiles.

6. With the **Material node** still selected, go to the **Texture** panel and in the first texture slot, create a new texture of type **Image or Movie** and name it `slate-tile`.
7. From the **Image** tab, open the `slate-tile.png` image you saved earlier.
8. Under **Image Mapping/ Extension**, select **Repeat** and set **Repeat** to **X** 9 and **Y** 6. That means the image will be repeated nine times in the X direction and six in the Y of the texture space.
9. In the **Influence** tab, select **Diffuse/Color** and set to 0.831. Also, select **Geometry/Normal** and set to -5.000. Finally, set the **Blend** type to **Darken**.

Save your work at this point, incrementing your filename number to `slate-roof-02.blend`.

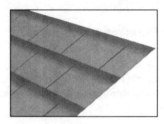

As you can see, a repeated pattern has been stamped on our flat surface with darker colors representing the slate tile separations and a darker top that currently looks like a shadow. This will be corrected in following recipes, along with the obvious clinical precision of each edge.

How it works...

The surface properties of slate produce a spread of specular highlight when the slate is dry. The best way of simulating that in Blender is to employ a specular shader that can easily generate this type of specular property. The Wardiso specular shader is ideal for this task as it allows a wide range of slope settings from very tight, below 0.100, to very widely spread, 0.400. This is different from the other specular shaders that use a hardness setting to vary the highlight spread. However, you will notice that other specular shader types produce a narrower range than the Wardiso shader. In our slate example, this particular shader provides the ideal solution.

Man-made materials are often made from repeated patterns. This is often because it's easier to manufacture objects as components and bring them together when building thus producing patterns. Utilizing simple tileable images to represent those shapes is an extremely efficient way of creating a Blender material simulation. Blender provides some really useful tools to ease the process, using repeats within a material as well as techniques to add variety and drama to a material.

Repeat is a really useful way of tiling an image any number of times across the object's texture space. In our example, we were applying the image texture to the object's generated texture space. That's basically the physical dimensions of the object. You can find out what the texture space looks like for any object by selecting the **Object** panel and choosing the **Display** tab and checking **Texture Space**.

An orange dotted border, representing the texture space, will surround the object.

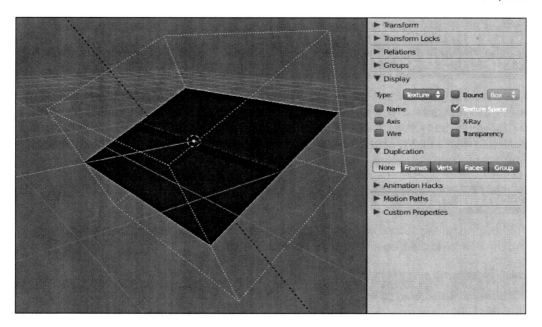

The plane object used for this material simulation is a square rectangle. If you were to scale the plane disproportionately, the texture would distort accordingly. If we were using this material for a roof simulation, where the scale may not be square, we may need to alter the repeat settings in the texture to match the proportions of the roof rectangle.

In our recipe, we started with a one blender unit square mesh then set the repeat pattern to **X** 9 and **Y** 6. The repeat settings have to be integer numbers so it may be necessary to calculate the nearest repeat numbers for the image you want to use. In our example, we didn't need to be absolutely accurate. Slates, after all, are often quite variable in size between buildings.

If you want to be absolutely accurate, scale your original mesh in **Object** mode to match to the image proportions. So, in our example, we could have scaled the plane to 2.60 (or 0.26) blender units on its **X** axis and 4.20 (or 0.42) on its **Y** axis, and then designed our repeats from that point.

See also

Later in this chapter:

► *Repeating a tiled texture to duplicated objects*

Warping a texture to disguise seams in a repeated texture

Slate, when cut, has irregular edges and duplicating this property will provide the observer with a very recognizable clue as to the material the slates are meant to represent. It's also a good idea to add just a little variation to the surface of the slate so that it looks like it has been split from a thicker slate stone. In other words, giving an indication as to how the slate was manufactured.

Getting ready

This recipe naturally follows on from the previous one. If you have not completed that recipe you can download the blendfile from the Packtpub website.

How to do it...

We will start by adding a procedural texture to warp the tiled image texture created at the end of the last recipe.

1. Load the file `slate-roof-02.blend` into Blender.

2. In the **Texture** panel, select the `slate-tile` texture slot and move the texture slot down one using the down button of the **Move texture slots up and down** buttons to the right of the texture slots as shown in the following image.

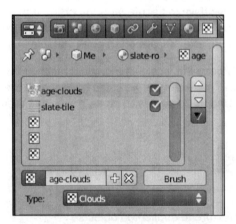

3. In the spare slot above the `slate-tile` texture, create a new texture of type **Clouds** and name it `age-clouds`. In the **Clouds** tab, set to **Grayscale** and **Noise** to **Soft**. Set the **Basis** to **Blender Original** with **Size** `0.60` and **Depth** `6`.

4. Under **Colors**, set the **Adjust/Brightness**, and the **Contrast** to `1.300`.

5. Under **Mapping**, set the **Coordinates** to **Global**, and the **Size X,Y,Z** to 3.00. The **Size** setting is important because the texture will map differently between object and global space.

6. Under **Influence**, only select **Geometry/Normal** and **Warp** and set them to 2.000 and 0.030 respectively.

Save your work as `slate-roof-03.blend` and perform a test render. You should see that the slate edges and surface now have a random variation to their appearance similar to that found on real slate tiles. However, their color is still rather light and the slates have no weathering marks. We will create that in the following recipe.

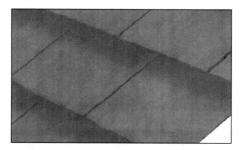

How it works...

Warping an underlying texture, using another texture mapped beyond the object space, is one of the most important ways of masking a repeated texture. Here, we mapped the age-clouds texture to the global co-ordinates, i.e., the world space. When you do this, the scale of the texture will need changing to re-adjust it back to the object space. We can do this approximately by multiplying the scale values by three. So, if you remap a texture to global, the scale reduces by about one-third. This is not meant to be an accurate difference, but in most cases, it will produce the desired affect.

This first texture, mapped to the global space, will **warp** the following texture across any of its tiled seams. This will give the impression that the repeats are more random as it will help hide any repeating imperfections. We might, after all, want to create several houses in a row and we wouldn't want each roof to be exactly the same. This method of mapping a warp texture modifier, to another co-ordinate system, means the warp will flow across all repeat seams and therefore each roof will look different.

However, this trick can only be used if the object doesn't move in an animation. If it did, the texture mapped to global would appear to stay still as the object moved. There are techniques that can be used to reduce this problem like mapping the texture to an **empty** parented to the mesh. Then, if the object moves the **empty** would move with the object and cancel this shortcoming.

Also, the object should not distort during an animation because, again, even if the warp texture were mapped to a parented empty, it's only mapping within the texture space and not directly onto the surface. In those circumstances, it is best to **UV** map a texture. However, it is possible to bake textures to a **UV** map and this will be described in later recipes. In our case, a slate roof wouldn't normally move so mapping the warp to global works perfectly.

The **warp** settings, shown in this recipe, warp the edge of our slate tile to produce a kind of ageing effect. This, together with the normal bump map settings, can be increased to make the tiles appear older. However, the warp setting should not be increased beyond approximately 0.05 as beyond this the warp will be too aggressive and produce an unnatural effect. The normal setting can be increased, to add a rougher surface to the slate, or made to look smooth and new, by lowering its settings.

See also

Chapter 1:

> ▸ *Creating a realistic pebble material using procedural textures*

Adding weathering by copying and reusing textures

In this recipe, we will add some weathering surface attributes by creating another material to represent nail rust running from underneath each slate as though rain has carried it down the roof.

Getting ready

This recipe picks up from the end of the last one. If you have not completed that recipe you can download the start blendfile from the Packtpub website: `slate-roof-03.blend`.

Open this file in Blender and continue with the following steps.

How to do it...

We first need to create a new material to provide the rust stains that will be applied in the material node tree. The easiest way to achieve this is to temporarily unlink the current material `slate-roof` from our object to create a new one. The `slate-roof` material still exists because it is assigned to the node material. Normally, objects can only have a single material assigned, although it is possible to have different materials assigned to vertex groups as will be shown in Chapter 8, *Assigning more than one material to a surface*.

In our case, it makes sense to temporarily unlink the `slate-roof` material, giving a clean slate to create a material to give weather and rust marks to the node material simulation.

1. With the roof mesh object selected, and from the **Materials** panel, unlink the material datablock by clicking the **X** by the material name. This will not delete the material, just temporarily unlink it from our object.

2. Create a new material and name it `slate-stains`.

3. Set the **Diffuse** color to **R** `0.39`, **G** `0.41`, and **B** `0.45`. Here, we use the default **Lambert** shader, which is fine for this part of the simulation.

4. Set the **Specular** color to **R** `0.57`, **G** `0.60`, and **B** `0.62`. Make it of type **CookTorr** with **Intensity** set to `0.087` and **Hardness** to `102`. The color settings produce a slightly blue specular shine. This is also the default specular shader that again is fine for this simulation.

Now, let us add some textures to produce the weathering required.

1. In the first slot of the **Texture** panel, select the `slate-tile` texture created earlier. Do this by clicking on the checker icon to the left of the texture name and choose from the list of textures displayed.

2. Under the **Influence** tab, de-select **Color**. Select **Geometry/Norm** and set to `5.000`. Set **Blend** to **Mix**, check **Negative**, **RGB to Intensity**, and **Stencil**.

3. In the next free texture slot, create a new texture of type **Distorted Noise** and name it `DistNoise`.

4. Under the **Distorted Noise** tab, ensure that **Noise Distortion** and **Basis** are both set to **Blender Original**. Set the **Distortion** to `1.000`, and **Size** to `0.25`.

5. Under **Influence/Diffuse**, check the **Color** and set to `0.833`. Set the **Blend** type to **Mix**, and from the color selector, set to **R** `0.31`, **G** `0.16`, and **B** `0.00`.

The next texture will add some more variety to the weathering look we are after.

1. In the next free texture slot, create a new texture of type **Musgrave** and name it `Musgrave`.

2. Under the **Musgrave** tab, select type **Multifractal** and set the **Dimension** to `1.175`, **Lacunarity** to `3.137`, and **Octaves** to `6.433`. Finally, set the **Basis** type to **Blender Original** with **Size** set to `0.09`.

3. Under **Mapping**, set the **Coordinates** type to **Global**.

4. Under **Influence/Diffuse**, select **Color** and set to `0.297`. Finally, set **Blend** type to **Mix**, set **RGB to Intensity**, and change the color selector to **R** `0.58`, **G** `0.69`, **B** `0.74`.

Save your work at this point, incrementing the file name to `slate-roof-04.blend`, and perform a test render.

The render should only show the effect of this material that produces a nice even slope to each slate with rust-colored stains that only begin from the point where the slates appear to overlap. It's also subtly mixed with some lighter streaking but again avoiding the places where slates overlap because of the stencil mask employed in the first texture.

How it works...

We utilized a method of reusing a texture between materials in this recipe, however, this is not the only method to do this. Blender allows you to copy or reuse textures in more than one way. Some offer the ability to copy and change settings while others will allow you to use a texture as a relative copy so that any changes you make to it, even if it's in another material, will change all occurrences within the blendfile.

In our example, we have used the same texture but in a new texture slot. As a result, we can make changes to the **Influence** settings separate from the settings in the other material slot. However, if you change the mapping in either texture, these settings will work across both textures. This is useful because we can have different settings for color, bump, or any of the influence attributes while only having to change the repeat setting in one of the image textures of the same name and the other will immediately match. Linking texture and materials, within and across blendfiles, will be discussed further in Chapter 4, *Managing Blender Materials*.

So, both of our materials share the same tiled image texture but we have added further procedural textures to alter the effect of the overall material to produce a weathered look. The **Distorted Noise**, and **Musgrave** textures add the rain and rust stains that once combined with our original `slate-roof` material will complete the material simulation.

Combining materials using nodes

In this recipe, we will combine two materials within a node tree to create the full slate roof effect.

Getting ready

This recipe starts at the end of the last one. If you have not completed that recipe you can download the blendfile from the Packtpub website.

How to do it...

Since two component materials have already been created, we only have to combine them within the material node to create the final result.

1. With the `slate-roof-04.blend` open, select the plane object and from the **Materials** panel, change the material to the `slate-roof` material created in previous recipes. Do this by clicking the **Browse Data ID** button to the left of the material name and select `slate-roof` from the displayed list. This will display the beginning node setup with the `slate-roof` material attached to an **Output** node.

2. In the **Node** editor, press *SHIFT+A* to bring up the **Add** menu and add a new **Input/ Material** node. Choose the `slate-stains` material from its **Browse Data ID**.

Now, we have two materials in the node tree. We will add a mixing node to combine them and send the mixed result to the **Output** node.

1. Add a **Color/Mix** node and connect the color output from `slate-stains` node to the **Color1** input of the **Mix** node.

2. Connect the color output of the `slate-roof` node to the **Color2** input of the **Mix** node.

3. Connect the color output of the **Mix** node to the color input of the **Output** node.

4. Finally, in the **Mix** node, change the mix type to **Multiply** and the **Fac** to 1.000.

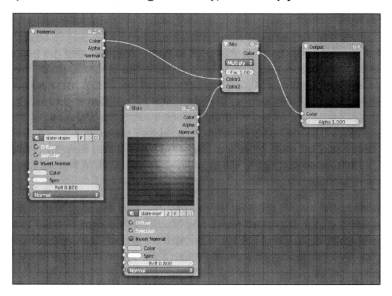

Save your work as `slate-roof-05.blend` and perform a final render, at a reasonable resolution, to view your completed slate-roof material.

How it works...

We have effectively created a complex man-made surface on the simplest of mesh objects. Remember there are only four vertices to our mesh. Another advantage of this material solution is that it will work even when rendered close up. So, if we were making an animation, where the camera has to travel across the roof, the material will hold up visually even if the lens appears to be very close to the slate. Yet, it only employs a very small image of 260 x 420 pixels, and only 321 KB in size, so the overhead, in processing terms, is quite small. This is very important if we were rendering an entire street or town of buildings.

Using materials to create complexity on simple meshes is an extremely useful skill to learn. Blender offers many tools to aid this process. Learning when to use them, and what weaknesses may hide within their use, will enable you to gain the most from Blender materials and textures.

There's more...

You will have noticed that we used the same texture `slate-tile.png` in both the `slate-roof` material and the `slate-stains` material. In each case, we used the texture as a bump map, as well as a mask, in one, and a color contributor in the other. However, the bump values in `slate-roof` are the opposite of those in `slate-stains`. This is because we had to use the negative setting within the **Influence/Blend** section of the `slate-stains` material to get the mask to work properly. As we need the bumps to work the same way in each material, it was necessary to reverse the bump direction in the other material. Without that, the two bumps would have canceled each other out. The good news is that Blender provides the tools to alter any of the **Influence** settings to either positive or negative. In this way, we can reverse the effect of any influence.

Why use the same bump map in the `slate-stains` material anyway? Well, because the stain marks supplied via the **Distorted Noise** and **Musgrave** textures needed to follow the bump direction of each slate. Using the same bump map in each texture ensures that when mixed in the node tree the stains will look as though they are on the slope of each slate tile.

Utilizing repeat textures

Use Google to search for instructions on how to tile textures using your favorite graphics program.

```
http://www.google.com/
```

Use a search term such as "creating tileable textures in GIMP", or your particular paint package. If you enter "creating tileable textures", hundreds of links will be displayed.

Because this recipe created a material based on slate tiles, you can use the image search engines to either give you reference or provide information as to pattern or style of laid slate tile roofs for your own interpretation of a slate roof:

- ► `http://www.google.com/images`
- ► `http://www.inspectapedia.com/roof/slatephotolib.htm`
- ► `http://www.fotosearch.com/photos-images/slate-roof.html`

Remember that these images are probably copyrighted. So don't use them directly in your work unless you have permission. If possible look for Creative Commons license photos.

To find out more about slate roof construction visit:

- ► `http://www.slateroofcentral.com/thinkingabout.html`
- ► `http://www.wikipedia.org/wiki/Roof`

As an individual exercise, see if you can create some more patterns to represent other slate roof types. Use these images below as a guide.

See also

In Chapter 3:

- ► *A barber pole with no moving parts*

Creating metals

Of all material surfaces, metals must be one of the most popular to appear in 3D design projects. Metals tend to be visually pleasing with brightly colored surfaces that will gleam when polished. They also exhibit fascinating surface detail due to oxidization and age-related weathering. Being malleable, these surfaces will dent and scratch to display their human interaction. All these issues mean that man-made metal objects are great objects to design outstanding material and texture surfaces within Blender.

It is possible in Blender to design metal surfaces using quite simple material setups. Although it may seem logical to create complex node-based solutions to capture all the complexity apparent within a metal surface, the standard Blender material arrangement can achieve all that is necessary to represent almost any metal.

Metals have their own set of unique criteria that need application within a material simulation. These include:

▸ Wide specularity due to the nature of metals being polished or dulled by interaction

▸ Unique bump maps, either representing the construction, and/ or as a result of interaction

▸ Reflection – metals, more than many other surfaces, can display reflection. Normally, this can be simulated by careful use of the specular settings in simulation but, occasionally, we will need to have other objects and environments reflected in a metal surface.

Blender has a vast array of tools to help you simulate almost any metal surface. Some of these mimic real world metal tooling effects like anisotropic blend types to simulate brushed metal surfaces, or blurred reflections sometimes seen on sandblasted metal surfaces. All these techniques, while producing realistic metal effects, tend to be very render intensive. We will work with some of the simpler tools in Blender to not only produce realistic results but also conserve memory usage and render times.

We will start with a simple but pleasing copper surface. Copper has the unique ability to be used in everything from building materials, through cooking, to money. Keeping up with a building theme, we will create a copper turret material of the type of large copper usage that might be seen on anything from a fairy castle to a modern day embellishment of a corporate building.

One of the pleasant features of such a large structural use of copper is its surface color. A brown/orange predominant color, when new, is changed to a complementary color, light green/blue, when oxidized. This oxidization also varies the specularity of its surface and in combination with its man-made construction, using plating, creates a very pleasing material.

Getting ready

To prepare for this recipe, you will need to create a simple mesh to represent a copper-plated turret-like roof. You can be as extravagant as you wish in designing an interesting shape. Give the mesh a few curves, and variations in scale, so that you can see how the textures deform to the shape. The overall scale of this should be about 2.5 times larger than the default cube and about 1.5 times in width at its widest point.

If you would prefer to use the same mesh as used in the recipe, you can download it as a pre-created blendfile from the Packtpub website.

If you create a turret-like object yourself, ensure that all the normals are facing outwards. You can do this by selecting all of the vertices in edit mode, and then clicking **Normals/ Recalculate** in the **Tools Shelf**. Also, set the surface shading to **Smooth** in the same menu.

Depending on how many vertices you use to create your mesh, you may want to add a **Sub-surface modifier** to ensure that the model renders to give a nice smooth surface on which we will create the copper-plating material simulation.

In the scene used in the example blendfile, three lights have been used.

A **Sun** type lamp at location **X** 7.321, **Y** 1.409, **Z** 11.352 with a color of white and **Energy** of 1.00. However, it should only be set to provide **specular** lighting. It is positioned to create a nice specular reflection of the curved part of the turret.

A **Point** lamp type set at **X** 9.286, **Y** -3.631, **Z** 5.904 with a color of white and **Energy** of 1.00.

A **Hemi** type lamp at location **X** -9.208, **Y** 6.059, **Z** 5.904 with a color of **R** 1.00, **B** 0.97, **B** 0.66 and an **Energy** of 1.00.

These will help simulate daylight and a nice specular reflection as you might see on a bright day.

Now would be a good time to save your work. If you have downloaded the pre-created blendfile, or produced one yourself, save it with an incremented filename as `copper-turret-01.blend`.

It will also be necessary for you to download, three images that will provide a color map, a bump map, and a specular map for the plated surface of our turret. They are simple grayscale images that are relatively easily created in a paint package. Essentially, one image is a tiled collection of metal plates with some surface detail, and the other is derived from this image by creating a higher contrast image from the first. This will be used as a specularity map. The third has the same outline as each tile edge but with simple blends from black to white. This will provide a bump map to give the general slope of each metal plate. All three, separate, are available for download from Packtpub website as:

- ▸ `Chapt-02/textures/plating.png`
- ▸ `Chapt-02/textures/plating-bump-1.png`
- ▸ `Chapt-02/textures/plating-spec-pos.png`

Once downloaded, save these files into a textures subdirectory below where you have saved the blendfile.

How to do it...

We are going to create the effect of plating on the turret object, tiling an image around its surface to make it look as though it has been fashioned by master copper smiths decades ago.

1. Open the `copper-turret-01.blend`. This file currently has no materials or textures associated with it. With your turret mesh selected, create a new material in the **Materials** panel. Name your new material `copper-roof`.

2. Change the **Diffuse** color to **R** `1.00`, **G** `0.50`, **B** `0.21`. You can use the default diffuse shading type as **Lambert**.

3. Set the **Specular** color to **R** `1.00`, **G** `0.93`, **B** `0.78` and the type to **Wardiso** with **Intensity** `0.534`, and **Slope** `0.300`.

That's the general color set for our material, we now need to create some textures to add the magic.

4. Move over to the **Texture** panel and select the first texture slot. Create a new texture of type **Image or Movie**, and name it `color-map`.

5. From the **Image** tab, **Open** the image `plating.png` that should be in the textures subfolder where you saved the blendfile.

This is a grayscale image composed from a number of photographs with grime maps applied within a paint package. Each plate has been scaled and repositioned to produce a random-looking, but tileable texture. Creating such textures is not a quick process. However, the time spent in producing a good image will make your materials look so much better.

6. Under the **Mapping** tab, select **Coordinates** of type **Generated Projection** and of type **Tube**.

7. Under **Image Mapping**, select **Extension/ Repeat**, and set the **Repeat** values of **X** 3 and **Y** 2.

8. This will repeat the texture three times around the circumference of the turret and two times on its height.

9. In the **Influence** tab, select **Diffuse/Color** and set to `0.500`. Also, set **Geometry/ Normal** to `5.00`. Finally, select **Blend** type **Multiply**, **RGB to Intensity**, and set the color to a nice bright orange with **R** `0.94`, **G** `0.56`, and **B** `0.00`.

Save your work as `copper-turret-02.blend`, and perform a test render. If necessary, you can perform a partial render of just one area of your camera view by using the _SHIFT+B_ shortcut and dragging the border around just an area of the camera view. An orange-dashed border will show what area of the image will be rendered. If you also set the **Crop** selector in the **Render** panel under **Dimensions**, it will only render that bordered area and not the black un-rendered portion.

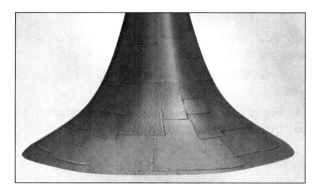

You should see that both the color and bump have produced a subtle change in appearance of the copper turret simulation. However, the bump map is all rather even with each plate looking as though they are all the same thickness rather than one laid on top of another. Time to employ another bump map to create that overlapped look.

10. With the turret object selected, move to the **Texture** panel and in the next free texture slot, create a new texture of type **Image or Movie**, and name it `plate-bumps`.

11. In the **Image** tab, open the image `plating-bump-1.png`.

12. Under the **Image Mapping** tab, select **Extension** of type **Repeat** and set the **Repeat** to **X** 3, **Y** 2.

13. In the **Mapping** tab, ensure the **Coordinates** are set to **Generated** and the **Projection** to **Tube**.

14. Finally, under the **Influence** tab, only have the **Geometry/Normal** set with a value of `10.000`.

Save your work, naming the file `copper-turret-03.blend`, and perform another test render. Renders of this model will be quite quick, so don't be afraid to regularly render to examine your progress.

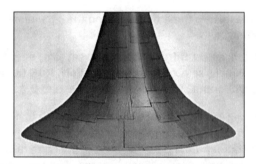

Your work should have a more pleasing sloped tiled copper look. However, the surface is still a little dull. Let us add some weather beaten damage to help bind the images tiled on the surface to the structure below.

15. With the turret object selected, choose the next free texture slot in the **Texture** panel. Create a new texture of **Type Clouds** and name it `beaten-bumps`.

16. In the **Clouds** tab, set **Grayscale** and **Noise/Hard**, and set the **Basis** to **Blender Original** with **Size** 0.11, and **Depth** 6.

17. Under the **Mapping** tab, set the **Coordinates** to **Generated**, and **Projection** to **Tube**. Below projection, change the **X,Y,Z** to Z, Y, X.

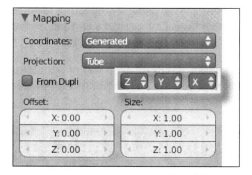

18. Finally, under the **Influence** tab only, select **Geometry/Normal** and set to -0.200.

Save your work again, incrementing the filename to `copper-turret-04.blend`. A test render at this point will not produce an enormous difference from the previous render but the effect is there. If you examine each stage render of the recipe so far you will see the subtle but important changes the textures have made.

How it works...

Creating metal surfaces, in 3D packages like Blender, will almost always require a photographic image to map the man-made nature of the material. Images can add color, bump, or normal maps, as well as specular variety to show these man-made structures. Because metals can have so much variety in their surface appearance, more than one map will be required. In our example, we used three images that were created in a paint package. They have been designed to give a tileable texture so that the effect can be repeated across the surface without producing discernible repeats.

Producing such images can be time consuming but producing a good image map will make your materials much more believable. Occasionally, it will be possible to combine color, bump, and specularity maps into a single image but try to avoid this as it will undoubtedly lead to unnatural-looking metals.

Sometimes, the simplest of bump maps can make all the difference to a material. In the middle image shown previously, we see a series of simple blends marking the high and low points of overlapping copper plates. It's working in a very similar way to the recipe on slate roof tiles earlier in this chapter. However, it is also being used in conjunction with the plating image that supplies the color and just a little bump.

We have also supplied a third bump map using a procedural texture, **Clouds**. Procedurals have the effect of creating random variation across a surface, so here it is used to help tie together and break any repeats formed by the tiled images.

Using multiple bump maps is an extremely efficient way of adding subtle detail to any material and here, you can almost see the builders of this turret leaning against it to hammer down the rivets.

Using specular maps to add age and variety to man-made surface materials

To help add that copper shine seen in newly installed copper roofing, we will add a specular map to increase the specular reflection but varying it to simulate what happens to copper when exposed to air for only a few days.

Getting ready

If you completed the previous recipe, load the `copper-turret-04.blend` saved earlier. Alternatively, you can download a pre-created blendfile from the Packtpub website.

How to do it...

We will now add a specular map to our copper material simulation. So, **Open** the `copper-turret-04.blend`, and select the turret object.

1. From the **Texture** panel, select the next free texture slot. Create a new texture of type **Image or Movie** and give it the name `specular-bump`.

2. In the **Image** tab, **Open** the file `plating-spec-pos.png`.

3. Under the **Image Mapping** tab, select **Extension** of type **Repeat** and set the **Repeat** to **X** 3, **Y** 2.

4. In the **Mapping** tab, ensure the **Coordinates** are set to **Generated** and the **Projection** to **Tube**.

5. Finally, under the **Influence** tab, only select **Specular/Intensity** and set to 1.000, and **Hardness** and set to 0.500.

Save your work once again, incrementing the filename to `copper-turret-05.blend`. Render a full-size image to see what our nearly new copper turret roof looks like.

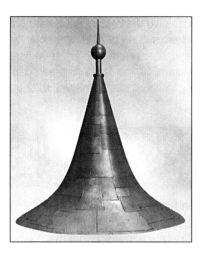

How it works...

When you are using images and procedurals, without UV mapping, you need to map them onto the surface of your mesh using one of the projection methods. Choosing which one can sometimes be tricky but a good rule of thumb is to look at your mesh and consider it as a simplified shape. So, in our case, the turret is not a cube or sphere, and it's certainly not flat. So, the nearest to its shape would be a tube.

Of course, you will inevitably get some distortion if your mesh is complex but providing it appears to work, it should be OK. In our case, the top of the mesh is narrower than the base so the tube projection will get smaller further up the model. However, that doesn't really matter as the plating would need to be smaller on these tricky to plate areas anyway.

We have also used an image to control both the intensity and hardness of the specular shine of the surface. Image maps are ideal for this purpose and can add an enormous amount of detail when light catches these changes in the specular effect provided by a simple grayscale image. It can be particularly effective if the light source or object move in an animation.

There's more...

The `plating-spec-pos.png` image is a positive higher contrast copy of the `plating.png` file. Just by playing with the levels command within your paint program, you should be able to extract portions of your image that could be used as a specular mask. The reason why I called this positive was because at the time I wasn't sure if I needed a positive or negative version of the image to create the specular variation I wanted. It was easier therefore to create two images by simply inverting one and saving it with another name. In the end, I didn't need the negative image but wanted to raise the issue here as it's very easy to produce positive or negative images for use as specular or bump maps in any paint package.

It is also possible to place lights to give interesting specular highlight to help frame the object. You can actually turn off the **Diffuse** setting of such a special light so that it will not light the whole of the object but just its specular areas. You are then free to move that light to give the best specular reflection. In this example, the lights suggested in the earlier recipe *Creating metals*, were positioned to give good specular highlights to show the variation across the plated copper surface.

Adding oxidization weathering to our copper material

Copper doesn't stay that pristine for very long. Oxidization will soon turn its surface green. Often, this will happen in varying amounts across the surface because of material differences between plates and because of damage to any protective coating, as well as natural variations in weathering. All these things can help add artistic interest to a copper material, so let's see how to add some copper weathering to our material simulation.

Getting ready

Reload the `copper-turret-05.blend` created at the end of the previous recipe or download a pre-created file from the Packtpub website.

How to do it...

We can start by applying a green color that blends with the copper color to give more oxidization on the top half of the turret. We can use the Blender procedural texture **Blend** to achieve this.

1. With the turret object selected, and the **Texture** panel active, select the next free texture slot and create a new texture of type **Blend**. You should name this `Blend`.

2. In the **Blend** tab, make the **Progression Linear**, and the direction **Horizontal**.

3. Under the **Mapping** tab, select **Coordinates Generated**, and **Projection Flat**. Just below this, set the **X,Y, Z** settings to `Z, None, None`.

4. Under the Influence tab, set **Diffuse/Color** to `1.00` and set the **Blend** type to **Mix**, and set **RGB to Intensity** with a color setting of **R** `0.51`, **G** `0.73`, and **B** `0.38`.

Always save your work after each stage of these recipes, incrementing the filename at each save. If you render at this stage, you will see a gradual change of color from our copper orange at the base of the turret through to a dull green at the top. However, metal weathering is never this even. Let us add another texture to produce some random variation to the green oxidization.

5. With the turret selected, move to the **Texture** panel and select the next free slot. Create a new texture of type **Image or Movie** and name it oxidization.

6. In the **Image** tab, **Open** the image plating-spec-pos.png.

7. In the **Mapping** tab, ensure the **Coordinates** are set to **Generated** and the **Projection** to **Tube**.

8. Under the **Image Mapping** tab, select **Extension** of type **Repeat** and set the **Repeat** to **X** 3, **Y** 2.

9. In the **Influence** tab, select **Diffuse/Color** with a value of 1.000. Set the **Blend** type to **Mix**, check **Negative** and **Stencil**, as well as **RGB to Intensity** with a color of **R** 0.51, **G** 0.73, **B** 0.38.

Save your work, once again incrementing the filename to copper-turret-06.blend, and perform a test render of the full height of the turret. You should see that the green oxidization varies across the surface giving a quite realistic oxidized copper turret.

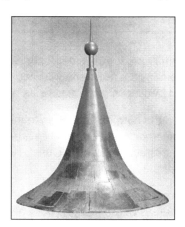

How it works...

In this recipe, we changed the mapping of the blend texture by remapping its coordinates to other axes and also to remove it from certain axes. We are able to remap any texture, image, or procedural onto other co-ordinates by employing the **Mapping** tab coordinate controllers. This is useful if you want a texture to appear on the sides of a model rather than the top. Of course, we can also set **Cube** mapping that will essentially copy the same image to each face of a theoretical cube. But, what if we would prefer to map the flat image to one side, rather than all round, or just the top? We can use the three controllers in the **Mapping** tab to remap the **X Y Z** coordinates to other surfaces. The following image illustrates what is required to map to the top (**Z** direction), the left side (**X** direction), or the right side (**Y** direction). Apart from remapping to other axes, we are also able to turn off any of the axes projections by selecting **None**. You may have to alter more than one of the remap co-ordinates to ensure the texture is not reversed.

Normal mapping X,Y,Z   Re-mapped Y,Z,X   Re-mapped X,Z,Y

The blend procedural is not a flat texture. It exists metaphorically in 3D space, so if it's applied to a cube that you are viewing from inside, the blend will occur across the entire internal space of that cube. Its direction, however, is controlled by its blend and mapping settings.

What we have done here is remap the normal X direction to the Z axis, which is basically up and down. We have turned off the other directions as they are not needed. That means we can employ the blend texture in all directions, which is useful in our example as we wished to add the oxidization from the top of the turret.

We also employed the specular map a second time. Here, it is used to paint the green oxidization onto only those black areas of the image. These are the parts that produce the least specular highlight as specified in the earlier specular-bump texture. The previous blend texture acts as a mask because of its stencil setting, which means that the green oxidization merges with the blend green, producing a more random distribution of the oxidization effect.

We have also applied the **stencil** for this repeated image texture so that both it and the blend will mask the following texture. Masks are always valuable and you don't need a node material to produce quick dramatic results. Here, it will be used to vary a following dirt type texture in the following recipe.

Adding grime and artistic interest to our copper material

The cooper turret created in the previous recipes may be accurate in terms of color, and aging of real copper, but sometimes it's useful to go beyond reality and add other textures to dirty a material simulation just because it looks better. We can do this with our simulation by adding two further textures.

Getting ready

This recipe uses the blendfile saved at the end of the last recipe. If you have not completed that recipe, you can download the following file from the Packtpub website: `cooper-turret-06.blend`.

How to do it...

We will begin by adding a repeated texture to mix a lighter green color to the areas of the turret not masked by the blend but controlled by the specularity image map.

1. With the turret object selected and from the **Texture** panel, select the next free texture slot and create a new texture of type **Clouds**. Name the texture `dirt-streaks`.

2. In the **Clouds** tab, select **Grayscale**, and **Noise/Soft**. Select **Basis** type **Blender Original** with **Size** `0.15` and **Depth** `6`.

3. Under **Mapping**, select **Coordinates** type **Generated** and **Projection** type **Tube**. Change the **Size Z** value to `0.50`.

4. Under **Influence**, set **Diffuse/Color** with a value of `1.000`. Set the **Blend** type to **Multiply** and the color selector to **R** `0.96`, **G** `1.00`, **B** `0.96`.

Save your work one last time as `cooper-turret-07.blend` and perform a render.

A copper turret material that can be applied to any shape tower you desire.

How it works...

The final `dirt-streaks`, is a simple **Clouds** texture with its **Z** size reset to `0.50`. This will essentially stretch the texture in the up and down direction to imitate dirt washed by rain, etc. It will also only form on those areas of the material not masked by the stencil command of previous textures. So, here it is masked by both the specular-bump, and blend textures to some degree or other. The result is random dirt that appears to collect mostly on those areas affected by oxidization.

Simple use of the stencil command can produce some quite dramatic results.

Creating a path or road material that never repeats

Creating a path or road material presents some really challenging issues for the material designer. We could just create an image and map it to the whole road surface. However, the image would need to be of sufficient size so that it would view correctly in either close-up or far away. Think of the yellow brick road with Dorothy, the Scarecrow, Lion, and Tinman seen at close shot dancing away along the road into the distance. Rather than have some enormous image applied to the whole road, is there some way we can create a repeating texture that appears not to repeat?

Another issue with applying an image to a path or road surface is that it will rarely be flat and straight. So, how do we make it curve and dip and rise as an interesting path might do in reality?

You may be asking why not just unwrap a curved road as a UV texture? Well, although theoretically possible, the mapping would be very distorted and would require a tremendous amount of work in a paint package to appear correct.

Fortunately, Blender has several tools that allow us to achieve a satisfactory path, or road, that can be twisted and undulated onto almost any landscape.

The recipe requires an image to map onto this mesh representing a cobbled path. You are encouraged to take your own photographs, of a suitable path, applying simple corrections to remove perspective distortions and create a tileable texture that can be repeated to represent a long path. Unfortunately, a description of how to do so in your paint package is beyond the scope of this book. However, all images used in this recipe are available for download so that you can experience the power of Blender's image-mapping capabilities.

Repeating a tiled texture to duplicated objects

You will have seen in previous recipes how tileable textures can be repeated within a Blender material. It is also possible to create a material that will appear to tile when the object is duplicated using one of the many Blender mesh duplication modifiers. Here, we will use it to extend the path to any length we require.

Getting ready

The following recipes use a simple mesh object representing a rectangular portion of our path. You will note that it is subdivided in its length by sixteen and by eight in its width. You may also note that it has a small thickness but no end faces.

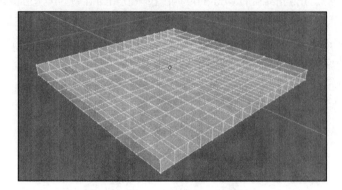

As this is a complex Blender model, I do not expect you to create it from scratch. You can, therefore, download a start blendfile with the mesh, and a special curve object, already created for all of the following recipes from the Packtpub website: `/Chapt-02/pathway-00.blend`.

You should also download the two image file used for the recipes in this section:

`Chapt-02/textures/path-color.png`

`Chapt-02/textures/path-bump-blur.png`

Save the blendfile to a suitable location on your hard drive and save the image files to a textures sub-directory below it. It is good practice to open the blendfile and immediately resave it as `pathway-01.blend`. In this way, you can always repeat the recipe from the start in the future.

How to do it

We will first apply an image texture to represent the cobbled path section. Ensure that you have opened the `pathway-01.blend` as saved in the getting started section.

1. With this mesh object selected, create a new material in the **Materials** panel and name it `path`.

2. Leave the default **Diffuse** color but change the **Specular** type to **Wardiso** with an **Intensity** of `0.000` and a **Slope** of `0.000`.

3. Switch to the **Texture** panel and in the first slot, create a new texture of type **Image or Movie** and name it `bump`.

4. In the **Image** tab, **Open** `path-bump-blur.png` saved earlier.

5. Under the **Influence** tab, only select **Geometry/Normal** and set to `-10.000`.

While we are here, look in the **Image Sampling** tab and see where the **Flip X/Y Axis** checkbox is. We might have to select this if we are creating such a project from scratch, depending on how you build the mesh. You don't have to worry with the downloaded blendfile but it is worthwhile if you need to quickly switch direction of an applied image.

1. In the next free texture slot, create a new texture of type **Image or Movie** and name it `color`.

2. In the **Image** tab, **Open** `path-color.png` saved earlier in the textures sub directory.

3. Under the **Influence** tab, select **Diffuse/Color** and set to `1.000` and under the **Blend** type, select **Multiply**.

Save your work as `pathway-02.blend` and perform a quick render.

Not bad, although, it's currently a very short path. We could at this point stretch the mesh in the direction of the path we want and use the repeat command in the texture to have it successfully fill a longer path. However, there is another and more versatile way of achieving this, particularly when we want our path to deform around objects, up, down, over hills, and dales.

1. With the path object selected, move to the **Modifiers** panel and **Add Modifier** of type **Array**.

2. Ensure the **Fit Type** is set to **Fixed Count** with **Relative Offset** of **X** `1.00`. Also, check the **Merge** checkbox, which will ensure you don't get nasty creases where each array item meets. Increase the **Count** value to about `5`.

3. Move the camera out to show all the arrayed repeats for the test render.

A quick render should show the path to be longer and the tiled textures exactly matching using the tileable texture.

There is just a little repeat in the textures caused by some level variation across the image's surface. We can hide that by employing another texture.

1. With the path object selected, switch to the **Texture** tab and select the next free texture slot. Create a new texture of type **Clouds** and name it mask.

2. Under the **Clouds** tab, select **Grayscale** and **Soft**, with a **Size** of 1.50, and a **Depth** of 3.

3. In the **Colors** tab, set the **Adjust/Brightness** to 1.200, and the **Contrast** to 2.000.

4. Under the **Mapping** tab, change the **Size X** 0.80, **Y** 2.00, and **Z** to 1.00.

5. In the **Influence** tab, ensure that only **RGB to Intensity** and **Stencil** are checked.

6. In the next free texture slot, create another texture of type **Clouds** and name it darkening.

7. Under the **Clouds** tab, select **Greyscale** and **Hard**, with a **Size** of 2.00 and a **Depth** of 4.

8. In the **Colors** tab, set the **Adjust/Brightness** to 1.400 and the **Contrast** to 1.200.

9. Under the **Mapping** tab, set the **Coordinates** to type **Global** and change the **Size** values to **X** 0.30, **Y** 2.10, and **Z** 0.30.

10. Finally, in the **Influence** tab, set the **Diffuse/Color** with a value of 0.585, and the **Specular/Hardness** to 2.000. Set the **Blend** type to **Multiply** and check **RGB to Intensity** with a color value of **R** 0.05, **G** 0.16, and **B** 0.00.

Save your work as pathway-03.blend and perform a test render. You should see that the repeats have been successfully masked with what looks like green moss or mold on the surface of the path.

How it works

The array modifier is a good way of repeating both a model and also tileable textures with such a project. Here, we had a very simple mesh but there is nothing to stop us creating a cambered road with an edge path arrayed into the distance. Such techniques are very efficient at memory usage.

Nothing beats a good tileable texture to fool the eye that it is seeing random patterns. Using a good paint package like GIMP to create these images will save you a lot of time in Blender. Here, our images are used to supply both the color and bump on our model. So, when we created the material we did not need to worry about its color. The image `path-color.png` was multiplied on top of the standard white of the default color producing the exact color of the image. You could also use **Mix**, which gives virtually identical results.

Deforming materials and textures in Blender

When using the standard, plane, cube, or sphere texture-mapping projections in Blender, you may feel you are limited to simple objects that approximate those shapes. However, you will frequently need to map a texture to complex twisting and turning shapes like a path, or road. Fortunately, Blender has some nice distortion facilities that will not only accurately curve or twist your object, but also do the same thing to the texture and material.

The previous recipes in this section have produced just a straight path, with no turns or meandering level changes. In reality, you would not find a real path to be this uniform.

Getting ready

Open the file saved at the end of the last recipe, or download a pre-created blendfile from the Packtpub website: `Chapt-02/pathway-03.blend`.

How to do it

Open the `pathway-03.blend`. This already contains a wild curve that is connected like a Möbius strip. We will use this to curve our arrayed path segment around its curving perimeter.

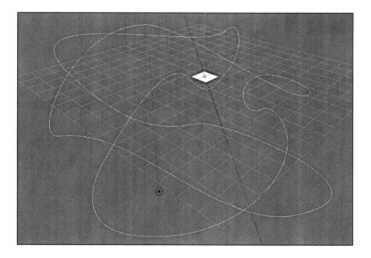

1. Select your path object and from the **Modifiers** panel, **Add Modifier** of type **Curve**. Two settings are required to get the arrayed path to follow the curve. First, we need to select the **Object** curve name from the list. There should only be one and its name should be **Curve**.

2. Finally, we need to set the **Deformation Axis**. In the blendfile supplied, it will be **X**. However, it may be different if you are creating your own curve or path object.

The path mesh should now follow the curve exactly. If you increase the count of the **Array Modifier**, it should be possible to create a never ending path that deforms both its shape and importantly the materials applied to it.

How it works...

One of the great attributes of the **Curve** modifier is that it not only deforms the mesh to match the curve, it also does the same with the materials and textures. It is important that the mesh has a few real subdivisions in it, otherwise, it will find it difficult to curve tight bends. Indeed, if any of the curve bends are too sharp, there will be some distortion. However, creative editing should avoid that problem.

There's more...

The photos used in this chapter were taken by me using an 8 megapixels Canon ED350D camera. This camera, although not expensive, produces exceptional quality pictures. However, you do not need a professional or expensive camera to take photos for use in textures. Even inexpensive mobile phones have remarkable cameras as standard these days. In fact, I have used images taken by my 1 megapixel old phone in several Blender creations. So, do not be afraid to take your own photos

See also

Chapter 3

▸ *Creating a burning sheet of paper*

This recipe uses a curve modifier to curl a sheet of paper as it apparently burns.

3
Creating Animated Materials

In this chapter, we will cover:

- ▶ How to move textures and create animation without moving a mesh
  - ❑ Using co-ordinates to move a texture over time
  - ❑ Manipulating the F-Curves of texture movement
  - ❑ Using an Empty as a dummy object to control texture movement over time
  - ❑ Creating barber pole with no moving parts

- ▶ How to alter the color of materials and textures over time
  - ❑ Creating a red hot iron bar
  - ❑ Changing the multiple settings within a color ramp over time

- ▶ How to animate transparency in a texture
  - ❑ A burning sheet of paper

- ▶ How to change textures during an animation
  - ❑ Creating a Red Alert sign using a sequence of images

- ▶ How to texture with movies
  - ❑ Creating a working TV material

Introduction

Blender is predominately a 3D animation suite. It contains some of the easiest to use animation tools available. These in turn enable the 3D artist to produce accurate movement in their mesh objects via a consummate set of armatures. The movements can be choreographed in action sheets just like the master animators have used for years in traditional animation.

However, we are not limited by only being able to manipulate mesh models in an animation. Blender offers some unique facilities to manipulate textures and materials over time. In fact, we will see that it is possible to animate a whole series of material properties that can produce apparent movement with none of the overheads of complex model manipulation. Combine these with the other mesh deformation tools and you will be able to produce some stunning animations.

You may wonder why we need to worry about changing textures when applied to an expertly animated model. Well, take a look at the back of one of your hands. You will see a variety of colors and bumps and surface specularity, all of which could be created in a decent paint package.

Still looking at the back of your hand, form it into a fist and examine the changed color of your knuckles, the bump on the back of your hand as the skin is stretched across the surface, and lastly, the change in specularity that happened when you performed that simple movement over time.

Walls become darker when the rain falls on them. TV screens get brighter when they are turned on. A chromed wing mirror on a car that is moving will have a moving reflection across its surface. All these things are natural and expected on surfaces that we see move or are expressing a passage of time. Adding this level of detail could help transform a good texture into an exceptional material simulation.

The types of texture and material animation tools in Blender

From version 2.5 of Blender, just about any of the material and texture settings can be animated over time. In order to appreciate their use, we need to consider the types of change that a material might make during an animated scene. Basically, we need to consider:

- Movement of a texture over time. This should enable us to alter the position of a texture applied to a material in each of the three axes, X, Y, Z.
- An attribute change over time, such as color, bump, or specularity. This should also enable us to change brightness and contrast, and any level associated with these type settings.

- ▸ Alpha value of a texture over time. Making it possible to animate transparency that can move across a mesh surface.

- ▸ Applying a sequence of images or even movies onto a surface over time.

- ▸ More exotic changes to things like the distribution of color across a texture or the normal direction as applied to a texture.

Understanding how to achieve these material and texture animation tasks will make you a much more accomplished 3D designer. You will see how each of the areas mentioned can be used in numerous ways to produce better material simulations. You will also see how exciting it can be to take a still high quality render and add the extra touch of movement to bring it alive.

How to move textures and create animation without moving a mesh

In the following recipes, we will see how a texture can be moved over time. We will examine the various methods to achieve this movement and then apply it to a real world example where the only thing that moves will be a texture.

Getting ready

For the first series of recipes, you will require the default scene with a cube mesh in the center. To this, add a plane mesh below the cube as though the cube is resting on its surface. Create a default material for this plane but set its **Shadow** settings to **Receive**, and **Receive Transparent**. This will ensure that some nice shadows will be cast as we work our way through the following recipes. Finally, move to the render panel and set the render dimension to 640 width and 360 height. We will be rendering several short animations and this smaller size will be more than adequate to observe the effect without extended render times.

Instructions within the text will indicate when it's necessary to add additional default mesh shapes such as a sphere, cone, etc. You are encouraged to alter the lighting to illuminate the scene to your own tastes. However, the default lighting as suggested in *Chapter 4, Managing Blender Materials* is perfectly adequate to demonstrate the versatility of texture movement animation.

Before starting any project, it's always a good idea to save your initial setup to a name-specific numbered blendfile. In this way, you ensure that you always have a start position to redo the exercise without the need to reset all over again. So, for this recipe, save your file as:

```
animated-materials-01.blend
```

How to do it...

1. With the cube mesh selected, move to the **Materials** panel and create a new material and name it `ani-mat-01`. Keep all the default settings for the moment.

2. Move to the **Texture** panel and create a new texture of type **Clouds** and name it `clouds`.

3. Under the **Clouds** tab, set **Grayscale** and **Noise/Soft**. Set the **Basis** as **Blender Original**, with **Size** `0.50` and **Depth** `3`.

4. In the **Mapping** tab, set **Coordinates/Generated** and **Projection/Flat**, with the default projection `X, Y, Z`.

5. Under the **Influence** tab, set **Diffuse/Color** and set to `1.000`. Set the **Blend** type to **Multiply** and change the color selector to white **R** `1.00`, **G** `1.00`, and **B** `1.00`.

Save your file as:

`animated-materials-02.blend`

and perform a test render.

As you can see from the screenshot above, the **Clouds** procedural texture has applied itself on all side of the cube. Each face looks much the same as the other but we have only projected this texture flat. The unique thing about Blender procedurals is that they exist in a virtual 3D state. Because they are mathematically generated and we have mapped them to `X`, `Y`, and `Z` axes, Blender will generate the texture at every pixel point of the surface of the object it's mapped to.

The best way to see this is by animating some movement into the texture. Before we do this, we should set up the start frame and the duration of our little animation.

6. In the **Timeline** editor, set the **Start Frame** to `1`, if it's not already set, and then set the **End Frame** to `100`. This will give a four-second animation that is perfectly adequate to see how the textures can be animated. Ensure you are on frame `1`.

In the **Render** panel, are all the other settings for **Dimension, Anti-Aliasing**, and **Output** format? You will find it better to render animations to PNG images and assemble them either in the Blender Sequencer or in an external creator like Quicktime. However, the Blender player is quite capable of playing any Blender rendered animation, even numbered still images like PNG files.

7. With the cube object selected, move over to the **Texture** panel and down to the **Mapping** tab. All of the **Offset** values for **X, Y, Z** should be 0.00 and the color of these settings, background should be light gray. Move your cursor to the **Z** value **Offset** box and *right click*. A menu will appear, *click* the first item on the displayed list **Insert Keyframes**.

The background color will change to a light yellow to show that a keyframe has been set for this setting and frame. If you examine the **Timeline** editor, you will see a vertical yellow line that also shows this is a keyframe. The current location of the viewing frame is indicated by a vertical green line:

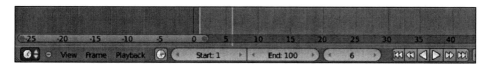

8. Move to the last frame, 100 and back in the **Texture** panel, alter the **Offset Z** value to -1.00. *Right click* this as in step 2 and select **Insert Keyframe**.

If you drag the cursor in the **Timeline** editor, you will see that the value in the **Offset Z** setting will vary as you drag between frames. You may also note that the background color in the **Offset** setting changes to light green when you're not over a keyframe. This shows you that these values have keyframes set within the Timeline. OK, save your work, incrementing the number to:

```
animated-materials-03.blend
```

Rather than render another still image, it's time to produce an animation. So, in the **Render** panel, click the **Animation** button. Rendering an animation will take a few minutes, however, at this size, 640x360, it shouldn't take too long. Perhaps, it's a good opportunity to stretch your legs or have a drink.

Once all the frames have rendered, click the play button in the **Render** panel to view your animation.

At the time of writing, the Blender Player was not enabled. However, by the time you read this, the developers should have completed the coding to enable this important feature.

The movement of the clouds texture appears to travel down each side of the cube and through its top surface. The apparent movement of the clouds starts slowly, builds to a speed, and then slows at the end.

How it works...

Setting keyframes is a fundamental task within Blender. If we were animating a cartoon character, we would need to create keyframes at any of the key points of action. It is just the same with movement of a texture applied to a mesh in a Blender material.

In our case, we have specified that on frame 1 the texture should start to move down the Z axis and continue doing so until coming to a stop 1 Blender unit down from its starting position on frame 100. Blender creates all the in-between movement based on those key positions. We therefore have a smooth transition from no movement in keyframe 1, building up to speed then slowing before stopping completely on key frame 100.

It is possible to apply keyframes to almost any of the settings within the material and texture panels. The most obvious are movement and size settings. We are not limited to single settings either. It's possible to have many keyframes across an animation with Blender smoothly inserting any necessary in-between actions as necessary.

However, it would be advantageous if we could control the smoothness of any of these animated material transitions. This can be achieved using the **F-Curve** editor.

Manipulating the F-Curves of texture movement

Finer control over the speed of transition from one keyframe to another is a useful tool to have at one's disposal. Blender has its own editor that treats these transitions as a fully editable curve.

How to do it...

Manipulating curves to control the overall speed of an action, or control variations in speed across time is easy in the **F-Curve** editor.

1. Open the following files, which you created earlier.

    ```
    animated-materials-02.blend
    ```

2. This will ensure we start with all the materials set up but no keyframes set yet. Make sure you are on frame 1 in the **Timeline**.

3. With the `Cube` object selected, move to the **Texture** panel and down to the **Mapping** tab.

4. Right click on the **Offset Z** setting and in the displayed list, choose **Insert Single Keyframe**.

5. Move to the last frame 100 and change the **Offset Z** setting to -1.00 and *right click* to set another single keyframe.

> Setting a single keyframe is useful if you need to limit or make individual changes to keyframe settings. It also makes it much easier to see an uncluttered **F-Curve** editor, if that's the only animated change you want.

6. To view the **F-Curve** editor, we need to change the current editor type in one of our Blender windows. So, click the editor type button in the bottom left-hand corner of the window header and choose **F-Curve** editor from the types displayed.

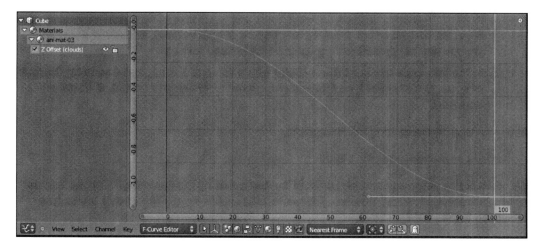

7. If you move the cursor within the **F-Curve** editor window and press the *Home* key, the curve will be expanded to fill the whole window making it easier to see and edit.

The curve looks just like a Blender bezier curve with handles and control points that can be moved to change the slope of the curve. The recipes in this chapter will cover many of the settings that can be changed in this editor but for now, let's look at one of the most useful when associated with procedural texture animation.

8. Make sure all of the control points are selected in the curve. You do this by pressing the *A* key on your keyboard, which will alternatively select all or none of the points. That is exactly the same as when editing mesh vertices.

9. From the **Key** menu in the Header, select **Extrapolation Mode** and choose **Linear Extrapolation** from the sub-menu.

The curve will immediately change to a straight line. This will ensure that the speed of the **Z** axis texture offset is constant. So, it doesn't matter if the animation is 10, 100, or 1000 frames long, the speed will always be constant.

Save your work at this point, naming the filename as:

`animated-materials-04.blend`

10. Move the Cube object over to right of the camera view in the **Y** direction.

11. Ensure your cursor is at the grid center by pressing *SHIFT+S*, for the **Snap** menu, and selecting **Cursor to Center**.

12. Add a new mesh of type **UV Sphere** keeping all the default settings apart from making the surface **Smooth** from the **Tools** panel.

13. Create a new material, naming it `ani-mat-02`, and set its **Diffuse** color as bright green, **R** 0.00, **G** 0.80, **B** 0.00. All the other settings in the material panel can stay as default.

14. From the **Texture** panel, create a new texture of type **Voronoi**, and name it `voronoi`. We can use the default settings of this nice cellular texture.

15. In the **Influence** tab, set **Diffuse/Color** with a value of 1.000, and **Geometry/Normal** of 5.00. Set **Blend** of type **Mix** and change the color selector to **R, G, B** 0.04, a dark gray.

Save your work, incrementing the filename to:

`animated-materials-05.blend`

We could at this stage animate the offset of the texture using the same keyframe method as used in the previous recipe. However, we can instead create a proxy object that the texture offset can follow.

How it works...

The **F-Curve** editor is incredibly useful, allowing us to alter the slope of a curve in multiple ways thus giving extreme control with what happens over time in an animation. Setting the curve type to **Linear Extrapolation** is very desirable with procedural textures. These types of textures never repeat so if we were to reverse the direction or size in an keyframe, it would look as if the texture changes were reversing, which will look very unnatural. It also means that our animation can be any length without affecting the speed of the texture translation.

You will find, when designing an animated texture, that you may not know the true length of the shot that will be used. Adopting straight line curves via **Linear Extrapolation** will always ensure you get the speed right rather than worry about the shot length.

There's more...

You can learn more about the **F-curve** editor in the release log on the Blender Wiki:

```
http://www.blender.org/development/release-logs/blender-250/f-curves-
actions-nla/
```

```
http://www.blender.org/development/release-logs/blender-250/
animation-editors/
```

See also

The **F-Curve** editor is used in other recipes in this chapter, and also chapter 6:

- ▶ Chapter 3, *How to alter the color of materials and textures over time*
- ▶ Chapter 3, *A barber pole with no moving parts*
- ▶ Chapter 3, *Creating a burning sheet of paper*
- ▶ Chapter 6, *Creating large scale water in Blender 2.5*

Using an Empty as a dummy object to control texture movement over time

Controlling movement of textures using individual keyframes within each texture can be time consuming, particularly when you may have several textures that need to move or scale together over time. It is possible to create a proxy object that can be animated, which in turn can control the offset, scale, and even rotation of a texture in a material.

How to do it...

Mapping material and texture settings to an object is easy in Blender especially if you use a non-renderable object like the Empty. An Empty object is one of the primary Blender objects like plane, cube, and sphere. It can be created anywhere in a scene but will never appear when rendered. Its purpose is to act as a proxy object to which renderable objects or textures can be mapped to. It is particularly useful when you want to control texture or material movement because you only have to map the material to the **Empty** and animate that rather than many material settings.

1. Open the blendfile `animated-materials-05.blend` saved at the end of the last recipe.

2. With the cursor still in the center of the grid create an **Empty** object by pressing *SHIFT+A*, for the **Add** menu, and selecting **Empty** from the drop down list.

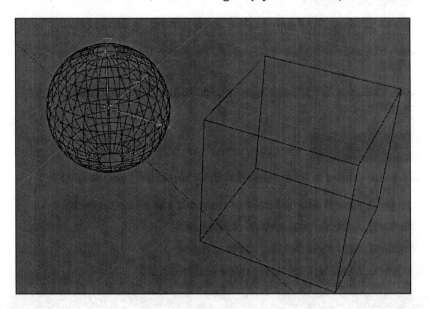

3. Re-select the `Sphere` and from the **Texture** panel **Mapping** tab select **Coordinates** of type **Object** and from the **Objects** list select the `Empty`.

4. Select the `Empty` and switch to the **Object** panel.

5. Under the **Transform** tab are settings for **Location, Rotation,** and **Size**. These should all be zero at this stage.

6. Move to the first frame and in the **Location Z** set to `0.000` and *right click* and **Insert a Single keyframe**.

7. Move to the last frame `100` and set the `Empty`, **Transform, Location Z** to `-1.00` and **Insert Single Keyframe**.

8. In the **F-Curve** editor, change the curve type to **Linear Extrapolation**. That's **Key, Extrapolation Mode**, and **Linear Extrapolation**.

That has produced a straight slope so that the speed of the offset will remain constant throughout the animation. Save your work before rendering the animation, remembering to increment the filename to:

```
animated-materials-06.blend
```

Render an animation and play the result. You should see that the textures on both the cube and sphere appear to be traveling down the objects at the same speed. However, the green voronoi texture is affecting the bump and color of the sphere making it look like green bubbles are flowing out of the sphere. Let's change the direction of the texture in the sphere.

9. With the `Empty` selected, move over to the **F-Curve** editor and select the center handle of the control point on frame `100`. If you press the *N* key, the properties panel will come up on the right of the editor. This will show the position and type of the control point selected.

10. In the **Active Keyframe** tab, alter the **Y** value from `-1.00` to `1.00`. If necessary, change the **Interpolation** type to **Linear** to ensure all handles for that keyframe produce a straight line. If a curve is produced, you may have to set the first keyframe `0` to **Linear** as well.

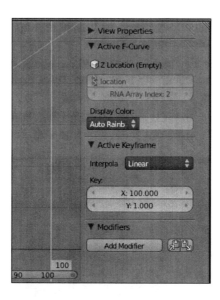

Save your work, incrementing the filename to:

```
animated-materials-07.blend
```

Render out and play another animation. You should see that the direction of the sphere texture goes up as opposed to the cube texture that goes down. Before leaving this recipe, we can show how creating keyframes for that proxy Empty can be made much easier than altering individual settings.

11. Select the `Cube` and in its **Texture** panel, select the **Clouds** texture.

12. In the **F-Curve** editor, select all keyframes by pressing the *A* key and press the *X* key to **Delete Keyframes**.

13. Now, back in the **Texture** panel and **Mapping** tab, select **Coordinates** of type **Object** and select the `Empty` previously created.

Now, both our cube and sphere object textures are controlled by the Empty.

14. Select the `Empty` object and move back to frame 1.

15. With the mouse cursor in the **3D** editor, press the *I* key, which will bring up the **Insert Keyframe** menu, and select **LocRotScale** to set a keyframe for all those settings on frame 1.

16. Move to frame 25 and scale rotate and move the empty to anywhere else within the camera frame. Press the *I* key and select **LocRotScale**.

17. Move to frame 50 and do the same with the Empty, i.e., move, rotate, and scale then press the *I* key to set another **LocRotScale** keyframe.

18. Move to frame 75 and perform the same task of moving, scaling, rotating, and setting another **LocRotScale** keyframe.

19. Finally, move to frame 100 and from the **F-Curve** editor, deselect all control points using the *A* key until no points are highlighted. Then, press the *B* key and draw a box around the control points on frame 1.

20. Copy the control points by pressing *Shift+D* and then immediately press *X* to copy and move along X axis and place them on frame 100. *Left click* to set them.

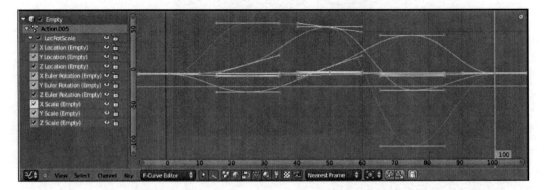

You should have a quite complex set of curves representing the movement, scaling, and rotation of the `Empty` within the scene. The smooth transition of the curves will help here as there are so many changes to the orientation of the Empty.

Save your work again, incrementing the filename to:

```
animated-materials-08.blend
```

Perform a new animation render and play the result. You will see that the textures in both materials swirl about in synchronization.

If you want to, create some other standard mesh shapes like tube and cone, and monkey and attach new materials to each with different procedural textures mapped to that `Empty`. If you render another animation, you should see the power of using a proxy object like the `Empty` to control texture orientation.

How it works...

Proxy objects are incredibly useful in Blender and when applied to textures, it makes it much easier to move them around. Combine with this the added advantage of scaling and rotation and you have a very versatile tool.

One of the greatest advantages is that you can see the `Empty` on the screen whereas you won't be able to see the textures unless you render. Getting an idea of how fast a particular texture should move within an animation becomes easy if you have a reference object visible in the edit screen. You can always perform a screen-based animated view of the 3D windows either by pressing the Play button in the Timeline editor, or by pressing *Alt+A* in any 3D window. The views will continuously animate until you press the stop button in the Timeline editor or press *Alt+A* again in the 3D view. Complex scenes may not display at full frames per second as shown in the top left of the window. You can perform a quick screen animation render by pressing *Ctrl+LMB*, the render button at the bottom of the 3D view to get a quick render from the viewport. You can play that quick screen animation by pressing *Ctrl+F11*. This will accurately show timing projected at the render frame rate.

A barber pole with no moving parts

Time to apply animating motion to textures in a real world example. We are going to produce a barber pole once seen on barber shops throughout the world. These display signs consist of a tubular striped pattern of either red and white, or white, blue, and red, that rotate to attract customers to enter and have a haircut.

Getting ready

As you can see from the above rendered image, I have taken the trouble of creating a quite complex mesh to represent the barber pole. However, it's not necessary for you to create this level of complexity. You can, if you want, just create a tube of similar proportions to that shown. However, you are welcome to add any level of extra detail that will make the result special.

Create the tube at the center of the grid and scale the `Tube` to be about 2 Blender units in diameter and 5.4 units tall. Also, create an `Empty`, also in the center position, and name it `barber-rotation`. Move your lights and camera to obtain a similar view to that above. My final render also set a white world background and also edge lines, which is a post processing effect. However, these just made the illustration appear better on a white sheet of paper.

The barber pole texture will also require a small texture to be created in a paint package.

This is a `256 x 128` pixel image with red, white, and blue lines. A grid was created in my paint package, dividing the image into four horizontally and vertically. As you can see, the middle red line is one division wide and is a diagonal across the width of the image. All other stripes are created to be parallel with each other in the sequence, red, white, blue, white, and then repeated. This image will tile in all directions and is therefore ideal for this recipe.

Save your completed tiled image in the textures directory below where you save your blender files. Save it as:

`barbers-pole.png`

Should you not wish to create this image yourself it is available from the Packtpub website

How to do it...

Animating a tiled textile is a simple and useful technique to learn in Blender.

1. In Blender, select the `Tube` mesh you have created for this exercise and from the **Material** panel, create a new material and name it `barber-pole`. We will keep all the default settings for this material.

2. Switch to the **Texture** panel and the first texture slot. Create a new texture of type **Image or Movie** and name it `barber-pole-tile`.

3. In the **Image** tab, **Open** your saved image `barbers-pole.png`.

4. In the **Image Mapping**, set the **Extension** to type **Repeat**. Now, set the **Repeat** values of **X** 4 and **Y** 1.

5. Under the **Mapping** tab, set the **Coordinates** to type **Object** and select the `Empty` created earlier called `barber-rotation`. Set the **Projection** to **Tube**. You may also find it necessary to change the **Size** values in this mapping tab to **X, Y, Z** `0.50` to make the band thickness look right in your renders. This depends on the size of the mesh tube you created.

6. Under the **Influence** tab, select **Diffuse Color** and set to `1.000`. Make the **Blend** type **Mix**.

If you haven't done so already, save your work, appending or incrementing a number at the end of the filename. If you render now, you should get a similar still render like that shown at the beginning of this recipe.

Time to create a continuous rotation of the barber pole.

7. Select the `barber-rotation` Empty and move to frame 1 of the animation.

8. From the **Object** panel under **Transform**, alter the **Rotation** of **X** to `90°` and **Y** and **Z** to `0°`. *Right click* on the **X** rotation and **Insert** a keyframe.

9. Move to frame 51 and alter the **Y** rotation to -90° and *right click* to **Insert** a new keyframe.

10. In the **F-Curve** editor, select all curves with the *A* key.

11. Press *SHIFT+E*, which is the shortcut for **Extrapolation Mode**, and select **Linear Extrapolation**.

The **Y** curve in the **F-Curve** editor should become an extended straight line. Now, make sure you set the animation length to 100 frames and save your work, incrementing the filename. If you render the animation, you will have a barber pole that will go on rotating forever.

How it works...

There are several tricks used in this animated texture example that you may have spotted as you went through the steps.

The texture was applied to the mesh using **Tube** mapping. This essentially maps the texture around the circumference of the tube as though projected from its center. However, because we are mapping via an Empty, it's necessary to alter its rotation to match that same projection. That is why we set the **X** direction to 90° to match the tube object's orientation.

You may have also noted that we set the second keyframe on frame 51. Because we set the slope to **Linear Extrapolation**, we know it will continue to rotate the texture to the end of the animation. However, when you are creating a cyclical animation you don't want the end of the cycle to be exactly the same as the beginning, otherwise you will get repeat frames every time the animation cycles. By setting the keyframe on frame 51, the rotation will be short on the last frame. This is ideal as the cycle takes it back to frame 1 when played, thus completing the rotation.

If you played the animation in the **3D** window by using the play button in the **Timeline** or pressing *ALT+A*, you should see that the rotation of the Empty travels through 180° rather than 360°. However, because the texture is tileable, we only have to render 100 frames to repeat the pattern. If we had rendered only 50 frames, the colors would swap on the cycle. If we rendered 200 frames i.e 360°, it would correctly repeat but would be wasteful as 50 frames produce the same result.

See also

The earlier recipes in this chapter show in detail how the **F-Curve** editor, as applied to materials, works.

▶ *How to move textures and create animation without moving a mesh*

  ❑ Using co-ordinates to move a texture over time

  ❑ Manipulating the F-Curves of texture movement

  ❑ Using an Empty as a dummy object to control texture movement over time

The technique is also used in the following recipes:

- Chapter 3, *How to alter the color of materials and textures over time*
- Chapter 3, *Creating a burning sheet of paper*
- Chapter 6, *Creating large scale water in Blender 2.5*

If you are interested in finding source material about barber poles, or you just want to find out about their history, these three links helped me to design the recipe you have just completed.

- `http://en.wikipedia.org/wiki/Barber%27s_pole`

  This is wonderful site giving a lot of information about the history and the design of barber poles.

- `http://www.barberpole.com/`

  The quintessential barber site with photos and history.

- `http://www.google.co.uk/images`

  Search for barber pole and lots of reference photos will be displayed. You may even see the inspiration for the design of barber pole used in the recipe.

How to alter the color of materials and textures over time

Being able to move, scale, and rotate a textures gives many opportunities to create some exciting textures. However, Blender offers much more within material and texture animation. One of the fundamental aspects of any material simulation is its color. We have seen how this can be changed in both the material and texture panels to produce a representation of any surface as it might appear in any slice of time. That means when we produce a leaf texture, we show it as it would be in the spring, summer, or autumn. We show a metal roof as it would appear after a few years of exposure to the elements. We see a rock on the seashore that changes its appearance every time the tide ebbs and flows.

Changes in surface color and specularity, over time, are natural and can be simulated in Blender. We will look at an interesting recipe that shows many of the color material aspects that can be animated over time. Each recipe will be a follow on from the preceding one. However, if you do not wish to undertake all of the associated recipes, at least read the getting ready part in this first section as it shows how to set up the mesh and default material upon which we will apply color change over time.

Creating a red hot iron bar

Nothing changes color more violently than heated metal. It can change from a dull gray to glowing white hot in a matter of minutes. In between these two extremes, multiple colors of ruby, then red through to golden yellow can be seen traveling along a metal bar as it is heated in hot coals in the blacksmith's forge. When it is fully heated, ready to be formed into an ornate gate detail on the anvil, it will physically glow.

All these extremes of color make it a good subject for an animated material. This time we will only use color settings to change these appearances. No image files will be used. However, we do need to create a default material to represent a strip of iron. We could also create the forge where the metal will be heated. However, in order to concentrate on the color animation aspects available with Blender, we will disregard these details and perhaps leave that as an extra project for you to explore outside of this chapter.

Getting ready

This recipe will require a simple extended cube that has been flattened to produce a bar-like object. Additional loops have been cut into the mesh to help model the bends and physical bumps found in forged metal. A little proportional vertex manipulation will help add the distortion found on such a surface through hammering.

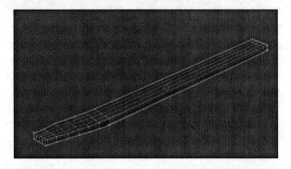

Once you have created this mesh, we can add a very simple material to represent the iron bar substance it is made from.

How to do it...

Creating a simple metal surface using procedural textures:

1. With the bar object selected, move to the **Material** panel and create a new material naming it `red-hot-metal`.

2. In the **Diffuse** tab, set its color to a dull gray **R, G, B** to `0.14`. Keep all the other material settings at default.

3. Move to the **Texture** panel, and in the second slot, create a new texture of type **Clouds**. Name this `iron-clouds`.

 You don't have to create textures in the first free slot available. It's possible to leave gaps when you know another texture may be needed there. If you don't know, you can always reorganize the texture positions later by using the **Move Texture slot** buttons to the right of the texture names.

4. In the **Clouds** tab set **Grayscale** and **Noise/Hard**, with **Basis** of type **Blender Original**, **Size** `1.00` and **Depth** `6`.

5. In the **Colors** tab **Adjust** the **Brightness** to `1.200` and the **Contrast** to `1.300`

6. Finally, in the **Influence** tab set **Diffuse/Color** to `1.00` and **Geometry Normal** to `5.000`. Set the **Blend** type to **Multiply** and select **Negative, RGB to Intensity**, and **Stencil**. Set the color selector to **R** `1.00`, **G** `0.88`, and **B** `0.96`.

That has created a fresh-looking iron bar material but we can make it just a little bit more interesting by adding rust.

7. In the next free texture slot following the `iron-clouds` texture create a new texture of type **Musgrave** and name it `rust-musgrave`.

8. In the **Musgrave** tab set the **Type** as **Multifractal** with a **Dimension** of `0.000`, a **Lacunarity** of `2.000`, and **Octaves** of `8.000`. Make the **Basis** type **Blender Original** with a **Size** of `0.25`.

9. Under the **Influence** tab set **Diffuse/Color** to `0.500`, and the **Geometry/Normal** to `-0.500`. Set the **Blend** type to **Mix** and the color selector to **R** `0.42`, **G** `0.11`, and **B** `0.00`.

Now is a good time to save your work with the filename:

`hot-iron-bar-01.blend`

If you render the scene at this stage, you should see a rusting metal bar.

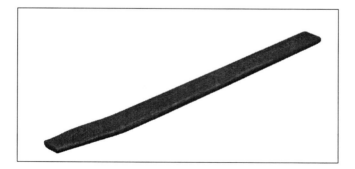

The image above was rendered with a white world background to help make it stand out on the page. However, for the animation, I would suggest that you alter the **World** background to black as it will help the heated metal stand out.

We will add the glow texture in its final position before we start to animate it.

10. With the metal bar object selected, move to the **Texture** panel and in the first slot, the one we left empty, create a new texture of type **Blend** and name it hot-blend.

11. In the **Blend** tab, set the **Progression** of type **Easing** and **Horizontal**.

12. In the **Mapping** tab, set the **Coordinates** to type **Generated** and **Projection** type **Flat**. Alter the **X** selector to Y, the **Y** selector to X, and the **Z** selector to None. Change the **Offset** of **X** to 0.10 and also change the **Size Z** value to 0.90. We will be using this tab to make the main color changes but for the moment let's complete the simple texture settings.

13. Under the **Influence** tab, set the **Diffuse/Color** with a value of 1.000. Set the **Shading/Emit** with a value of 1.000. Finally, set the **Blend** type to **Mix** and change the color selector to **R** 1.00, **G** 0.75, and **B** 0.00.

That has created the initial settings for this material. However, if you were to render at this point, a rather disappointing straw colored band will cover the back half of the iron bar. We need to set up a more color-varied blend that should place the hot end of the metal at the left side of the scene.

14. Move back to the **Colors** tab and select the **Ramp** checkbox. This will display the default **Blend** as transparent on the left of the ramp and white and solid on the right side of the ramp. We will be adding control points and changing color and alpha values to create a red hot end to our iron bar.

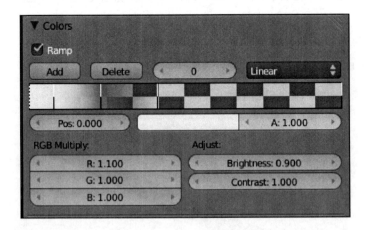

15. In the **Colors** tab, ensure that the **Choose active color stop** is displaying 0. This means the first **color stop** in our ramp. The active **color stop** also shows a dotted line in the ramp.

16. Change its color from the default black to a light yellow. You can achieve this by using the color selector just below the ramp. Change it to **R** and **G** 1.00, and **B** 0.31. Also change its **A**(lpha) value to 1.00.

17. Click the **Add** button to create a new color stop. The number displayed should now show 1 and the dotted line will have moved to the middle. We need to change its color and position.

18. In the **Pos**(ition) box, change the value to 0.079 and in the color selector, change the color to **R** and **G** 1.00 and **B** 0.00. This produces a bright yellow. Alter the **A** value to 1.000.

19. Add a new color stop and position it at 0.231, with a color setting of **R** 1.00 and set **G** and **B, to** 0.00. A bright red. However, alter its **A** to 0.900.

20. Add yet another color stop at position 0.413, with a color setting of **R** 0.55 and **G** and **B** to 0.00. Set its **A** to 0.000.

21. Using the **Choose active color stop** indicator, click the right arrow to move to the default right-hand color stop, which in our case is number 4. Its position should be at 1.000. Change its color to **R** 1.00, and **G** and **B** to 0.000. Set its **A** to 0.000. Finally, in the **RGB Multiply**, set **R** to 1.100 and **Adjust/Brightness** to 0.900 with a **Contrast** of 1.00.

Time to save your work, incrementing the filename to:

`hot-iron-bar-02.blend`

If you render now, you will see a still image of a red hot poker.

We can move this over time by creating a couple of keyframes altering the X mapping position of the hot-blend texture.

22. Ensure that the animation length is `150` frames and that you are on the last frame `150`.

23. With the metal bar object selected, move to the **Texture** panel and select the first texture slot `hot-blend`.

24. In the **Mapping** tab, move the mouse cursor over the **Offset X** setting, which should be `0.10`. *Right click* and from the displayed menu, select **Insert Keyframes**.

25. Move to the first frame and alter the **Offset X** value to `1.00` and set another keyframe.

We will alter the curve of these two keyframes in the **F-Curve** editor to produce a more dynamic movement.

26. In the **F-Curve** editor, select the first keyframe control handles. You will find it best to select the middle handle. Press *R* to start rotating the handle until the curve looks close to that in the following image. It doesn't have to be that precise.

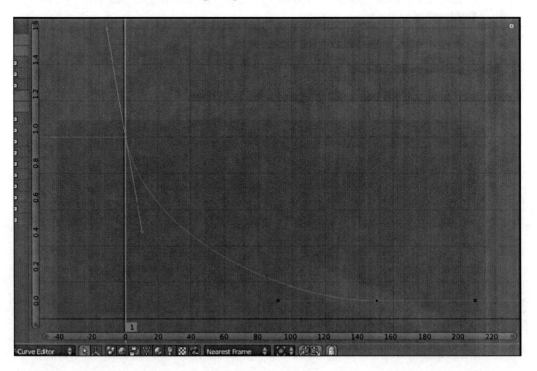

Save your work, incrementing the filename to:

`hot-iron-bar-03.blend`

If you wish, you can render an animation of this scene. However, with 150 frames to render, ensure that you choose a small image size or you will have to wait a long time for the whole animation to render. However, the completed animation should show the Blend texture moving up the iron bar, slowing towards the end of the animation.

How it works...

The ramp shader is an incredibly useful tool for producing complex color and alpha settings within a single texture. We have used it here to add variation in both color and emit levels. It has made the Blend procedural even more versatile by allowing us to vary the texture transparency as well as color so that the underlying textures can show through.

Moving the Blend texture with a series of keyframes makes it look as if the metal is being heated in a forge. However, a simple color transition even with this nice texture, produces a rather lame animation. Wouldn't it be better to vary the color of each stop as well as their individual positions within the ramp to produce a much more dynamic animation?

Changing the multiple settings within a color ramp over time

In this recipe, we will animate multiple settings in a color ramp to simulate the varying color and speed changes associated with an iron bar heating in a forge.

Getting ready

This recipe uses the file created from the last recipe. If you have not completed that recipe, you can download the file from the Packt Publishing website.

How to do it...

Adding finer control over simple color movement requires a little more attention to the detailed control offered by the **F-Curve** editor or Key Frame animation in Blender.

1. Open the file `hot-iron-bar-03.blend`.

2. With the iron bar mesh selected, move to the **Texture** panel and select the `hot-blend` texture in the first Texture slot. Move to frame `150` and you should see in the **Preview** tab and the **Colors** tab, the settings of the **Ramp** for the end of the animation.

3. Drag the green current frame indicator either in the **F-Curve** editor or the **Timeline** editor back to frame `1`. As you do so, the Preview will update showing the movement of the color ramp that was animated in the last recipe. However, you will note that the **Ramp** itself remains unchanged over the animation. Let us change that.

4. Ensure you are still on frame 1. In the **Color ramp**, select **color stop** 1 using the **Choose active color stop** button. Change its color in the selector to **R** 1.00, **G** and **B** 0.00. Now, change its **Pos**(istion) to 0.011. *Right click* the **Pos** value entered and from the menu, choose **Insert Keyframe**. This will record the position, color, and alpha at this frame for that ramp color stop.

5. Select color stop 2 in the ramp and alter its position to 0.102 and color to **R** 1.00, **G** and **B** 0.00. *Right click* the position and insert a new keyframe for this color stop.

6. Move to frame 100 and select color slot 1 in the color ramp. Alter the **A**(lpha) value to 1.000 and insert a new keyframe.

We have now set all of the ramp changes required to create a better animation of the iron bar heating up. Save your work at this stage, incrementing the filename to:

```
hot-iron-bar-04.blend
```

You can now render an animation and when you play it, you should see that the iron bar begins to get ruby red at its tip. This redness increases and spreads along the bar for a certain distance. The red begins to change to a yellow and finally to bright yellow as the metal apparently gets to its correct temperature for being worked by a blacksmith.

How it works...

Not only have we moved a color along our mesh material, we have been able to vary the speed and color of a whole range of positions to simulate more accurately the way metal heats up. Using a **Ramp** shader in a texture is very easy, animating it is easier still. We have ultimate control over the way the curves expressing the changes in the color stops is edited in the **F-Curve** editor. For instance, you may find it necessary to alter the slope of a particular curve if the speeds don't quite work in test animations. In fact, you will find it necessary to run test animations as you develop any animation. You can save yourself considerable time by rendering to a smaller size than the finished animation will be. The render panel allows you to reduce a full size animation by a percentage. You may find it useful to therefore render to 25% or 50% for these test animations.

At times, the **F-Curve** editor can become crowded, particularly when you have a lot of animated curves. You can bring order to the **F-Curve** editor by un-checking the checkbox against any curve you don't need to see in the left panel of the editor. You are also able to highlight the curve of interest by just selecting it in this panel. It is also possible to lock any curve you do not want to accidentally edit by clicking the lock symbol in the same panel.

See also

You can download example animations for each of the Chapter 3 recipes from the Packt Publishing website.

How to animate transparency in a texture

Using the color ramp shader to change color over time has been shown to be very useful. Previous recipes demonstrate how alpha values within the ramp can help textures show through the ramp colors. We can take this one stage further and apply full transparency animated across the material.

This is very useful to the 3D designer. Using this tool enables us to create many objects that would be difficult using direct modeling. Adding the chance to animate the transparency over time provides even more opportunities.

We could use the technique to animate a bug eating its way through a leaf, or the autumn season progressing across the same leaf. What about a seamless portal opening on a spaceship smooth sphere? Or even a sheet of paper burning away to nothing.

Creating a burning sheet of paper

In this recipe, we will create a sheet of paper that will start to burn until it is consumed.

Getting ready

Preparation for this recipe is very simple. Just create a ground plane to act as a base and a smaller subdivided plane to be our sheet of paper. Ensure the sheet of paper mesh is set as smooth.

As you may see from the image below, two curves have also been created. One in the X axis and one in the Y. These are not strictly necessary but provide a way of getting the paper to curl as it apparently burns. This can be achieved by adding two curve modifiers to the mesh and animating the curves to move in the X and Y direction as the animation progresses. Since we are here to learn animated textures, I will leave that exercise for you to complete if you want to.

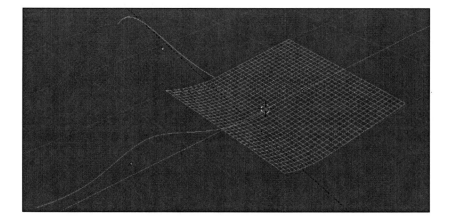

Save the blendfile as:

```
paper-fire-01.blend
```

How to do it...

We will start by creating the un-animated materials and textures for the recipe:

1. Since it would be nice to see our paper separated from the background plane, raise it slightly and add a curl to the edge of the paper mesh. You can do this by proportional mesh editing or by employing a curve modifier.

2. Create a material for this background plane making it a light blue, again to help separate the paper sheet from the surface. By default, the material should be set to receive shadows. However, you should check this in the **Shadows** tab of the **Materials** panel in case it has been turned off. This will help separate the paper from the surface.

3. Select the paper mesh and create a new material naming it `paper-burn`.

4. In the **Specular** tab, set its type to **CookTorr** and its **Intensity** to `0.000`, with a **Hardness** of `50`.

5. Click the **Transparency** tab to set it, and set to **Z Transparency**, and turn the **Specular** setting to **0.000**.

6. Switch to the **Texture** tab and create a new texture of type **Musgrave** and name it `burning-musgrave`.

7. In the **Musgrave** tab, select type **Multifractal** with **Dimension** `1.000`, **Lacunarity** `6.000`, and **Octaves** `8.000`. Set **Basis** to type **Blender Original** with a **Size** of `0.65`.

8. In the **Mapping** tab, set the **Projection** as type **Sphere**.

9. Under the **Influence** tab, set **Diffuse/Color** to `3.000` and **Alpha** to `1.000`. Set the **Blend** type to **Multiply**.

Now is a good time to save your blendfile, incrementing the filename as:

```
paper-fire-02.blend
```

Time to set up a color ramp shader and animate it.

10. With the paper mesh selected and from its **Texture** panel, select the `burning-musgrave` texture created in the last step.

11. Move to the **Colors** tab and check the **Ramp** box. We will create 4 more color stops and color and position them. To make this quicker, I will deal with each color stop in turn.

12. Select the first color stop 0. Ensure that it is at **Pos**(ition) 0.000 and its color is **R, G, B** 0.00 and it's **A**(lpha) is 0.000.

13. Click the **Add** button to create a new color stop. Set its position as 0.233 with color **R, G, B** 0.00 and **A** of 1.000.

14. Add a new color stop. Set its position as 0.396 with a color of **R** 1.00, **G** 0.44, and **B** 0.00. Set its Alpha value to 1.000.

15. Add yet another color stop and position at 0.588. Change its color to **R** 1.00, **G** 1.00, and **B** 0.00. Set its **Alpha** to 1.000.

16. Add a fourth color stop with position 0.743 and color **R, G, B** of 1.00. Set **Alpha** to 1.000.

17. Move to the last texture slot and confirm it is position 1.000 color white and **Alpha** 1.000.

18. Ensure that the animation length is 100 frames by altering the **End Frame** number if necessary. Move to frame 1.

19. Back in the **Texture** panel, **Colors** tab, alter the **Adjust /Brightness** to 2.000, and the **Contrast** to 5.000. *Right click* on each of these settings in turn and choose **Insert Keyframe**.

20. Move to frame 50.

21. Back in the **Colors** tab, alter the **Brightness** setting to 0.200 and *Right click* on that selector and choose **Insert Keyframe**.

22. Move to frame 100 and change the **Contrast** value to 0.010 and set a **Keyframe** for just this setting.

Time to save your work once again, remembering to increment the filename:

`paper-fire-03.blend`

Render an animation and when you play the result, you will see the paper burn and disappear before your eyes.

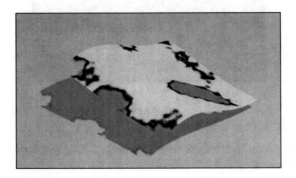

How it works...

This effect is actually very simple. We are merely changing the **Brightness** and **Contrast** of the **Musgrave** texture over time. We start on frame 1 with the brightness and contrast up to maximum. At frame 50, we fix the Brightness at 0.200. However, the Contrast will continue to fall as we approach frame 100, where a keyframe sets the contrast to a very low value.

There's more...

I mentioned earlier that it is possible to animate two curves to distort the paper sheet as though it is curling when heat is applied to paper, driving out any moisture. There are example movies and also blendfiles available where you can explore these possibilities.

It's also possible to create a Node Compositor system to extract those parts of the texture that are supposed to be hot and create a glowing red ring effect just as a real burning paper has. Again, an example blendfile is available for you to examine.

See also

The blendfiles and example movies for this exercise can be downloaded from the Packt Publishing website.

How to change textures during an animation

It's possible in Blender to apply a sequence of images as a texture over time. This may not seem immediately practical but it offers a really economical method of mapping image textures at set times in an animation. It is particularly useful for creating changing signs, or hoardings that change over time. From traffic lights to airport arrival and departure boards, sequence textures is the way to go.

Creating a Red Alert sign using a sequence of images

This recipe shows how to create a Red Alert sign worthy of any star trip universe.

Getting ready

This recipe requires a flattened cube and three texture images for the sequence. The cube should look something like that shown in the following image:

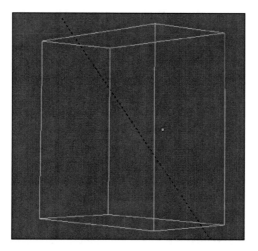

You will also need to create three identically sized images in a graphics program. The examples I used were all 1024 x 768 pixels but they can be smaller if required. If you do not wish to create these yourself, they are downloadable from the Packt Publishing website.

Just unzip these to the textures directory below where you save your blendfiles.

Each image is black and white and should be saved in the same location with the filenames as specified. If you are going to produce images for a texture sequence, they must be named the same with the correct sequence number at the end of the filename preceding the image format. No color is required in these images as we are going to add that within the material design.

How to do it...

Creating the initial materials for the Red Alert sign:

1. When you have created the cube as suggested, select it and move to the **Materials** panel.

2. Create a new material and name it `red-alert`.

3. In the **Diffuse** tab, set the color to black **R, G, B** `0.00`.

4. In the **Specular** tab, select type **Phong** and set the **Intensity** to `1.000` and **Hardness** to `14`.

Save your work at this point naming the file:

`red-alert-01.blend`

5. Move to the **Texture** panel and create a new texture in the first slot of type **Image or Movie**. Name the texture `red-alert-seq`.

6. In the **Image** tab, **Open** the first numbered image `RA-001.png`. An information area will appear in the tab telling you how many frames are in the **sequence (3)**, and also the **Start, Offset, Fields, Auto Refresh**, and **Cyclic**. Select **Auto Refresh** and **Cyclic**. We will change another setting here a little later.

7. In the **Colors** tab, set the **RGB Multiply R** setting to `2.000`.

8. In the **Mapping** tab, change the **X, Y, Z** mapping to **Z, X, Z**.

9. Finally, in the **Influence** tab, set the **Diffuse/Color** to `1.000`. Set the **Blend** type to **Screen** and change the color to bright red **R** `1.00`, **G** and **B** `0.00`.

Save your work again, incrementing the filename to `red-alert-02.blend`.

If you were to render an animation now, the change between textures would happen on every frame, which is too fast. We need to slow the changes down to a more reasonable interval. Let's set an animation length for the whole sequence of this Red Alert sign.

10. Change the **End Frame** of the animation to `120`. That's `5` seconds at `24` fps.

11. With the mesh selected, move back to the **Texture** panel and the `red-alert-seq` texture.

12. In the **Image** tab, change the **Fields** entry to `80`. That was arrived at by dividing the number of frames by the number of frames of the sequence `120/3=40`. Now, you probably noticed that the Fields initial figure was `2` and that's because every frame in a sequence must have at least `2` Fields. We, therefore, multiply `40` by `2` to get `80`.

Save your work again, incrementing the filename and perform a test animation render of your Red Alert box.

The resultant animation should change the words on the sign in succession, repeating forever until you stop the playback.

How it works...

You can apply sequenced images just like any other image as a texture. Here, we **Color** tab **RGB Multiply R** setting to force the image to be more than fully illuminated when applied to the black material box. We also used the **Screen** mix method to make sure only the words would affect the black box material. Remember, **Screen** will mix light colors but ignore dark colors. The black of the image backgrounds will therefore have no affect on the box material.

Getting the timing right for the transitions of the sequenced images can be a little tricky. However, using the simple formula used in the recipe should make it a little easier. The formula is:

Fields setting = (animation length/sequence length) * 2

The images that you use for a sequence do not have to be the same size or resolution. Just as long as their filenames have an incrementing number at the end preceding the format name. That means if you wanted a black frame between any sequenced images, you could just use a one pixel black image, named in sequence, and that will be applied like all the other images in the sequence. A 1 pixel image takes up almost no room in computer storage terms.

There's more...

In the animation we produced, each sequence changed abruptly every 40 frames. It is possible to animate the images so that they will fade in and out between changes. To do this, it's necessary to set keyframes on the **RGB Multiply R** setting in the **Colors** tab of the **Texture** panel. Altering the value from 2.000 to 0.000 will make the images fade out.

At the time of writing, although one can animate these settings, no keyframes are shown. So, you may need to be careful when performing such an animation because it becomes difficult to see what you have done. Perhaps by the time you read this book that slight deficiency might have been corrected.

A completed blendfile using this technique is available on the Packt Publishing website.

You may have noticed that when we created the initial material setting, we used the **Phong** specular shader and set its intensity value to 1. Phong is an excellent specular shader and although lacking some of the features of more modern shader types, it produces excellent clinical specularity. Here, it's used to help give some shape to an otherwise completely black surface.

See also

See Chapter 9, *Special Effects Materials* and *Using billboard fire renders to produce a complex effect without the render overhead*.

How to texture with movies creating a TV screen

Since Blender is a 3D animation suite, it stands to reason that it can produce movies. In fact, Blender has an excellent video editor that can be used to edit and render entire films if necessary. Bearing this in mind, it would be advantageous if we could use movies as textures in material simulation. After all, if you have to produce an animation of a working TV set, you would really require a video image to be painted on the surface of the TV screen. Fortunately, Blender allows us to use movies, as well as still images, as a texture source.

We will create a simple scene of an old TV set and apply a short movie sequence as a texture. In the examples that I show here, I have used a short sequence created by me a few years ago. The file is available for you to use in the recipe but there are other examples of open source movies that could be used also. I will give reference to this in the *See also* section of the recipe.

Getting ready

You will need to create a mesh to represent an old cathode ray tube TV. If you start with the default cube and in edit mode create some additional loops, it should be possible to form the curved front of these old TV set screens using the proportional editing within Blender.

Apply a Subsurf modifier to the mesh to give nice rounded corners to this old TV.

You can also create a box to surround the TV tube representing the case that houses our TV screen. Texture this box to represent a plastic monitor case with a few bumps. I will leave you to do that but it is not vital to what we will achieve in this recipe.

Save your work as:

    tv-screen-00.blend

How to do it...

Applying a movie as a texture is actually quite simple and follows the same principles as applying a still image to a surface.

1. With the TV tube mesh selected, move to the **Material** panel and create a new material and name it TV-screen. In the **Diffuse** tab, set the color to **R**, **G**, and **B** all to 0.11. This will create a dull gray material color. Leave all other material setting at their default.

2. Switch to the **Texture** panel and in the first texture slot, create a new texture of type **Blend** and name it TV-glow-blend.

3. In the **Blend** tab, set the **Progression** to type **Linear** and **Horizontal**.

4. In the **Colors** tab, check the **Ramp** checkbox and using the **Choose active color stop**, select stop 0, which should be at position 0.000. Change the **A** value to 1.000. This changes the alpha from transparent to fully opaque.

5. Add a new stop by clicking the **Add** button and **Position** it at 0.841. Set its color to black **R, G, B** 0.00, and its **Alpha** to 1.000.

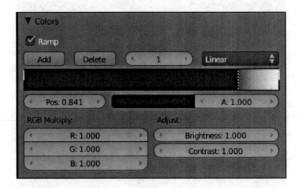

6. Under the **Influence** tab, uncheck all **Diffuse, Shading, Specular**, and **Geometry** settings. However, set **RGB to Intensity**, and **Stencil**.

7. Move to the next free texture slot and create a new texture of type **Image and Movie**, and name it movie-texture.

8. In the **Image** tab, **Open** the movie you want to place in this texture. In my case I opened colin-litster_FXWARS(634x270).mov, which is a 1 minute 27 second, Quicktime format movie.

9. When the movie is loaded, an information line will appear below the filename location giving details of the loaded movie. Take note of how many frames the movie is. You are able to change settings of when and what frame the movie should start. In our case, we can leave these at default but click the Cyclic checkbox so the video will just repeat if our animation is longer than the movie texture.

10. Under the **Mapping** tab, set **Coordinates** to **Generated** and **Projection Flat**. Change the **X,Y,Z** settings to **Z, Y**, and **None**.

11. In the **Influence** tab, set **Diffuse/Color** to 1.000 and **Shading/Emit** to 2.000. Finally, set the Blend type to Mix.

Save your work as:

tv-screen-01.blend

Before rendering the animation, you may like to increase the number of frames to match the movie length found in step 9. Be cautious, however, 1,500 to 3,000 frames, is only 1 to 2 minutes at 25 fps, but that's a lot of rendering.

My animation was 1,880 frames long at 24 fps and was rendered at 75% of 1920 x 1080 resolution. Each frame took approximately 6.12 seconds to render. So, the whole animation took over 3 hours to complete. I would, therefore, suggest you render no more than 2,000 frames and set the size lower than I did.

However, at the end of the render, you should have the movie texture animating within the TV screen.

How it works...

Applying a movie texture is a clever way of adding movement to any object. Specific examples like a TV screen are obvious but the technique can be used to create complex-looking objects from simple meshes. It could, for instance, be used to create a changing billboard in a city street at night, or to add detail to space captain's comm port. All of which could be a movie texture on a simple plane mesh.

You will undoubtedly require other textures to complete the effect. In our TV screen material we use a Blend texture to limit the movie to the front of the screen and also add a slight graying at the edges of the tube, thus making it look older. The Blend is being used as a stencil, therefore the black areas of the blend will stop the following texture showing and the white will allow it to appear on the front of the screen. The slight blend at the edges produce the graying effect.

When opening a movie, a texture information will appear to tell you its length, in frames, and its dimensions.

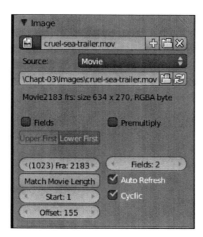

Below that are a series of controls to set how the movie will be applied to the texture over time. So you can set it to start the movie texture a certain number of frames into your animation via the **Start** number.

You can set an **Offset** so the movie texture will start from some other point rather than its first frame.

You can also set up **Cyclic** to allow the movie to repeat if the animation is longer than the movie texture.

There are other controls like **Auto Refresh** movie texture at each frame change, and **Fields** to help deal with interlaced video. However, you should find it easy to open a movie as a texture and map it to your object.

In our texture we have set the **Influence** to **Emit** to a level greater than 1.00. In this way we make the movie texture that is not masked by the preceding blend texture, almost glow just like an old TV. This technique of being able to set values greater than 1.00 may seem to be incorrect because how can you make it more than its supposed maximum? Well, Blender has solved this and setting values above their maximum can make it easier to achieve some special effects like this glowing TV tube.

There's more...

If you are going to use a movie as a texture, ensure it is of a short length, e.g., trying to load a full-length feature film for a 10-second shot would be rather wasteful of resources. Also, don't use copyrighted material unless you have permission. Bearing these two points in mind, using movies as textures can be really useful to the 3D material designer.

The format of the movie that you wish to use can be any of the formats that Blender can render itself. So, AVI and Quicktime are popular codecs that Blender can accept as movie textures. There are other formats that Blender will accept as textures but be aware that some of the more exotic codecs may not be supported. If this is the case, you should convert it to an acceptable format prior to using it. Codec conversion is a complex subject but there are plenty of free tools available that can perform the appropriate transition to a Blender readable format. A way of finding out if the format can be read by Blender is to attempt to load it into the Blender sequencer. If it is viewable there, you can use it within a Blender material.

See also

See *Chapter 9, Special Effects Materials and Adding complex FX without the render overhead* Although that recipe uses a sequence of still images, you could substitute a looping movie to generate the same effect.

There are plenty of open source movies available via the Internet that you could use to create a TV screen showing a movie. Some of the best and highest quality are available from the Blender Foundation in various formats. Currently, this consists of the three open source movies created by talented artists through the Blender Institute in Amsterdam:

- Elephants Dream: `http://orange.blender.org/download`
- Big Buck Bunny: `http://www.bigbuckbunny.org/index.php/download/`
- Sintel: `http://durian.blender.org/`

4

Managing Blender Materials

In this chapter, we will cover:

- ▸ Setting a default scene for materials creation
- ▸ Additional settings for default scene
- ▸ Creating an ideal Blender interface for material creation
- ▸ Creating an ideal texture animation setup
- ▸ Naming materials and textures
- ▸ Appending materials
- ▸ Linking materials
- ▸ Making blendfiles stand alone

Introduction

Organizing your work, as you develop any project, will ensure that you achieve your task sooner and more efficiently. How to do this in Blender may not be immediately obvious. However, Blender has a raft of tools that will make your life, as a materials creator, so much easier. This chapter deals with the techniques that can be used to organize your textures and materials, and thus encourage some order to complex tasks.

While Blender can be a very flexible 3D suite, allowing the designer more than a single approach to a simulation, it is better to develop a more ordered strategy to your material and texture creations.

We will explore several recipes that attempt to show how to control material creation. However, apart from the inbuilt tools, there are several setups that will be dependent on personal preference. You are therefore encouraged to modify any of these recipes to suit your own approaches to organizing material production.

Setting a default scene for materials creation

It's always a good idea to set the initial state of Blender to suit your needs. For us, the primary task is to explore materials and texture creation. When you first install Blender, a default layout will be presented. From here, you can perform most tasks, such as modeling, and rendering, as you create your desired objects. We can aid the process of surface creation by improving the lighting in the default setup. Adding a second light can give better definition to objects that are rendered.

Getting ready

When you first download Blender, the default factory settings provide a simple cube illuminated by a single light. Even if you have already changed some of these defaults, you will be able to apply the suggested changes in this recipe on top of your personalized settings. So, you can either start with the factory settings or your own.

How to do it...

1. Start Blender, or select **New** from the **File** menu. This will ensure that any previous default settings are loaded.

2. Move the mouse cursor into the main 3D view and press *SHIFT+A* to bring up the **Add** menu and select **Lamp** of type **Hemi**.

3. Move, and rotate the lamp so that it will illuminate the shaded side of the default cube. Try to adjust its height and distance from the object similar to the default lamp.

4. From the lamp menu, set the **Energy** value between **0.200** and **0.500**. Render a quick scene and adjust as necessary.

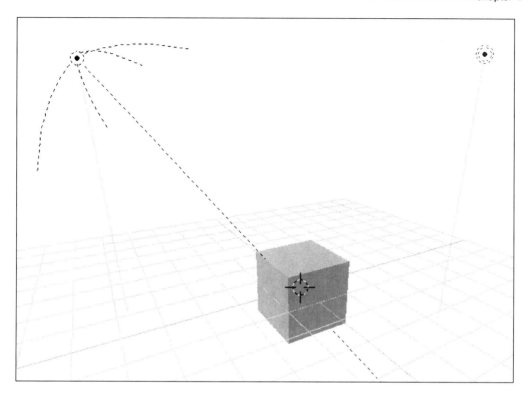

5. Move to the **Render** panel.

6. In the **Dimensions** tab, select **Render Presets**. From the list, select **HDTV 1080p**. This will give a render size of 1,920 x 1,080 square pixels. However, alter the **Resolution** percentage slider to 25%. Just below the **Aspect Ratio** settings are two buttons, check **Border** and then **Crop**. Now, uncheck **Border**. This might seem strange but although the **Crop** checkbox is grayed out it is still set.

7. Ensure the **Anti-Aliasing** tab is selected, and the figure below that is set to **8**, with the anti-aliasing method set to **Mitchell-Netravali**. Ensure that the **Full Sample** is **NOT** set.

8. Under **Shading**, ensure **Textures**, **Shadows**, **Ray Tracing**, and **Color Management** are set, while **Subsurface Scattering** and **Environment Map** are not.

9. Move down to the **Output** tab and from the list of choices select **PNG**. You can also change the Compression percentage to between 0% for a loss less saved image or up to 100% for full compression. I usually set to 0% to produce the clearest images.

10. Finally, in the **Performance** tab, ensure that **Threads** is set to **Autodetect**.

11. You can save these settings as the default scene by pressing *CTRL+U* and selecting **Save User Settings**. Now, whenever you restart Blender, or select a new scene, you will have a better lit setup with render settings providing an ideal environment to create materials.

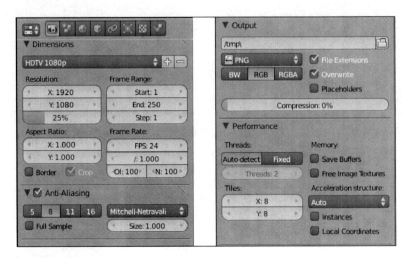

How it works...

The recipe provides a relatively simple set of changes to the factory default scene. However, they are ideal for materials creation because they make it easier to judge the surface characteristics as you develop the material.

We started by improving the default lighting by adding a second light to give a little more illumination to the shaded side of the objects you will be creating materials and textures for. Being able to set this as the default scene means we don't have to worry about special light setups every time we create a new material. It also helps with consistency because the levels of light will be very similar between every new material you create. It is not there to provide the finished lighting for every scene you create, but just to give a more even illumination when you test render materials you are developing.

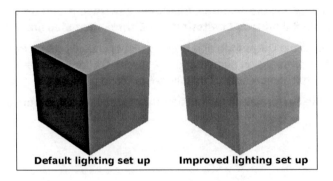

Default lighting set up   **Improved lighting set up**

What we have done is produced a key light and a fill light, which is the minimum in almost any 3D lighting arrangement. The **Hemi** light offers a nice broad illumination but will not cast shadows. This is ideal for a fill light as it can represent bounced light off of ceilings, or walls, or even the outside world. The **Point** light source acting as our key light will cast shadows just as the strongest light in a natural environment would.

When you have developed your materials, you can light the actual scene with a more complex or artistic lighting setup if you wish.

For the majority of digital work, we need to use square pixels and a resolution that matches the size we wish to render to. Here, we have set the render size and resolution from the presets to **HDTV 1080p**. This produces a relatively large render area with square pixels. Square pixels are really important when developing objects or materials for digital work. It's possible to set different aspect ratios that would alter the screen and render proportions, which are of no value when creating models or developing and placing textures on them. If you eventually want to render out to these none square pixel ratios, do so only when all you're modeling and scene creation is finalized.

> The render panel offers several useful presets. These are based on screen resolution and pixel aspect ratio to exactly match the desired output. Be careful not to inadvertently select one of the non-square pixel ratios, like HDV 1080p.

In the same step, we set the render resolution down to 25%. This will still give a render size of 480 x 270, which is OK for initial quick renders to check how a material is progressing. You can easily scale that up to 50% or 75% for more detailed renders. However, these will obviously increase the render times.

If you create a border in the camera view, by pressing *SHIFT+B*, and dragging the orange dotted border, Blender will only render what's inside that rectangle. This is why we also checked the **Crop** checkbox so that Blender automatically crops the rendered image. If you perform a bordered render without the **Crop** set, the unrendered part is filled with black pixels. Therefore, setting the crop checkbox will ensure it will be cropped if selected. This will save valuable render time and also smaller image saves.

Anti-aliasing

Even if we are rendering to a large size, we should set Blender to anti-alias the resultant render to remove the jagged edges that would otherwise appear. Here, we have set the anti-aliasing method to **Mitchell-Netravali**. This is probably the best of the available options. It will give very reasonable anti-aliasing at the relatively low setting of 8 without unreasonable render times. For final render, you might want to consider raising the level to 16.

Turning off unneeded render settings

Subsurface scattering and **Environment map** are not always required so can be turned off in the default scene. They can always be turned on for a particular material simulation that might require them. However, normally, they are not required and render times will be reduced by having them turned off.

If you are working on a material that requires environment mapping or subsurface scattering, you can set these, then save your first file of the simulation. Saving a blendfile will save all additional settings as well as objects and materials.

Blender offers an enormous range of output formats for your rendered still or animation masterpieces. You will not need to use them all so which should we choose as a default?

PNG (Portable Network Graphics) has lossless data compression, as compared to JPG which is lossy, and therefore, the picture is degraded every time you save. However, PNG can efficiently compress images without the subsequent loss of quality. It can also handle alpha channels. It can be read by most web browsers so is suitable for the Internet. Because Blender can render an animation as a series of still images, it is ideal for producing animations as well. Several video editors, including Quicktime, Adobe Premiere, and of course Blender, can take these sequenced still PNG images and combine them into movie formats like `.mov`, `.avi`, `.mp4`, `.mpeg`, and so on. I would therefore suggest that PNG is probably the best all-round image format to set as default.

> If you're primary work is in either the game development, or print, fields you might want to consider using TGA (Truevision Advanced Raster Graphics Adapter), or TIFF (Tagged Image File Format). However, windows-based systems will not display thumbnails of TIFF formatted images at this time.

There's more...

There are other settings that you may want to consider as appropriate in a default scene. You can set locations of often used resources from the **Blender User Preferences** window, *CTRL+ALT+U*. Under the file menu of this preferences window, you can set file paths for such things as Fonts, Textures, Render Output, and so on.

Many of these locations will be specific to your operating system and where you choose them to be. Blender defaults are fine, but if you want to be specific go to this window and enter your appropriate choices. To ensure they are saved as default, click the **Save User Defaults** button, or press *CTRL+U*.

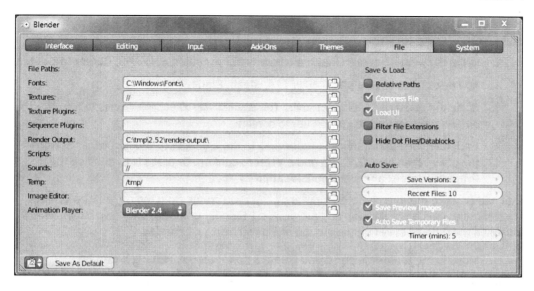

Additional settings for default scene

If you have a powerful enough computer system, you might want to consider setting some more advanced options to make your test renders look really special. In some ways, what you will be doing with this recipe is creating a more production-ready materials creation environment. However, each render will take longer and if it is a complex mesh object with transparency and multiple large-scale image textures, you may have to wait several minutes for renders to complete. Although this may not seem to be a significant disadvantage, the extra render time can build up as you produce multiple renders to test the look of a material simulation.

The renders reproduced in this book, and online, were created with these additional settings. The majority of development work also used these additional settings. While the majority of the simulations only took a few minutes to render at maximum resolution, one or two took a little longer. If that is the case it can slow down your material development, just turn some of these additional settings off before your first save of the blendfile. Any settings will be saved with the blendfile.

Getting ready

As we are adding additional settings to the default scene, ensure you have either just started Blender, or selected **New** from the **File** menu. This will set Blender back to the default scene ready for you to append the additional features suggested here.

How to do it...

1. In the 3D window, ensure that the cursor is at the center. *SHIFT+S*, **Cursor to Center.**

2. Add new object of type **plane**. *SHIFT+A*, **Mesh, Plane.**

3. Scale the plane by 50 Blender units. The easiest way to achieve this is to type *S*, enter 50 and press the *ENTER* key to confirm.

4. Grab the plane and transpose it down -1 in the **Z** direction. You can either select the plane, then type *G, Z, -1*, and *ENTER* to confirm. Or press *N* to bring up the **Properties** panel and alter the **Z location** to -1.000.

That has ensured that the plane is below any object you create from the origin. New objects are created at the cursor position and are always 1 Blender unit from their own origin, which will mean they should stand on the ground plane you have just created.

5. Move to the **Materials** panel and create a new material, naming it **ground**.

6. Under the **Diffuse** tab, change its color to **R, G, B** 1.000 or pure white.

7. In the **Specular** tab, change the type to **WardIso** with an **Intensity** of 0.250, and a **Slope** of 0.300.

8. Under the **Shadow** tab, select **Receive** and **Receive Transparent**.

That has set up the ground ready to act as a shadow-receiving backdrop to our material creations. However, we need to set up a better shadow than that in the default key light setup.

9. Select the key light.

10. From the **Light** panel, select the **Shadow** tab and set **Ray Shadow** with **Sampling** set to **Adaptive QMC**, with **Samples** set to 6, and **Soft Size** of 1.000 and **Threshold** 0.001.

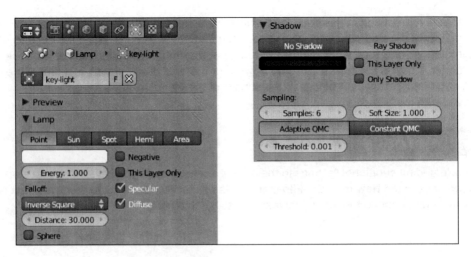

Finally, we will set up ambient occlusion to give our models a little more shape.

11. Move to the **World** panel and select **Ambient Occlusion**. Set its **Factor** to 1.30 and its **Mix** type to **Multiply**.

12. In the **Gathering** tab, select **Approximate**, with **Attenuation/Falloff** selected and its **Strength** changed to 0.900. Set **Sampling/Passes** to 6.

13. Select the **Render** tab, then save this as the new default setting by pressing *CTRL+U*.

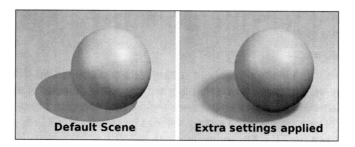

How it works...

The plane is there just so that any shadows will have somewhere to fall. Shadow casting is normally created as a default once an object has a material assigned. In step 19, we also said let the plane receive transparent shadows. That means that objects casting shadows with an alpha component such as windows, or transparent materials, will have accurate shadows showing that transparency.

We also set up soft raytrace shadows by turning on this feature for the key light. The important setting here is the number of samples. Too low and the shadow will look fake. Too high and the render times will become rather lengthy. Setting this to 6 is a good compromise for accuracy and speed.

Finally, we have set up ambient occlusion, which simulates the darkening of shadows in crevices and shaded portions of a model. The higher the **Factor** level, the darker the ambient occlusion will become. Essentially, the darkening is being multiplied on top of the rendered image, although it can also be set to **Add**.

Full raytraced ambient occlusion can take some time to compute, so it is good news that Blender has an excellent **Approximate** method, which is very quick. The **Attenuation** and **Passes** can be tweaked to give the best balance between accuracy and render time. Too low a setting will produce a spotty darkening that is not very real. We set **Passes** at 6, which is another excellent compromise. Ambient occlusion is only available if you render with raytrace enabled.

To save all these extra setting as the default, we only had to press $CTRL+U$. Now, whenever you start a new scene, these settings will be pre-set.

There's more...

Occasionally, you may go too far with default settings and find that render times become too long when you only want to check how a material is progressing. Another common problem is that users will sometimes inadvertently save a pre-created scene as the default. If this happens, you can always return to the factory settings by pressing $CTRL+N$ or choosing the **Load Factory Settings** from the **File** menu.

As you will be doing this regularly, the default light setup is perfectly adequate. However, for a 'hero' render, I would recommend the following settings:

Lights

Your key light, the one to the right of frame, should be set to **Energy** 0.500. Under the **Light** panel, set **Shadow** to **Ray Shadow**. Under **Sampling**, set to **Adaptive QMC** and **Soft Size** to 5.318, and **Samples** to 6. This will create a nice soft shadow, which is more realistic than the sharp ray shadows produced by the default settings.

Ambient occlusion

Ambient occlusion can produce a nice darkening of overall illumination around those shaded parts in our renders. It adds a decent approximation of how real light and shadow spread through an environment giving a render depth.

In our example, a **Blend** sky has been set in the **World** panel, with a **Horizon color R and G** set to 0.80, and **B** set to 0.69. The **Zenith** color has been set to **R** 0.69, **G** 0.75, and **B** 0.80.

Ambient Occlusion has been selected with the following settings: **Factor** 1.00, and **Multiply**. Under **Gather**, **Raytrace** is selected and **Sampling** is set to **Adaptive QMC**, with **Samples** 24. **Threshold** and **Adapt To Speed** are all set to defaults. Under **Attenuation**, **Distance** is set to 10.000 with **Falloff** and **Strength** set to 0.220.

Creating an ideal Blender interface for material creation

Blender comes equipped with several pre-configured windows to help you in your mesh creation, animation setups, and sequencer editing tasks. These pre-defined setups are available from the main Blender Information header.

You are not limited by these factory defaults as it is possible to design new ones and add them to this menu. One notable omission from the factory defaults is any kind of material creation screen. In this recipe, we will create such a screen and save it in the menu of our default scene so it will always be available whenever we start a new scene.

Getting ready

From the Blender screen, select **New** from the **File** menu to ensure you have the unmodified default screen loaded.

How to do it...

Rather than create a brand new screen from scratch, we can copy one of the preset window types that most closely matches what we wish to have in a materials creation screen. For this recipe, we can use the **Default** setup, which offers most of what will be required to create a material.

1. Select the **Default** screen from the **Browse ID data** selector in the Blender Information Header.

2. From the same selector, click the + icon to create a copy. The header should display **Default.001** to show it's a copy.

3. Click inside the name and change it to **Materials**.

The layout of our new **Materials** screen has a large area set to 3D view, a **Timeline** window below this, and a vertical window to the right that has a **Outliner** window at the top and a **Properties** window below that. We need to change the 3D view to create a few more window types to make it easier to work with **Materials**.

4. Move your mouse cursor over the top right corner widget of the 3D window until it changes to a cross-hair. Drag the cursor down and release about half way down the current window. This will essentially divide the 3D view into two identical windows.

5. In the top window header, change its editor type to **Node Editor**.

6. Divide the window below this into two vertical divisions by dragging the corner widget to the left about half way. You will now have two 3D windows below the **Compositor** window.

7. In the left hand 3D window, change its editor type to **UV Image Editor**.

8. In the right hand 3D window, change the 3D view to **Camera**. You can quickly achieve this by pressing the Keypad *0* key while your mouse cursor is over that window. Also, remove the **Tool Shelf** by pressing the *T* key.

The general location of each element is now set but we can do some fine adjustments to make it easy to work with materials.

9. In the vertical **Properties** window, select the **Render** panel if not already selected.

10. Under the **Render** tab, select **Display** type **Image Editor**.

11. In the **UV Image Editor** window, to the left, click on the little render icon and select **Render Result**.

12. In the vertical **Properties** window, select the **Materials** panel.

13. Finally, we can save this new screen setup. Reselect the **Default** screen from the **Browse ID data** selector in the Blender Information header. Press *CTRL+U* and **Save User Settings**.

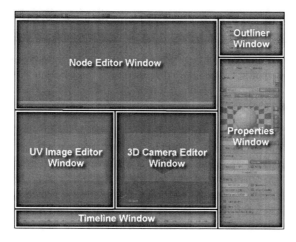

How it works...

Blender offers total flexibility in how the screen can be configured for any editing task. However, consistency in window location will lead to an improved working environment. Almost inevitably, the Blender beginner will use the factory default screen for most of their work. Your mouse hand will become used to the vertical properties window on the right of the screen. So, duplicating this in this materials screen makes sense.

The large node area gives us a good work area if we need to create texture or material node setups.

The Camera view allows us to see what part of the model will be rendered and the UV Image Editor will show the rendered image beside this camera view. Indeed, when rendering, the window focus will remain with this screen rather than switching to a separate render window requiring the *ESC* key, or re-clicking on the editing window, to recapture focus.

We have access to the Object browser, allowing us to select or hide from render view an object in the rendered view.

You can hide an object, from rendering, by de-selecting the render icon in the object browser window. This can be useful if you have a busy scene, with lots of different objects, when you just need to concentrate on the object material you wish to create.

Having the timeline at the base of the screen is also of value because the object, or camera, may move in an animation. You may wish to develop a material and render from different viewpoints. Setting these up with a camera or object rotation can make this possible. Therefore, you only have to drag the timeline until the camera shows the side of an object you wish to test render.

Creating an ideal texture animation setup

In Chapter 3, we explored animated materials and textures. We can create a screen setup to aid us in that process as well.

Getting ready

Ideally, you should have created the previous recipe because we will use that to act as a template, applying a very simple modification to transform it into an animated materials layout. We will run through this recipe quite quickly so if you do not understand the interface controls to change and position Blender windows, complete the previous recipe, which should take no longer than 15 minutes. If you do this, the current recipe can be completed in less than 5 minutes.

How to do it...

You will need to begin by either starting Blender, to ensure the default scene is loaded, or to select **New** from the **File** menu.

1. Select the **Materials** screen from the Browse ID data selector in the Blender Information header. This was the screen created in the previous recipe.

2. From the same selector, click the **+** icon to create a copy. The header should display **Materials.001** to show it's a copy.

3. Click inside the name and change it to **Animated materials**.

That has just created an exact copy of the materials screen but with a different name. We will change the top node window to something more appropriate for materials animation.

4. In the top **Node Editor** window, change the editor type to **Graph Editor** from the header bar. This is at the bottom of the window in this screen. Click on the **Displays current editor type. Click for menu of available types**.

5. In the displayed header, ensure the **F-Curve Editor** is selected.

There are ten buttons to the right that can be turned on, by clicking and revealing a darker background, or turned off, by clicking to display a lighter background. Not all of these are required for materials or texture animation, so let's turn some off.

6. Select the first button, the arrow icon button, and click until its background is dark, showing it is selected.

 This button when set will ONLY include channels related to the selected objects and data

7. Do the same with the second button, the axis icon.

 This button when set will Include visualization of object-level animation data (mostly transform)

8. The next eight buttons only have three turned on. The Node icon.

 Which will Include visualization of node related animation data

9. The material icon.

 Which will Include visualization of material related animation data

10. The texture icon.

 Which will Include visualization of texture related animation data

Time to save this to our user settings, remembering to switch back to the default screen before pressing *CRTL+U* **Save User Settings**.

How it works...

All we have done here is copy the materials screen, change the top screen from Node Editor to Curve Editor, and remove a few unnecessary display settings that are not relevant to material and texture animation.

You can create as many of these screens as you like. Once saved as user settings, they will be available every time you start a new scene.

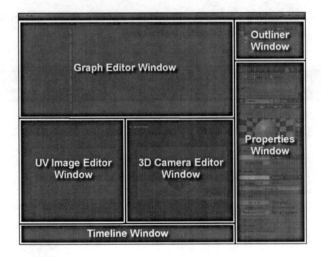

See also

Chapter 3, *Creating Animated Materials*

Chapter 3, *Manipulating the F-Curves of texture movement*

Chapter 3, *Using an empty as a dummy object to control texture movement over time*

Chapter 3, *Creating a red hot iron bar*

Naming materials and textures

Blender gives you total control over how you name materials and textures. Although this freedom may be liberating, your material naming style can soon become messy or confusing. This is particularly so if you are working in a production environment where many blendfiles may need to be produced, and several months may elapse between working on a particular material, or object that uses a material.

Even if you are working as an individual, it is amazing how quickly one forgets how a particular material was named. Unfortunately, there are no easy buttons in Blender to automatically organize materials and textures. You will have to develop your own methods that suit your type of production. However, we can discuss, and begin to develop good practice, through this recipe, and show some guidelines for material and texture naming methodologies.

These are not set rules, and you are encouraged to adapt them to your own requirements. However, the following methods have been found useful in my own productions.

How to do it...

Blender has certain restrictions that should be respected. However, they will help you develop better naming strategies.

1. Start Blender, or select **File/New** to create the default scene. We will use this to experiment with material and texture naming.

2. With the default cube selected, create a new material and name it 0123456789012345678901. That is 21 characters long.

3. Click the + sign at the right of the newly created material to produce a copy. You should see that the name will have reduced to 20 characters in length.

4. Click the + sign again and see that the name reduces to 19 characters.

5. Do this a few times until the name changes to 12345678901234567.001

6. Rename the texture using some of the less common keys on your keyboard ! " £ $ % ^ & * ( ) { } [ ] @ ~ # ?. You will notice that almost any key is accepted in a material or texture name. Rename it **Mat & Tex Names**.

7. Move to the **Texture** panel and create a new texture of type **Clouds**. You will notice that the name will automatically be named **Texture**.

8. Create a new texture, in the next available slot, of type **Marble**. The name of this texture will automatically become **Texture.001**. Rename it **marble**.

You do not need to save this blendfile.

How it works...

Although Blender allows a maximum of 21 characters in a material or texture name, when you copy a material or texture, it will attempt to add a dot followed by a numbered extension from 000 to 999. Therefore, if the name is longer than 17 characters it will remove one character for every copy until it comes to 17 characters. To make naming of materials and textures consistent, limit their length to no more than 17 characters. In fact, keep names as concise as possible while making their meaning obvious.

`Tyrannosaurus-skin` is too long.

`TRex-skin` is well within the max of 17 characters, yet makes just as much sense.

Don't be tempted to use all 21 characters for the name. You may need to make copies of materials or textures in a production and using the automatic dot number addition to the copied name is quite a neat way of organizing them.

`TRex-skin.001`

`TRex-skin.002`

`TRex-skin.003`

You will have noticed that it's possible to use almost any character in a name. Although this may sound useful, you should avoid these characters as they can be confusing when searching for a particular material or texture several weeks or months later. Try to only use alpha numeric characters, although spaces or dashes can be used to separate items within a name.

There is also no restriction on using lower case or capital characters in a name. Blender does not distinguish between the two. Personally, I prefer to use lower case names, although if you want to differentiate important names, you could enter these as capital letters.

Texture names are automatically created every time you create a new texture. However, these give no idea as to what the texture is so it is recommended that you name them to give some idea as to their origin. Procedural textures have so many settings within them that you may find it best to just name them after the procedural type. However, if you need the same procedural with different settings within a single material, you may find it better to append some text to show how the procedural texture will be used in your material, such as:

```
marble-color
```

```
marble-bump
```

```
marble-spec
```

See also

The majority of the recipes within this book have applied the principles outlined here. However, if you are interested to see how large-scale Blender productions have approached materials naming you can examine the Creative Commons entire studio backups for the three Blender Foundation animated films:

- Elephants Dream

  http://blender-mirror.kino3d.org/peach/
- Big Buck Bunny

  http://video.blendertestbuilds.de/download.blender.org/ED/DVD1/

  http://video.blendertestbuilds.de/download.blender.org/ED/DVD2/
- Sintel

  Not yet known but should be available by 2011

Appending materials

Once you have created a large range of materials and textures, it stands to reason that you could possibly use them in more than one blendfile or production. This may save you a lot of time in not having to recreate things you have already successfully created.

You may also be able to use a previously created material or texture as a basis for a new one. Fortunately, Blender provides some very useful tools to make this possible.

Getting ready

You will need access to a blendfile that has materials created. Why not use one that you saved from a previous recipe? We will not be modifying this blendfile, merely using or appending some of its materials into a new scene we will create. For the purpose of illustration, I have appended materials from the *Creating a realistic copper material* recipe from Chapter 2. The specific file is `copper-turret-04.blend`. You can use whatever blendfile you have access to.

How to do it...

Blender allows us to append objects, materials, world settings, and a whole host of other Blender attributes from one blendfile to another. When you append an object, all of its attributes like materials and textures are appended along with it. However, Blender allows us to choose what we are going to append.

1. Start Blender or choose **File/New** from the **File** menu.
2. Delete the cube if that is what is in your default scene.
3. Add a Cone Mesh in the center of the grid, *SHIFT+S* **Cursor to Center**, *SHIFT+A*, and select **Mesh Cone**.
4. Now, scale it four times *S 4 ENTER*.
5. From the **File** menu, select **File/Append**, or *SHIFT+F1*. The screen will change to the browser and from here you can browse to find the blendfile you wish to append a material from. In my case, I chose `copper-turret-04.blend`.

6. You will be presented with 11 folders, select **Material**.

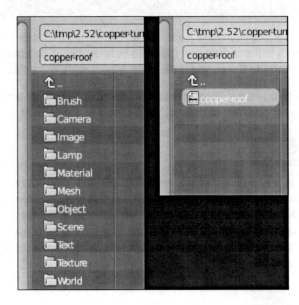

7. A list of available materials will be displayed. In the copper-turret example, there is only one called **copper-roof**. Select it and click **Link/Append from Library**. You will be returned to your Blender scene.

8. Blender will not automatically apply this appended material to your object. So, with the cone object selected, switch to the **Materials** panel and click on the **Browse ID Data** button to display a list of available materials and you should see copper-roof. Select this and the material will load.

Save your work as `append-01.blend`. Perform a test render and if you appended the same material as I did, you should see the copper-roof material now applied to the cone.

How it works...

Append essentially copies the part of the source blendfile to your current blendfile. The material in our case will be a direct copy of the material data from the source. However, it is now totally independent of that source file. You can modify the material or textures in any way and it will have no affect on the source file. This is great because it is a good way of saving time if you want a material similar to one you created earlier.

This also re-emphasizes why a good naming strategy is so important. In my example, I named the original material copper-roof, which gives a good indication of what the material is. Something like **material.004** tells us nothing of what the material is meant to simulate.

Linking materials

Blender offers many methods of bringing materials into a new blendfile. One of the most useful is the ability to bring in a material or texture from a source blendfile but have it retain a link to the source file. If we were to link a material in this way to multiple blendfiles and then find out that the material needs changing in some way, we wouldn't have to edit all occurrences of the material in each blendfile. All we would have to do is change the material in the source blendfile and as soon as we save it, all other linked materials would take on the same changes.

This can be incredibly useful in a production environment, where we would frequently have to work with both proxy objects and maybe proxy materials and textures as a production is being developed. We could get to the point that hundreds of shots are completed before a final material is decided upon. Linking materials and textures allows us to make a single change to a material and all linked blendfiles with that material will be updated.

Getting ready

We will need to create four blendfiles for this recipe. The first is the source blendfile, which we can pretend is a new blender logo material, will be applied to each shot of a multi-shot animation. However, the logo is not finished, so we will use it linked to three other blendfiles as though they are shots from the animation.

How to do it...

We will first create the source blendfile.

1. Create a new scene made up of the default cube. Make sure it is selected.

2. From the **Properties** window, select the **Materials** panel and create a new material. Name it `Blender-rocks-logo`.

3. Change its **Diffuse** color to a bright orange **R** `1.00`, **G** `0.38`, **B** `0.00`. Leave all the other material settings at their default.

4. In the **Texture** panel create a new texture in the first slot of type **Image** or **Movie**.

5. In the **Image** tab, open the file `blender-rocks-LOGO1.png` and check **Premultiply**. This screenshot (`blender-rocks-LOGO1.png`) is available in the code bundle present on the Packt Publishing website.

6. Under the **Mapping** tab ensure **Coordinates** is of type **Generated** and **Projection** is **Flat**. Below that alter the **X Y Z** coordinated to **Y Z None**. This will ensure the logo will appear on the front of the object.

7. Under the **Influence** tab, check **Diffuse/Color** and set to `1.000`. Leave all other settings at their default.

8. Save your work as `blender-rocks.blend`

Now, let us create three other blendfiles that we will link back to `blender-rocks.blend`

9. Create a new blendfile and delete the default cube.

10. Create a **UV Sphere** in the center and change it to **Smooth Shading** in the **Tools** panel.

11. Temporarily save this as `001-Blender-AD.blend`.

12. From the **Files** menu, select **Link**. From the browser, select `blenderrocks.blend`, and choose **material**. From the displayed materials list, select `Blenderrockslogo`.

13. In the **Materials** panel, click the materials icon next to the **New** button to **Browse ID data**. From the displayed list, select `Blender-rocks-logo` to attach it to the object.

14. Save the file once more so that the linked material is saved.

15. Create two more blendfiles following the same steps 8 to 13. However, substitute the object for a **Cube**, linking the **Blender-rocks-logo** material, and saving as `002-Blender-AD.blend` in the second file, and substitute a **Cylinder**, without capped ends, linking the **Blender-rocks-logo** material, and saving as `003-Blender-AD.blend` for the third.

The three files created, that represent different shots from a fictitious advert, are now all linked to the original blendfile. Any changes you make to the source file will be duplicated in all linked files.

If you open `blender-rocks.blend` and alter the diffuse color of the material and then save the file, when you open any of the `nnn-Blender-AD.blend` files and render, they will have the same changed color as the source.

How it works...

Every time you open a linked blendfile it will try to locate the source file and load the material or textures that were linked. You will notice that all the material and texture commands are grayed out and unavailable to any linked materials or textures. The only things you are allowed to do in the textures panel is refresh the link or search for the source file should it not be in the location expected by Blender.

Blender even offers the facility to report missing files, or find missing files, via the **File/External Data** menu item.

Making blendfiles stand alone

Even if you are the super-organized type there will be times when you will have gathered many textures from various locations on your computer and used them within a single blendfile. Great, as long as the blendfile or those textures never move from their original location. But what happens if you want to move the blendfile to another computer?

This is a common occurrence in a production environment, particularly where contributors may be scattered across not only a country but maybe across the world.

Blender offers a neat way of collecting all the separate texture elements within a blendfile and packing them into the file.

Getting ready

You will need a blendfile that has an external image file used as one of its texture elements. If you completed the last recipe, you have such a file named `blender-rocks.blend` If not, use one of your own blendfiles.

How to do it...

We start by opening the blendfile in Blender in the normal way.

1. From the **File** menu, select **External Data** and **Pack into .blend file**. Although nothing much will appear to happen, the external files will be added within the blendfile the next time it is saved.

2. Save the blendfile, either overwriting, or giving it a new name to keep the original untouched. The save may take a little time as it is compressing all the external image textures into the blendfile.

That file can now be copied onto external media and taken to any computer where on loading, it will be renderable. Should you wish to extract the images for further editing on the external computer, you can unpack the data into a separate directory.

1. From the **File** menu select **External Data**, and **Unpack into Files**.

The image textures will be unpacked into a subdirectory, below where the blendfile is saved, called **Textures**. You can edit these files just like any image and re-pack them into the blendfile for onward transmission to another contributor if required.

How it works...

Packing the external image files in this way is a very quick way of bringing together all of the resources in a particular animation or still production. Be warned, however, that if your blendfile contains many large textures the size of the blendfile can become enormous. This can be particularly true if you expect to e-mail the file to anyone. The compression algorithms used are quite efficient however so, hopefully, you will not need a 48GB USB drive to copy your file to.

See also

Some of the blendfiles available for this cookbook are packed to make it easier for you to download. These are highlighted in the *Getting Started* sections of the relevant recipes. Once downloaded, I would recommend that you unpack them, so they are directly available in the created Textures directory.

These files are available for download at the Packtpub website.

5

Creating More Difficult Man-made Materials

In this chapter, we will cover:

- ▶ Creating rust on iron-based metals
- ▶ Creating a mesh object to provide good reflective surfaces
- ▶ Using environment map textures to simulate reflection
- ▶ Varying environment map reflections to simulate corrosion or wear
- ▶ Using raytrace reflections to simulate polished metals
- ▶ Varying raytrace reflections to simulate dirt and grime

Introduction

In Chapter 2 we looked at man-made objects and discovered ways to simulate their properties. However, man-made objects frequently have characteristics that require more complex solutions for the materials designer. Both the process of manufacture, and handling of objects, often introduces smoother and more reflective surfaces. As a result we should explore its reflectivity and how it can be simulated in Blender. We can also look at what happens to man-made materials over time, exploring rust damage, and simple abuse. All of these things will help add interest to the materials and textures we create in Blender.

Some of these attributes may seem quite difficult to achieve, however through the recipes in this chapter we will experience together the many ways in which Blender can help us achieve more difficult man-made material simulation.

Creating rust on iron-based metals

Simulating rust on iron-based metals is a really useful skill to learn in producing convincing urban metal objects. If you look around you at the real world you will see many examples of how red oxide rust will overrun metal surfaces, giving a certain drama to their look. This is because most metal manufactured items are derived from iron ore in varying proportions. In moist climates rust will form very quickly even under surfaces that have been protected with paint and other rust-inhibiting compounds. However, although a great problem to most bridge builders, rust is an extremely useful surface attribute to the 3D designer as it adds drama to a metal object. Rust is cool.

Getting ready

For this recipe we will simulate an old sea mine similar to those that can still be found dangerously floating in many seas around the world. Fortunately, our mine is simulated and therefore requires no special handling or mine disposal.

The main mesh object is a standard UV sphere of 32 sections and 16 rings. The mine detonators were created as a single object, dupliverted onto a five-sectioned, five-ringed, UV Sphere, with the top and bottom vertices removed. This was the same size as the main UV Sphere so that any dupliverted objects will uniformly rest on the mine surface. To the main sphere I have also added a little detail to represent the access plate. However, since we are not here to learn Blender modeling I will leave you to explore how that might be achieved. You can download the start blendfile from the Packt Publishing website.

How to do it...

We will start by creating a material to represent the general color and specularity of a mine surface. Now, as it happens, I do not have a ready reference to mine color, or specularity, at hand so we will have to use a little imagination to come up with a suitable approximation.

Both the mine sphere and the mine detonator objects share the same texture. We will create it on the mine sphere then apply it later to the detonator objects.

1. Open the `mine-01.blend` blendfile and select the main UV Sphere object, which is named **mine**.

2. Create a new material in the **Materials** panel, naming it **Mine**.

3. In the **Diffuse** tab set the **Color** to **R** 0.175, **G** 0.238, **B** 0.300. Leave the type as **Lambert** and the other settings at their default.

4. In the **Specular** tab ensure that the color is pure white, **R,G,B** 1.000. Keep the default **CookTorr** type but change the **Intensity** to 0.900, and **Hardness** to 103.

We have created a dark grey-blue base material with a spread specular highlight. The color may not be what original sea mines were painted but it looks good as a contrast to the rust texture we will create next.

1. With the mine object selected switch to the **Texture** panel and create a new texture in the first slot. Make this of **Type Clouds** and name it **Bumps**.

2. In the **Clouds** tab set **Grayscale**, and **Noise** to **Soft**, with a **Basis** of **Improved Perlin**. Set **Size** to **0.44**, and **Depth** to **3**.

3. Move to the **Influence** tab and check **Diffuse/Intensity** and set to -1.000. Check **Color** and set to 1.000. Check **Geometry/Normal** with a setting of -0.500. Set the **Blend** type to **Mix** and change the **color** to **R** 0.217, **G** 0.250, **B** 0.216.

Save your work as `mine-02.blend` and perform a test render. Do not be surprised if the result looks not much different from the default material. This first texture is quite subtle but will add to the overall effect.

1. In the next free texture slot create a new texture of type **Clouds**, and name it **rust mask**.

2. In the **Clouds** tab set **Grayscale**, **Noise/Soft**, and **Basis Improved Perlin**. Set the **Size** to 1.00, and **Depth** to 6.

3. Under **Colors**, **Adjust/Brightness** to 0.793, **Contrast** to 3.142, and **Saturation** to 1.000.

4. Under **Influence** set **Diffuse/Color** to 1.000. Set **Geometry/Normal** to 1.500. Set the **Blend** type to **Mix** and ensure **RGB** to **Intensity** and **Stencil** are both checked. Finally, change the color selector to **R** 0.000, **G** 0.083, and **B** 0.051.

Save your work, incrementing the filename to `mine-03.blend`. A render will show some dark green/blue blotches. However, the main point of this texture is that it will mask the following texture using its **Stencil** setting.

1. In the next free texture slot create a new texture of type **Musgrave** and name it **rust**.

2. Under the **Musgrave** tab set the **Type** to **Multifractal**, and set **Dimension** to `0.378`, **Lacunarity** to `3.066`, and **Octaves** to `6.514`. Set the **Basis** to **Blender Original** with a **Size** of `0.25`.

3. In the **Influence** tab set **Diffuse/Color** with a value of `1.000`, **Geometry/Normal** with a value of `2.000`. Ensure the **Blend** type is **Mix** and alter the color selector to **R** `0.400`, **G** `0.183`, and **B** `0.000`.

We need to attach the material to the detonator spikes. Because they are dupliverts we only need to change the main detonator object and all the copies will inherit the same texture.

1. Switch to wire frame view in your 3D view. You can do this by pressing the *Z* key.

2. If you zoom up on the mine center you should see an upright detonator object in the center of the mine. Select it and from the **Materials** panel click the little icon next to the material name to **Browse ID data**. Select the **Mine** material just created and it will be applied to this object and all the duplicated ones around the mine.

Save your work as `mine-04.blend` and perform a final render. You should see rust damage to the sea mine, showing all the indications of significant damage even beneath the protective coating.

How it works...

This relatively simple material uses many of the techniques identified in other recipes throughout this book, particularly the masking of one texture by another using the Stencil command within a texture setting. This has restricted the rust Musgrave texture to varying parts of the surface. Because of the Clouds' texture random nature the rust location appears across the surface as it might for an object that is bathed in seawater constantly.

The Musgrave texture that represents the rust is ideal for the relatively sharp-edged nodules of natural iron rust that it is used for in our material example. The single color setting of a dull orange when mixed with the other texture colors produces the rust-like colors one would expect. As the Clouds rust mask texture has graduated edges the rust and its associated orange color fade out as though the rust is forming below the paint surface. The dark green color that we applied with the rust mask also has an influence on the color of the rust.

The very first texture **Bumps**, added color, and color intensity, along with a small bump value. Although these settings did not make a huge difference when viewed in isolation, the cumulative effect has added some subtle color and bump variations to the surface. These are best viewed when you see the mine in motion. If you have experimented with any of the animation techniques in Chapter 3, why not have a go at animating the mine so that it spins slowly around? If you do so you should see all those subtle variations as the light catches the surface of our sea mine material.

There's more...

You will have noticed that we did not use any of the textures to modify the specular color or intensity, even though one might think that the specularity of painted metal and rust might be quite different. Well this mine is meant to be wet. That oily and dirty wet associated with such nasty objects. This demonstrates that we do not need to simulate every possibility within a material simulation for it to capture the essence of a surface.

I have used this model and material within a current animated short I am developing. I have used the **Edge** post processing effect, from the **Render** panel, in that production setting with the **Threshold** at 90 with an edge color of black. This gives the render a nice technical illustrative look that I personally like. The renders in this book show this outline.

You can see some examples of the mine animated in the code bundle provided for the chapter at the PacktPub website.

Animated examples of the mine rotating showing the surface variations not easily visible in a still image can be seen in `mine-06-rust.mov`.

Two animations of the mine in seawater are `mine-surface_480x270.mov` and `7x-new_960x405.mov`.

See also

Later in this chapter are two recipes that employ the Stencil command:

- ▶ *Varying environment map reflections to simulate corrosion or wear*
- ▶ *Varying raytrace reflections to simulate dirt and grime*
- ▶ Chapter 1, *Creating a gray limestone pebble*
- ▶ Chapter 2, *Creating a slate roof node material—Adding weathering by copying and reusing textures*
- ▶ Chapter 2, *Adding oxidization weathering to our copper material*
- ▶ Chapter 2, *Creating a tileable image of a cobbled path using a paint package*
- ▶ Chapter 3, *Creating a red-hot iron bar*
- ▶ Chapter 3, *Creating a working TV material*
- ▶ Chapter 6, *Creating realistic large-scale water in Blender 2.5*
- ▶ Chapter 6, *Adding a non-repeating bump to the leaf material*
- ▶ Chapter 6, *Adding color complexity to the leaf material*

Creating a mesh object to provide good reflective surfaces

One area of material simulation that has not been covered so far in this book is reflections. Manufactured metals often exhibit reflective surfaces. We have seen how specularity can simulate a certain amount of bright light reflection but to be really accurate we need to develop ways of creating reflections on our surface simulations. Fortunately, Blender has several methods that can be applied to simulate reflection and this recipe will create an ideal mesh to synthesize reflective materials.

Getting ready

Some of the later recipes in this chapter will use this object to demonstrate various methods of reflection in Blender 2.5. However, such an object is very useful to create any reflective material simulation because of the complex curves and shape of the surface. The object is a representation of a faucet or tap as might be seen in a designer catalogue for bathroom fittings.

How to do it...

The object was designed to illustrate reflections across lots of interesting curved surfaces. It was created by extruding a 16-vertex circle mesh to form the central shape then extruding portions of the mesh to form the outlet and the stopcock. A subdivision modifier was added to help smooth the whole surface.

This is a complex model and I do not expect you to recreate this from scratch, unless of course you want to. A prepared blendfile, and associated texture files for all exercises, is available from the Packt Publishing website.

However, to use this model, as a basis for reflective material creation, following the simple steps will ensure it is always available for use for your reflection material projects.

1. After downloading the `faucet-blank.zip` file to your computer unzip the file to a suitable location on your hard drive.

2. The base location you have chosen will have a `faucet-blank.blend` blendfile and a subdirectory below it called textures with some image files that can be used to test reflections in your own material creations, as well as several step files and images for several of the later recipes in this chapter.

3. If you use this file for your own reflective material tests I would suggest you open the `faucet-blank.blend` blendfile and immediately save it with a new project-specific filename. Doing this will ensure the `faucet-blank.blend` is always available for future use.

If you create any special blendfile for the purposes of testing materials always open and resave with a unique name. That means you will be able to go back to the base blendfile. Later recipes use this technique to rename and save at the beginning before you explore the material topics covered. This will ensure you do not overwrite any other recipe exercises completely.

How it works...

The mesh model has many curved surfaces that will generate a large range of reflective possibilities. It uses a simple smoothed mesh that was generated from a low-quality 16-vertex circle and then extruded to form the shape. A sub division surface modifier has been added to this simple model to create a very smooth curved surface that provides multiple reflection possibilities, including self reflection, and the possibility of reflection of every point of the world in which it sits.

See also

Later in this chapter:

▸   *Using environment map textures to simulate reflection*

▸   *Varying environment map reflections to simulate corrosion or wear*

Using environment map textures to simulate reflection

Blender provides several methods of simulating reflection. The first uses a technique that has been in Blender since the old days. Essentially, a texture is used in a material slot that is a 360-degree representation of the reflected world. This is mapped onto the surface as a reflection. The texture type is known as an **Environment Map**.

It is possible to generate environment maps directly in Blender, and this is most useful if you want to have multiple objects in a scene that need to reflect each other. However, nowadays raytrace reflection is an easier way of achieving that goal. We will look at raytrace reflection later. Here we will explore how easy it is to create a totally configurable reflection.

Getting ready

You will need to download the `faucet-blank.zip`, as mentioned above, and unzip to a suitable location.

For this recipe rename the blendfile `faucet-environment-map-01.blend`

How to do it...

Open the blendfile `faucet-environment-map-01.blend`

1.   Select the faucet object, which is named `faucet-no.2`, in the **Object** panel and **Outliner**.

2.   Move to the **Materials** panel and create a new material, naming it **old copper**.

3. In the **Diffuse** tab change the color to **R** `0.644`, **G** `0.859`, and **B** `0.630`. Ensure the type is set to **Lambert** with an **Intensity** of `1.000`.

4. In the **Specular** tab ensure the color is **R, G, B** `1.000` and the type set to **Wardiso**. Set the **Intensity** to `0.000` and **Slope** to `0.100`.

5. Move to the **Texture** panel and in the first slot create a new texture and name it **Environ-map**. Make it of type **Environment Map**.

6. In the **Environment Map** tab choose **Image File** type. Open the file `environmap-test18.png` that you unzipped earlier. It should be in the **Textures** directory below where you saved the blendfile.

7. Under the **Preview** tab select the **Sphere** preview type and **Both** so that you can see the texture displayed on the curves of a sphere and as the raw projected texture.

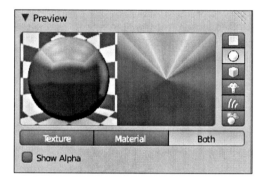

8. In the **Colors** tab change the **RGB Multiply** to **R** `1.500`, **G** `0.600`, and **B** `0.000`.

9. Under the **Influence** tab select **Diffuse/Intensity** with a value of `0.250`, and also check **Color** and set its value to `1.200`. Finally, set the **Blend** type to **Multiply**.

Save your work, remembering to increment the filename to `faucet-environment-map-02.blend` and perform a test render. The following screenshot is just a portion of the whole image render to show the reflection on the surface:

We can see that we have reflection on our faucet. However, we can add a little variation to it, reproducing the undulating nature of most metal surfaces. After all, very few metals are perfectly smooth.

1. With the faucet object selected move to the **Texture** panel and select the first texture slot that contains the **Environ-map** texture. Using the up and down buttons, next to the slot names, click the down button to move this texture down one slot. That will leave an empty texture slot above the **Environ-map** texture.

2. Select that new first slot and create a new texture of type **Clouds** and name it bump.

3. In the **Clouds** tab set **Grayscale** and **Noise** to **Soft**. Chose **Blender Original** and the **Basis**, and set the **Size** to 1.00, and **Depth** to 5.

4. Under the **Influence** tab only check the **Geometry/Normal** selection and set its value to 1.000.

Save your work, remembering to increment the filename to faucet-environment-map-03.blend and perform a test render.

How it works...

Environment maps are images that have six square representations of the left, back, right, bottom, top, and front sides of a box. If you were standing in the middle of that box the view around you would look like a 360-degree view of the world. This type of box mapping is frequently used in game construction as it can quickly generate reflections without computing overheads of raytrace calculations.

LEFT	BACK	RIGHT
BOTTOM	TOP	FRONT

Environment maps can be in any of the image formats that Blender can accept, although their dimensions should be in multiples of two. This is because game engines can manipulate binary data much faster than floating point data. The image used in the recipe is 1536 x 1024.

As you can see it is a very simple image with a six-light ceiling and one window on the right side. Window frames are frequently used as a shortcut reflection device in all kinds of animation. Disney and other early animators used it as a quick way to show eye reflection in some of their characters. Here a very simple frame has been cut into the wall background with a simulated sky color to give it a bit more shape. You do not need to hand-draw environment maps. You can use real photos and arrange them in the order indicated to produce an environment map. Just make sure that the edges match to create the illusion of a 360-degree environment.

Obtaining the color of copper in recipe uses an interesting method of color application. You will have noticed that the main color of the faucet was created by applying color variation within the texture rather than within the material settings. Essentially, you have been adding a color wash over the environment map. This is very similar to how oil paint artists create a mirrored copper object. First employing a grayscale under paint, to represent the shadow, and highlights, and then applying an orange/yellow thin wash to make it look like copper. So even in the digital world we can learn from the masters.

In setting those colors we used a red value above 1.00. Blender allows us to enter many values above what is apparently their maximum. In this case it ensured the red channel of the image really dominates the render, which is how copper actually appears. We further increased the **Influence/ Color** value to 1.200. The **Influence** mix method is also set to **Multiply,** which means that the environment map colors are multiplied on top of the underlying material diffuse color. Interestingly that light green, apart from influencing the overall material color, is the color of copper oxidization, which we will exploit further in the next exercise.

Applying color in this way ensures that the environment map itself could be used for any colored metal surface. We just need to change the colors, in the **Texture/Colors,** tab to match the metal to be simulated. You might like to experiment with that yourself to produce bronze or steel examples.

There's more...

A disadvantage of the way we have used an environment map here is that the surface will not reflect any other objects should they be in the scene. It is possible to use Blender to generate an environment map from the location of an object. However, it is easier to create such other-object-reflections using raytrace techniques, which we will explore later. However, if you are interested in investigating the steps necessary you can read about it in the Blender Wiki.

A further disadvantage is that if the object were to move in an animation the reflection would appear to move with it. However, environment maps are a quick and controllable method of simulating reflections.

Should you not have time to create your own environment maps a search on Google should discover Blender, and other cube environment maps. Just remember that unless these images are Open Source you should not use them without copyright clearance from the owner. Apart from the simple map used in this exercise I have included a range of simple environment maps available from the same location as the zipfile on the packt website.

See also

▶ *Using environment map textures to simulate reflection*

▶ *Varying environment map reflections to simulate corrosion or wear*

Varying environment map reflections to simulate corrosion or wear

Reflections will frequently be inconsistent across a surface. Wear and tear will smudge, or remove, reflection from those damaged sections of an object. With environment map reflections we have to develop strategies to simulate that variation because there is no simple command or button to do this for us. However, we can employ masks to achieve some really quite realistic results using environment maps.

Getting ready

You will need to extract the `faucet-blank.blend` file from the `faucet-blank.zip`, downloaded in the earlier recipe *Creating a mesh object to provide good reflective surfaces*. If you have already downloaded and unzipped that file, open it in Blender and rename it as `faucet-old-copper-01.blend`. Save this file before continuing with the recipe.

The recipe uses the same environment map as used for the previous exercise. This should be located in the textures sub-directory below where you extracted the zip file. Please read the earlier recipe *Creating a mesh object to provide good reflective surfaces* of this chapter, which gives all necessary details.

How to do it...

We will first create the underlying color for the copper. If you have already completed the previous recipe you will see some similar settings. However, we will make some modifications to aid the coloring.

1. With the **faucet-no.2** object selected move to the **Materials** panel and create a new material, naming it `old-copper`.

2. In the **Diffuse** tab change the color to **R** `0.086`, **G** `0.220`, and **B** `0.099`. This will create a darker green background color than that in the previous recipe. Set the **Intensity** to `1.000` and the type to **Lambert**.

3. In the **Specular** tab change the color to **R** `1.000`, **G** `0.949`, and **B** `0.688`. Select the type as **Wardiso**, with an **Intensity** of `0.235`, and a **Slope** of `0.300`.

That has produced a darker green with a dull yellow specular highlight. Time to set up textures to create an old corroded copper faucet appearance.

1. Switch to the **Texture** panel and select the first texture slot. Create a new texture of type **Clouds** and name it `mask`.

2. Under the **Clouds** tab ensure the **Grayscale** and **Noise/Hard** are selected. Choose the **Basis** as **Blender Original**, with **Size** `0.70`, and **Depth** `6`.

3. In the **Colors** tab change **Adjust/ Brightness 0.800, Contrast 1.700**.

4. Under the **Influence** tab check **Diffuse/Color** and set to `0.500`. Check **Specular/ Intensity** and set to `0.500`. Set the **Blend** type to **Mix** and check **Negative**, **RGB** to **Intensity** and **Stencil**. Change the color to **R** `0.774`, **G** `1.000`, and **B** `0.730`.

That has readjusted the background color to a more realistic oxidized copper look. It has also set a mask for all following textures. Save your work at this point, incrementing the filename to `faucet-old-copper-02.blend`. There is no need to render at this point as the material magic only really develops with the next two textures.

1. In the **Texture** panel select the next free texture slot below **bump** and create a new texture of type **Musgrave** and name it `rust-damage`.

2. Under the **Musgrave** tab select **Type Multifractal**, with **Dimension** at `0.000`, **Lacunarity** `2.400`, and **Octaves** `6.000`. Make the **Noise Basis Blender Original** with a **Size** of `1.50`.

3. In the **Colors** tab check the **Ramp** checkbox and create a new color stop in the ramp at **Pos** 0.911. The color should be white by default and the **Alpha** at 0.44. If not, then just click on the color band and enter those settings.

4. Under the **Influence** tap check the **Diffuse/Color** set to 1.000. Check **Specularity/ Intensity** set to 2.000 and **Geometry/Normal** to -0.100. Set the **Blend** type to **Mix** and ensure **RGB to Intensity** and **Stencil** are both checked. Finally, change the color to **R** 1.000, **G** 0.730, and **B** 0.000.

Once again save your work, incrementing the filename to faucet-old-copper-03.blend. If you were to render now you would see a broken yellow/orange color on top of the green material color. To make this into a reflective metal we shall add our environment map.

1. In the next free texture slot create a new texture of type **Environment Map** and name it **Environ-map**.

2. In the **Environment Map** tab select **Image File** and open environment-test18. png from the textures folder.

 This file should have been created when you unzipped the faucet-blank.zip download following the instructions at the beginning of this section.

3. Under the **Colors** tab change the values in **RGB Multiply** to **R** 1.600, **G** 1.000, **B** 0.500. Also change the **Adjust** values of **Brightness** 1.300, **Contrast** 1.700 and **Saturation** 1.200.

4. In the **Mapping** tab set the **Coordinates** type to **Reflection**.

5. And finally in the **Influence** tab check **Diffuse/Intensity** to 0.250 and **Color** 1.200. Change the **Blend** type to **Multiply**.

Save your completed material simulation as faucet-old-copper-04.blend and perform a final render. Not bad for a simple environment map reflection.

How it works...

Using the Stencil command within a texture is a great way of masking parts of the surface. However, sometimes it can be tricky to work out what will be covered or revealed. It also can be complex when you wish to use other attributes within the stencil texture such as color. That is why the material color was made a little darker than the previous recipe. Because when we used the Clouds texture in mask we had to make it negative to mask out the correct part of the faucet. By setting the color to a light green the mixing effect actually lightens the background material color, while still giving some color variation across the surface.

The rust-damage is the Musgrave, which is also used as another stencil for following textures. You can therefore use one mask to restrict portions of your textures and another, or more, to restrict further within that mask. Because the settings of the Musgrave are set with a high contrast we create a sharp-edged mask for the environment map texture that follows.

You will also see that we have changed the color to a ramp within the texture. These will change the way the texture appears, depending on the angle the object is rendered. So the edges will have less reflection than the faces seen directly by the camera. This will further help give a prominent copper-like appearance to the material.

Finally, we applied the environment map changing the color, brightness, contrast and saturation to amounts higher than 1.000. This will really make the color of the reflection prominent. This is important because with real reflection of things like window frames the range of brightness levels is much higher than an ordinary image can represent.

There's more...

For the initial render shown at the beginning of this recipe I added a composite node set up to provide a little depth of field. If you would like to try this I have included that blendfile for you to explore.

Animating settings to produce a time-lapse of copper aging

It is possible to animate a kind of aging process of this faucet oxidizing as time progresses. If you have explored Chapter 3, *Animating Blender Materials*, you will have discovered that any of the texture or material settings can be animated over time. Under the **Colors** tab of the rust-damage texture you could set keyframes for the **Contrast** and **Brightness** values, above or below 1.000, and then animate over time. If you would like to see the effect of such an animation you can view a short sequence on which I have added further textures to take the faucet from bright and shiny to corroded and dull over about seven seconds.

```
http://vimeo.com/13779512
```

See also

Chapter 4, *How to alter the color of materials and textures over time*

Using raytrace reflections to simulate polished metals

Environment map reflection is OK for quick simulation of a reflective surface. However, for true reflection we need to use raytracing to generate physically accurate reflections just like we would see in real life. Raytrace rendering has been used for many years in 3D applications such as Blender. However, until recently the processing required producing a raytrace generated render was beyond 3D animation tasks because of the long render times involved. Fortunately, the power of computers has moved on as has the algorithms that are required to calculate such complex physical light properties. Blender has a really efficient raytrace engine. All of the renders you will undertake in this book were actually raytrace renders. We were just not using many of the facilities such as ray mirror reflection. Raytracing is switched on by default in Blender.

In this recipe we will explore the ease of ray mirror to produce very accurate reflections in another man-made appliance.

Getting ready

This recipe uses another faucet design to demonstrate ray mirror. This is again a complex mesh that I do not expect you to manually duplicate as part of the recipes. I have included the start file for the next two recipes in the `faucets-blank.zip` file that can be downloaded from the Packt Publishing website.

The blendfile required for this recipe is `faucet-mirror-blank.blend`.

You are advised to open this file and immediately save it as `faucet-mirror-gold-01.blend`. This will ensure you do not overwrite the start file for future exercises.

All of the image textures required for this exercise will be found in the Textures folder below the directory you unzipped to.

How to do it...

As with any reflection it will be necessary to create a world to reflect in our object. Once again we do not have to build this world in Blender. We can use the **World** setting, with a special image type, that makes these ray mirror reflections so attractive.

1. Open the blendfile `faucet-mirror-gold-01.blend` as discussed earlier.

2. Select the **faucet-no.1-base** object. You will notice that there are three objects in this scene.

3. From the **Materials** panel create a new material and name it `mirror`.

4. Change the **Diffuse** color to **R** `1.000`, **G** `0.570`, and **B** `0.200`. Leave the other **Diffuse** settings at default.

5. Under the **Mirror** tab set **Reflectivity** to `1.000`. Set **Fresnel** to `1.700`, and **Blend** to `1.250`. Change the color to **R** `1.000`, **G** `0.973`, and **B** `0.444`. Change the **Depth** to `4`, and under **Gloss** change the **Amount** to `0.977`, **Samples** to `18` and **Anisotropic** to `0.459`.

The preview should show the sphere reflecting a background grid.

Now that we know our faucet will mirror the outside world, it's time to create the world it reflects.

1. Switch to the **World** panel and without changing any of the settings immediately select the **Texture** panel. This will bring up the same texture panel you can use in materials but this time it is in world context. So any texture here will be applied to the world.

2. Create a new texture in the first empty slot of type **Image or Movie**, and name it `HDR-world`.

3. In the **Image** tab **Open** the file `Church_HarvestLobby.hdr` from the Textures folder.

4. In the **Mapping** tab select **Coordinates** of type **View**.

5. Under **Influence** check both **Horizon** and **Zenith** both with a setting of `1.000`. Leave all the other settings at default.

You should see in the world preview a panoramic interior.

Its time to save your work, remember to increment the filename to `faucet-mirror-gold-02.blend`. Perform a test render and you will see both this background image and the reflection in the faucet base.

Although we have a gold-looking reflection we can clean this render up a little to remove the distracting background and also make the reflection a little sharper.

6. Switch to the **Render** panel and select the **Layers** tab. Under **Include** un-check the **Sky** box. Collapse the **Layers** tab so that it does not take up too much room. Click the down triangle next to the **Layers** tab name.

7. Move down to the **Anti-Aliasing** tab and alter the **Size** setting to `0.500`.

8. We can now attach this material to the other components of this faucet.

9. Select the `faucet-no.1-lever` object and from the **Materials** panel click the material icon **Browse ID Data** and select the material mirror for this object.

10. Do the same thing for the `faucet-no.1-joint` object. The **Materials** panel mirror material should show that three objects now share the same material.

Save your work, incrementing the filename to `faucet-mirror-gold-03.blend`. A test render will show the whole faucet on a black background but with the world still reflected on the surface of our object. A nice clean reflection but it would be nice to make this faucet the most expensive available, so let us add a little solid gold surface ripple.

11. Select the `faucet-no.1-base` object and select the **Materials** panel. Immediately select the **Texture** panel and in the first free slot create a new texture of type **Clouds** and name it gold-bump.

12. In the **Clouds** tab select **Greyscale** and **Noise Soft**. Change the **Depth** to 2 and leave all other settings at their defaults.

13. Under the **Influence** tab uncheck all checkboxes apart from **Geometry/Normal** and change its value to `0.075`.

Save your finished solid gold faucet blendfile as `faucet-mirror-gold-04.blend`. Perform a final render to see your completed work.

How it works...

The main color settings of this material simulation created a nice orange/yellow diffuse color and light yellow mirror color for any reflections. The Diffuse color is more apparent on the surface facing the camera because we set up a Fresnel-like effect in the material mirror tab. Reflectivity is set to maximum to give a very reflective surface. The depth was set to four meaning that the raytrace calculations will trace reflected ray across four bounces or reflections. This ensures that reflections of reflections are also included. It can be set much higher but there is little point as with each reflection the mirror effect will dim anyway. However, if you set it too low the resultant reflections can look a little odd.

Of course, a reflection is only as good at what is being reflected. Here we used an image mapped to the world view. However, this image is rather special as it holds much more than just the straight image you can see. High Dynamic Range Images hold an enormous range of light levels within the file. Blender can read these and as a result sunlight through a window pain looks incredibly bright just like it would in reality. You can also see detail in the shadow areas. These images are fantastic for the purpose of world creation without the need for complex modeling. However, such images are hard to produce yourself. Luckily, there are some excellent examples available online that can be used freely in your creations. The image used here, and others are available from: `http://www.hdrmill.com/Freebies.htm`

This company also offer a paid-for service that you may be interested in exploring.

You are not limited to just `.hdr` images. As with environment maps Blender can accept a large range of image formats for textures. A search in Google should turn up a number that might be useful in your own creations.

The final texture added to our material was a simple Clouds texture applied as a bump map. You will have noticed that the level of bump was very small. You will find that when applying bump maps to a reflective surface, only small amounts of the normal are required to give the effect. Reflections really emphasize any surface bumps.

There's more...

The renders I have used in the book have a white background. This was achieved by creating a simple Compositor node setup. The render layer was passed through an **Alpha Over** node with a white color in the upper image input. I have also set up **Ambient Occlusion** to add a little darkening to the components of the faucet. All these settings are available in your finished `faucet-mirror-gold-04.blend` file you saved at the end of the exercise. Just go to the **World** panel and turn on **Ambient Occlusion**. The settings will be the same as I have used.

See also

Chapter 6, *Creating realistic large-scale water in Blender 2.5* and *Creating an ocean surface material*

Varying raytrace reflections to simulate dirt and grime

As we all know, nothing stays clean for long. Dirt and grime will quickly form on any object given time and interaction with the atmosphere and we humans. Simulating this on raytraced mirror surfaces is quite difficult. However, we will attempt to turn the spectacular gold faucet created in the last recipe to one that might be found in a rather disreputable establishment.

Getting ready

This recipe uses the finished blendfile from the previous recipe. If you have not completed that you can download the blendfile from the Packt Publishing website.

How to do it...

We can start by turning down the mirror settings for the material. This is to imitate dust on the surface.

1. Open up the blendfile `faucet-mirror-gold-04.blend`, and immediately resave it as `faucet-dirty-gold-01.blend`.

2. With the `faucet-no.1-base` object selected move to the **Materials** panel and the **Mirror** tab. Reduce the **Reflectivity** setting to `0.6`.

Now let's add some additional textures to represent human interaction.

1. Move to the **Texture** panel and select the free slot below the `gold-bump` texture and create a new texture of type **Clouds** and name it `mask`.

2. In the **Clouds** tab select **Greyscale** and **Noise Hard**. Set the type as **Blender Original** with a **Size** of `0.85` and a **Depth** of `6`.

3. Under the **Colors** tab **Adjust** the **Brightness** to `1.100` and the **Contrast** to `3.000`.

4. In the **Influence** tab de-select all of the checkboxes apart from **RGB to Intensity** and **Stencil**.

5. In the **Texture** panel select the next free slot and create a new texture of type **Image or Movie** and name it `fingerprints`.

6. In the **Image** tab **Open** the image `fingerprints.png` that you will find in the Textures directory.

7. Under the **Mapping** tab change the **Z** size to `0.70`.

8. In the **Influence** tab check **Shading/Ray Mirror** and set to `-1.500`. Select **Specular/Intensity** and set to `-1.000`. Set the **Blend** type to **Multiply** and check **RGB to Intensity** and **Negative**. All other Influence settings should be unselected.

9. In the **Textures Panel** select the next free texture slot and create a new texture of type **Musgrave** and name it water-spots.

10. Under the **Musgrave** tab select **Type Multifractal** and change the **Dimension** to `0.400`, **Lacunarity** `3.900` and **Octaves** `8.000`. Set the **Noise Basis** to **Blender Original** with **Size** `0.08`.

11. In the **Colors** tab **Adjust** the **Brightness** to `1.500`, and **Contrast** `1.700`.

12. Finally, in the **Influence** tab check **Diffuse/Intensity** and set to `1.000`, and **Color** `2.000`. Set **Shading/Emit** to `1.000`. Set the **Blend** type to Mix and check **Negative** and **RGB** to **Intensity**. Change the color to **R** `0.821`, **G** `0.874`, and **B** `1.000`.

Save your work as `faucet-dirty-gold-02.blend` and perform a render. I think this bathroom needs a clean.

How it works...

Reducing the reflection setting in the material immediately dulls the metal. Of course, the reflection still stays crisp because raytracing is so accurate. To reduce this pristine look we need to add some other textures to change color, specularity and intensity of color. This was achieved by first adding a simple mask and then a series of textures to represent the kind of interaction such an object would pick up.

The first texture is an image map of fingerprints. It was obtained by using a series of Gimp brushes that are freely available on the Internet. An image was created and made to tile. This is then simply mapped to the surface, with specular and ray mirror settings, to alter the appearance of the reflection. There was no point in accurately placing that image to the surfaces as even if it stretches some fingerprints it makes it look like fingers have been dragged across the surface.

The Musgrave texture has been used to represent water drops or soap splashes. By varying the **Dimension, Lacunarity,** and **Octaves** it is possible to produce a few or many such drop shapes. So Musgrave has proved to be a useful procedural texture once again.

There's more...

Once again I used Ambient Occlusion in my renders for the book and also a Compositor node tree to simply create the white background. All those settings are in the default file. You just need to turn them on and they will be part of your renders.

The textures used in this recipe have used Brushes created for use in Gimp or Photoshop. These are extremely useful to the Blender materials designer. Fortunately, like Blender, Gimp is an Open Source product and as a result there are a lot of freely available brushes and tools for creating all kinds of images. The fingerprints used a series of brushes available from: `http://hawksmont.com/`.

They are also available in Photoshop versions.

6
Creating More Difficult Natural Materials

In this chapter, we will cover:

- Creating realistic large-scale water in Blender 2.5
    - Setting up an environment to represent an ocean vista
    - Creating a wave surface using textures
    - Creating an ocean surface material
    - Creating wake around objects in water
- Creating image and bump maps, with alpha channels
    - Using images as the basis for a leaf material
    - Adding non-repeating bump to the leaf material
    - Adding color complexity to the leaf material

Introduction

Natural materials can be quite good fun to produce in Blender. However, sometimes, they require some quite tricky approaches in order to obtain the surface simulation that tells the viewer what they are looking at. Transparency and reflection are both difficult natural surface properties to simulate. Transparency exists in all kinds of natural surfaces from holes in plant life caused by insect damage, to natural transparency of elements such as water. Water, and wet surfaces, also require reflective elements to make them convincing. In this chapter, we will cover both of these challenging surfaces.

Creating realistic large-scale water in Blender 2.5

Water is one of the most difficult of natural substances to simulate in any 3D design system. Blender comes with some extremely good fluid tools that can make an excellent physically based fluid simulation possible. However, unless you have an extremely powerful computer, and plenty of time, simulating large-scale water surfaces is better achieved using materials and textures.

While the following recipes can produce some excellent still renders, water really comes alive when it is seen in motion. In the following recipes, we will create an entire ocean, with water interacting with objects, as well as waves in motion. Fortunately, you will not require a super fast computer to complete these exercises, although renders will take between 5 and 15 minutes per-frame, depending on the resolution required for the final animation. Creating a realistic ocean material is quite complex and for that reason, we will break the process into several recipes. However, you don't have to follow them in a sequential order to produce the completed animation. Start blendfiles are available for each stage of the simulation.

For those of you who may have followed some of my earlier cogfilms.com, ocean and seascape tutorials, you will find in these recipes new ideas on how to conquer this apparently difficult natural material simulation.

Getting ready

If you completed Chapter 1, *Creating a sea rock material*, you may notice that the rock recipe mesh is used in this simulation. Some of the settings in that recipe are used to texture the rock. However, additional textures have also been applied to correctly place the rock in water. These include specular and reflective maps, along with a little interaction from our seagull friends. As we covered rock material simulation in some detail in Chapter 1, I don't intend to cover the rock here as a recipe. However, you can explore the texture in combination with those original recipes to see how the seagull droppings and masking was applied.

There are also a series of special textures used to create the wash around the rocks, which were prepared from images obtained from within Blender, but modified in GIMP. I will give instructions on how they were produced later. You can download a special zip file called `large-scale-ocean.zip` containing all of the images and start blendfiles for this entire section from the Packtpub website.

If you are going to run through each recipe in this section, be prepared to spend a few days to gain the most from them.

How to do it...

In this initial recipe, we will need to set up the correct working environment to help generate our ocean.

1. Unzip the `large-scale-ocean.zip` to a suitable location on your hard drive. A series of blendfiles and a textures directory will be produced with all of the image files for these recipes.

2. The start file is called `large-scale-water-00.blend`. Open this file in Blender and immediately save it as `large-scale-water-01.blend`. This will ensure you can always return to the start file should you wish to complete these recipes again in the future.

3. You should also create a sub-directory to store the animation files ready for later recipes in this chapter. I would suggest creating a sub-directory below where the blendfiles are located called `animations`.

How it works...

When you need to create either an animated render, in one of the Blender-supported animation formats like `.avi`, `.mov`, or as a series of `.png` frames, ensure that you create a unique sub-directory to store them. Blender allows you to save files virtually anywhere on your system. However, the default location will probably be the same directory as the blendfile. This is not the best place to store them as such files can easily be lost amongst all of your blendfiles. I recommend always setting up a specific sub-directory for individual blendfile animations. In this way, you can keep the animated files separate and, therefore, easier to find for post processing work or for the editing tasks later in the production pipeline.

There's more...

To help you understand what can be achieved by completing all the recipes in this section, you can view a final rendered animation at the following location:

`http://vimeo.com/13763186`

[The animation not only uses all of the ocean recipes in this chapter but also one from Chapter 8, which paints some additional skyline detail by post processing.]

Setting up an ocean vista environment

Before we can start creating ocean-like materials, we need to set a scene that will enable our materials to work over what will be very large scenes in Blender. The camera will be able to see to its limits many hundreds of Blender units up to the horizon. Therefore, lighting and background will be important to help place our material into a world-sized environment.

Getting ready

This recipe picks up from the last, so you will need to open the blendfile `large-scale-water-01.blend` created at the end of the last recipe, or unzip the file from the zip file.

How to do it...

In this recipe, we will set up the initial scene to make the most of the ocean simulation.

1. Open `large-scale-water-01.blend` that you completed from the last recipe, or unzipped earlier.

You will notice that the rocks mesh object is selected, and the camera has been moved somewhat from the recipe where we created some nice rock simulations in Chapter 1. This is to produce a more pleasing layout to give plenty of sea area to show the waves as well as the rock interaction with the water. The base plane has been renamed `sea-distant` and the lights have been repositioned and turned off in this initial blendfile. This is so that we can turn each on individually to explore their effect on the scene one by one.

2. Select the point light behind the `rocks` object that is named `back-light`.

3. Under the **Lamp** tab, check both **Specular** and **Diffuse** to turn this lamp back on.

4. Perform a test render at 25%. This will produce a dark image with an obvious back light illuminating the top and back of the rocks. It also casts a shadow. Note the intensity of this lamp at **Energy** `1.000`.

5. Select the hemi light at the front of the rocks, called `fill-hemi`, and check just the **Diffuse** checkbox.

6. Perform a test render and you will see that the dark fronts of the rock have been slightly lightened. Note the intensity of this lamp with an **Energy** setting of only `0.040`. And, of course, it casts no additional shadows.

7. Select the spot light on the left of the rocks called `key-light` and check both its **Specular** and **Diffuse** settings in the **Lamp** tab.

8. Perform a test render and you should see that we have a more interesting lighting setup ready for our new rock texture.

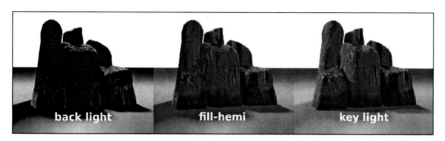

So far, we have just examined the lighting within this scene. Let us create a world background to help place our ocean scene.

9. Select the **World** panel and in the **World** tab, check **Blend Sky** and **Real Sky**. Change the **Horizon Color** to **R** `0.938`, **G** and **B** `0.940`. Change the **Zenith Color** to **R** `0.284`, **G** `0.617`, and **B** `0.912`.

10. In the **Texture** panel, create a new world texture of type **Clouds** and name it `Stratocumulus`.

11. Under the **Clouds** tab, set **Grayscale**, and **Noise Hard**, **Basis Blender Original**, with a **Size** of `1.10`, and **Depth** of `6`.

12. In the **Mapping** tab, change the **Coordinates** type to **View**.

13.. And, finally, in the **Influence** tab, check **Blend** and set to 3.000, select **Blend** type **Mix** and set the color to **R** `1.000`, **G** and **B** `0.947`.

Save your work, incrementing the file name to `large-scale-water-02.blend`.

How it works...

The setup of this blendfile has some interesting features. Firstly, the lighting is quite subtle and low key. However, it produces some nice shadows on the rock even before we add a material. You will also notice that two of the lights cast shadow. The key light and the back light both cast shadows in different directions. You may think that this would produce problems when we are trying to simulate a daylight scene. However, both have been set to produce soft shadows and since most of the shadow will be on the surface of the water, it will be masked by the textures used for the water surface. Bounce light from clouds is also common in sun cloud environments. This bounce light also casts shadow. However, in real life, these secondary shadows would be washed out by the stronger sun key light. Here, we have magnified that secondary shadowing effect to help give shape to the rocks. If the opposing shadow becomes too prominent, we could either turn the shadow off, on the back light, or blur it even more.

The fill light is important here because it helps lighten the dark shadows that would be produced without it. Because default lighting in 3D systems does not generate any global illumination, we have to fake it. A simple hemi light that will not cast shadows performs this function admirably. Blender has a new environment lighting function in the World panel. Although we could have used this, the resultant render times would have produced a very long animation process for such a large scene. We will be employing raytrace reflection for the waves so anything we can do to avoid unnecessary render complication should be encouraged.

The sea-distant plane is a large four-vertex plane that stretches beyond the vision of the camera thus giving the effect of the horizon. However, because we are only illuminating the rocks, the distant areas currently look rather dark. You will see that once we add some texture to this plane that horizon darkening will not adversely affect the rendered animation.

Lastly, you may have noticed that the objects in the scene have been arranged on different layers. Selecting only the appropriate layers for any stage in the materials development can save time in rendering. In this setup, we have the camera and lights on layer 1, the moving waves will be on layer 2, the rocks on layer 3, the sea-distant object on layer 4, and some empties, we will use to aid animation, on layer 5. Organizing your scene assets this way, especially with complex scenes, will ensure that you can concentrate on creating individual materials without being encumbered by having all the other objects appear when you are creating, or test rendering. This can be important because a test render, on just one of the objects, will take several minutes at full resolution. Whereas, limiting it to one object could half those test render times.

See also

If you haven't done so yet, you may find it useful to examine the rock example materials in Chapter 1. You could also explore the copper turret recipe in Chapter 2 that uses the same world settings to produce a semi-cloudy sky.

Creating a wave surface using textures

In this recipe, we will create the waves that will wash against the rocks. To make it a little easier, we will base the wave motion on slack water so that we don't have to worry about tide movement. Although we can generate all kinds of weather, we will keep this wave motion relatively calm.

Getting ready

You will need to open the saved file from the last recipe or if you are undertaking this out of order unzip the `large-scale-water-02.blend` from the zipped file download following the instructions at the beginning of this section.

How to do it...

We will first create a simple plane upon which our waves will be created.

1. With the `large-scale-water-02.blend` opened in Blender, select layer 2 in the header of the **3D view**. Move the cursor to the center of the grid *SHIFT+S*, **Cursor to Center**.

2. Create a new plane mesh. *SHIFT+A*, **Add**, **Mesh**, **Plane**. In the **Object** panel, name it `sea-closeup`.

3. Scale this new plane by ten, S key, `10`, and *ENTER*. You can achieve the same by bringing up the **Transform** properties panel in the **3D view**, by pressing *N*, and changing the scale figures for **X**, **Y**, and **Z** to `10`. While in this properties panel, we will numerically lower the plane in the Z axis to get it into a nice position to add the waves. Change the **Location Z** value to `-0.195`. Close this panel by pressing *N* key once more.

4. Switch to mesh edit mode by pressing the **Tab** key, and subdivide the mesh five times by pressing **Add/Subdivide** button in the **Tool box**. Also, select **Shading/Smooth**.

5. Press *Tab* to exit mesh edit and from the **Modifiers** panel, **Add Modifier** of type **SubSurf** with **View** set to `1` and **Render** `3`. Check **Subdivide UVs**, and **Optimal Display**. You should also select each of the four buttons, **Camera (Use modifier during rendering)**, **Eye (Realtime display of modifier)**, **Mesh cube (Use modifier while in edit mode)**, and **Mesh triangle (Apply modifier to editing cage during Edit mode)**.

Save your work at this stage, incrementing the filename to `large-scale-water-03.blend`.

To complete this stage of the ocean simulation, we need to apply a displacement modifier to create the wave shape. To do so, we first have to create a texture within a material so it can become available to the modifier stack.

6. With the **sea-closeup** object selected, move to the **Materials** panel and create a new material. You don't need to name it, or change any of its default settings, it is merely being used as a temporary holder for the texture we need.

7. In the **Texture** panel, create a new texture of type **Clouds** and name it `wave-bump`.

8. In the **Clouds** tab, select **Grayscale** and **Noise Hard**. Set the **Basis** as **Blender Original** with **Size** `1.00`, and **Depth** `6`.

9. In the **Colors** tab, change **Adjust/Brightness**, and **Contrast** to `1.300`.

10. Move back to the **Modifiers** panel and **Add Modifier** of type **Displace** and name it `waves`. In the **Texture** selector, click the little checker icon and it will display any textures currently in the Blendfile. Select the `wave-bump` texture we just created.

11. Select **Direction** type **Normal** and **Texture Coordinates Object**.

Currently, we have no object to use here. However, let us change the remaining settings in the Modifier stack before we set the object up.

1. Change the **Midlevel** to `0.500`, and **Strength** to `-0.05`.

Rather than animate the texture setting within a material, we can map the displacement texture to another object such as an Empty. Then, it becomes easy to scale it and move the empty over time to get the movement we require.

2. Move to the layer **5** where you will find several empties already created. These will be used with the ocean and rock materials. However, we will create the one for the wave movement to show you how easy they are to create and use.

3. Move the cursor to the center of the grid *SHIFT+S*, Cursor to Center. Press *SHIFT+A*, **Add Empty**. Name it `wave-movement` in the **Object** panel.

4. Scale this empty by six, S, 6, *ENTER*.

5. Shift select both layers **2** and **5** so that you can see both the **Empty** and the **sea-closeup** object in the camera view.

6. Select the `sea-closeup` object and move to the **Modifiers** panel.

7. Under the `waves` **Displacement** modifier, click the **Object** icon and from the displayed list, select `wave-movement`.

The displacement is now controlled by the position of the empty. If you select that empty, `wave-movement`, and move it in the view, you should see the surface of the **sea-closeup** move just like waves on the surface.

Save your work, incrementing the filename to `large-scale-water-04.blend`.

Let us set up a quick animation by creating an animated movement of the `wave-movement` empty. The settings that we will use were worked out following a little trial and error. However, although they may seem arbitrary, just follow the directions and I will explain how you can find the correct speeds yourself.

8. Move the **wave-movement** empty back to its start position. If you moved it, press *ALT+G*, which returns it to the location it was created.

9. Set an animation length starting at `1` and ending at `250`. That is the default anyway. That will give a 10-second animation at 25 fps.

10. Move to frame `241` and in the **3D** view, bring up the **Transform** panel by pressing *N*.

11. Right click on the **Location Z** value that should be `0.000`, and select **Insert Single Keyframe**.

12. Move to frame `50`, and in the **Transform** panel, change the **Location Z** value to `-8.000`. Then right click on this and **Insert Single keyframe**.

13. Change the bottom view to the **Graph** editor and you should see a curved line representing the animation of the empty between frame `50` and `241`.

We need to change that to a straight line so that the movement will be constant.

1. From the **Key** menu of the **Graph** editor, select **Extrapolation Mode**, and **Linear Extrapolation**. The graph should change to a straight continuous line.

Save your work, incrementing the filename to `large-scale-water-05.blend`. Rather than do a render at this time, we can see what the movement might be like using the camera view.

2. Select layers 1, 2, and 3, so that we can see the rocks as well as the sea. Enlarge the camera view to full-screen, *CTRL+UP ARROW*, and press *ALT+A* to play the animation. It might be best to view in solid mode by pressing *Z*. In the top left of the screen, you will see a red FPS readout showing how fast the view is playing.

3. Press *ESC* to cancel the live preview.

How it works...

We explored animation, and the graph editor, in Chapter 3. To produce constant movement, we need to use linear extrapolation to the curve created. By mapping the displacement to the empty, it was possible to play with the empty and see on screen the kinds of movement we could obtain.

This technique has been used in many special effect facilities for feature films. An Oscar-winning example was seen in Peter Jackson's *King Kong* (2005). Weta Digital created a scene of the venture boat crashing into the rocks at Skull Island. The animators had to search through digital waves to find the right one to make the shot. You can almost see the animator moving the empty around the scene until they found the correct wave. In our example, the waves are less violent than those in *King Kong*. However, we can still use a similar technique to set the perfect speed for our waves.

When you played the timeline by pressing *ALT+A*, a red the fps indictor is displayed in the top left of the screen. The speed will be affected by the power of the computer you are using, as well as the complexity of the scene, and the screen draw method you have adopted. The PC I am using displayed at about 14/15 fps, which is half the speed of NTSC, which is approximately 30 fps, or nearly 60% of the correct speed at 24 fps. By adjusting the slope of the empty in the graph editor, you can adjust the speed up or down. You can either adjust the slope of the graph until the speed looks OK at 15 fps (my Computer) then reduce the slope by 50% or 60% and you should be close to the correct speed.

You will eventually have to perform a short rendered animation to double check that the speed works. Do it at this stage before you have complex materials attached that slow down your renders.

Two good tips to produce fast test animations

1. Create a render boarder, *SHIFT+B* in the camera view, around part of the waves and only render that section over 50 – 100 frames.

2. Render out an OpenGL render of the camera viewport by clicking the little clapperboard icon on the 3D view header.

Be careful to give a different output name for such renders. It is very easy to overwrite full render images without realizing you are doing it.

See also

If you haven't done so already, explore Chapter 3, *Creating Animated Materials*. Here, you will see the kind of animations possible within Blender.

Creating an ocean surface material

In this recipe, we will create the ocean surface material to add finer waves or wavelets and also wave foam under the surface. This type of interaction is frequently seen in shallower water where the wave action interacts with the plankton waste materials to produce tiny air bubbles that eventually rise to the surface near the shoreline. It will be used to add a nice contrast to the material to give a semi-transparent look to the simulation.

Getting ready

You will need the `large-scale-water-05.blend` saved at the end of the last recipe. Or unzip it from the `large-scale-ocean.zip` you downloaded at the beginning of this section.

How to do it...

We will first set up the color and reflectivity of our waves surface material.

1. Open the `large-scale-water-05.blend` and select the **sea-closeup** object on layer 2.

2. From the **Materials** panel, create a new material and name it `waves`.

3. In the **Diffuse** tab, change the color to **R** `0.052`, **G** `0.107`, **B** `0.185`. Ensure that the shader type is **Lambert** and the **Intensity** is set to `0.800`.

4. Under the **Specular** tab, change the color to pure white **R, G, B** `1.000`. Set the shading type to **CookTorr** and set the **Intensity** to `0.821`, with a **Hardness** of `164`.

5. In the **Mirror** tab, check the **Mirror** checkbox and set the **Reflectivity** to 0.100. Set **Fresnel** to 0.400, and the **Color** to pure white **R, G, B** 1.000. Set **Blend** to 1.250. Set **Depth** 4, and **Amount** 1.000.

Save your work, incrementing the filename to `large-scale-water-06.blend`. A quick render will show a rather unconvincing reflective wave. We need to add more detail to the surface with a few textures. We will start by adding some small and tiny waves.

6. With the `sea-closeup` object selected, move to the **Textures** panel and create a new texture of type **Clouds** and name it `tiny-waves`.

7. In the **Clouds** tab, make it **Grayscale** with **Noise/ Soft, Basis Blender Original**, with a **Size** of 1.46, and a **Depth** of 2.

8. Under the **Mapping** tab, set **Coordinates** to type **Generated, Projection Flat**, and **Size X, Y,** and **Z** to 50.00.

9. In the **Influence** tab, deselect everything apart from **Geometry/Normal** and set to 0.100.

Save your work, incrementing the filename to `large-scale-water-07.blend` and perform a quick render. You should see that the surface has been broken up just a little. We can add another small wavelet to further break the surface.

10. From the **Texture** panel, select the next free texture slot and create a new texture of type **Clouds** and name it `small-waves`.

11. Make all the settings the same as `tiny-waves` apart from **Mapping** tab **Size X, Y, Z,** which should be set to 25.00.

Save your work, once more incrementing the filename, which should be `large-scale-water-08.blend`. If you render now, you should have nice detailed wave shapes on top of the displacement waves created earlier.

This is fine except we want these little wavelets to also change over time. If we didn't, it would look like semi-frozen water. Rather than create an empty to animate theses textures, we will employ the direct approach by animating the settings within the texture panel.

12. Move to frame 1 in the **Timeline**, and with the **sea-closeup** object selected, change to the **Texture** panel and select `tiny-waves` texture.

13. In the **Mapping** tab, change the **Offset Z** value to `0.75` and right click on the setting and **Insert Single Keyframe**.

14. Move to frame `250` on the **Timeline** and in the **Mapping** tab, change the **Offset Z** value to `0.25`, and right click the setting and **Insert Single Keyframe**.

15. Change one of the larger windows to the **Graph** editor and change the **Key** values to **Linear Extrapolation** to produce a straight line.

We need to do the same process with the small-waves texture. However, with that we will create a different direction to the slope.

16. Repeat steps 12 to 15 substituting the **small-waves** texture and changing the **Offset Z** value at frame 1 to `-0.75`, and `-0.25` at frame `250`. Don't forget to change the **Key** values to **Linear Extrapolation**.

Save your work once more, incrementing the filename to `large-scale-water-09.blend`.

No need to perform an animated render at this time. Before doing that we will add the remaining textures to produce the water surface.

17. With the `large-scale-water-09.blend` open and the **sea-closeup** object selected, move to the **Texture** panel and in the next free texture slot, click the checker icon to **Browse ID Data** and load the texture **wave-bump** into that slot. This was what we used for the original displacement.

18. Under the **Influence** tab, select **Geometry/Warp** and set to `0.500`. All other influences should be unchecked. However, select **Blend** type **Mix**, **RGB to Intensity**, Check **Negative**, and **Stencil**.

19. In the next free texture slot, create a new texture of type **Clouds** and name it `wave foam`.

20. In the **Clouds** tab, select **Grayscale** and **Hard, Basis Blender Original, Size** `1.00`, and **Depth** `6`.

21. Under the **Colors** tab, select **Ramp** and create new color stops a follows.

22. Stop 0, at **Position** `0.000`, with **RGB** at `1.000` and **Alpha** `1.00`.

23. Stop 1 at **Position** `0.512`, **RGB** at `1.000`, and **Alpha** `1.00`.

24. Stop 2 at **Position** `0.712`, **R** `0.000`, **G** `0.570`, and **B** `0.257`, with **Alpha** `0.36`.

25. Stop 3 at **Position** `1.000`, **RGB** `0.000`, and **Alpha** `0.00`.

26. **Adjust** the **Brightness** `1.900`, **Contrast** `1.800`, and **Saturation** `1.000`.

27. In the **Influence** tab, check **Diffuse/Intensity** 1.500 and **Color** 1.500. Also, check **Shading/Emit** 1.000, and **Ray Mirror** 1.000. Set the **Specular/Intensity** to -2.000, and check **RGB to Intensity** with a color of **RGB** 1.000.

Finally, we will set another animated texture setting to give a little movement to this wave foam.

28. Move to frame 1 in the **Timeline** and in the **Mapping** tab for this texture slot, right click on the **Z Offset**, which should be 0.00 and **Insert a Single Keyframe**.

29. Move to frame 50 and change the **Z Offset** to 0.10 and right click to **Insert a Single Keyframe**.

30. Move to the **Graph** editor and make the **Key Linear Extrapolation**.

Save your work as large-scale-water-10.blend. Running a small animation render of this will produce wave movement and foam as well as some color variation as time progresses. However, the sea currently only goes a short distance away from the rocks where it stops. A true ocean would continue to the horizon. We can add that very quickly without adding any new materials or longer renders.

31. Move to layer 4 and you will see that there is another plane called **sea-distance**. It is scaled to 100 Blender units.

32. Select it and assign the **waves** material by clicking on the **Browse ID Data** material icon in the **Materials** panel, to the left of the materials name. Choose the material **waves** and it will now be assigned to this object as well as the **sea-closeup**.

Save your work for a final time in this recipe incrementing the filename as large-scale-water-11.blend.

How it works...

It is possible to have a displace texture within a material. However, you will only see the displacement when you render. The displace modifier stack allows you to see in real time how the texture will displace the mesh. Controlling its movement using an empty becomes a great tool to experiment with timing and motion. This is particularly important when creating difficult surface structures like water. Being able to see the result without rendering can save an enormous amount of time.

However, this displacement will only provide the larger-scale wave movement. To make ocean-like water, it is necessary to add finer detail to simulate wind variation across the surface. We used Cloud textures with quite small depth values to simulate smaller concave wavelets, simply animating these directly in the texture settings. You may remember in an earlier chapter that I talked about the scaling of textures when mapped to the texture space of the object. That results in an apparent problem when we map the same material to the much larger object like the sea-distance. However, although the small and tiny waves will be enlarged on this surface, they are so far away from the camera lens that we will not notice the disparity.

We used the same wave-bump displace texture to create a warp for all following textures in our material. Because it is being moved by the empty, the warp will vary over time. This produces another variation to the surface and in fact produces a below surface-like effect on the foam texture that follows it. This texture also has a high emit value because this type of foam tends to be a much lighter contrast than the surrounding water color. Making it emit like this means that it will also show through some of the darker reflections in the water, again giving the impression of foam below the surface. It has one more advantage in that when applied to the sea-distance object, the emit values in the foam will create the illusion of distance lighting like global illumination without the render overhead of such a facility.

Although this has been one of the most render-intensive recipes so far, you may have noticed that the render times of a 50% HD image are not too long. Blender raytrace rendering has improved to the point where it can be used for such rendering tasks. Most of this development has been achieved in the last few months with the completion of the Durian Project, Sintel, and the Blender 2.5 development.

See also

This recipe was based on one produced by me several years ago. However, this recipe, and the one that follows, uses new techniques to produce an even more realistic result. If you are interested in reading that older approach to producing large oceans in Blender, you can download a free PDF tutorial from:

`http://www.cogfilms.com/`

Creating wake around objects in water

So far, the ocean water surface has produced a reasonably realistic result. However, at the moment, the rocks are producing no wake where they meet the water. This would be OK in a lake or pond with less wave disruption but, in the ocean, a wake would be produced as foam would form as the seawater splashed onto the rock. Of course, since this is not a physical simulation, the rock and water materials have no idea that either is there. To produce that interaction, we have to cheat to produce both surface tension, to raise the water as it interacts where it meets the rock, and foam that will distort as the wave flows up and down against its surface.

Getting ready

This recipe follows on from the previous. You therefore need to open the `large-scale-water-11.blend`. If you are starting this before completing the previous recipe, unzip the blendfile from the zipped file you downloaded at the beginning of this section.

How to do it...

We need to apply two textures, one as a second displace modifier and the other as a wake foam texture within our previous material. But, first, we have to make them available by temporarily creating textures within the material.

1. With the `large-scale-water-11.blend` opened in Blender, select the **sea-closeup** object and move to the **Texture** panel.

2. Select a free texture slot and create a new texture of type **Image** or **Movie**, and name it `surface-tension`.

3. In the **Image** tab, **Open** the image `foam-mask-bump2.png`, which should be in the **Textures** directory below where you unzipped the `large-scale-ocean-default.zip` file.

No other setting are required as this texture will only be used as a displace modifier.

4. Move to the **Modifier** panel and **Add Modifier** of type **Displacement** and name it `surf-ten`.

5. Click the checker icon below **Texture** and select the `surface-tension` texture.

6. Select **Direction Normal**, and **Texture Coordinates Object**. From the scroll list below, select `surfaceT-POS`. Set **Midlevel** to `0.100` and **Strength** to `0.005`.

7. From the **Outliner**, select `surfaceT-POS` empty and change to layer 5. You will see that the selected empty is some distance above the rock position and is larger than the default empty.

8. In the **3D** view, press the *N* key to bring up the **Transform** panel. You will notice that the **Location** is locked at **X** `0.155`, **Y** `0.504`, and **Z** `8.348`. The **Scale** is also locked at **XYZ** `3.400`. These were found to be the best scale and location to make the image be directly under the rocks.

9. Reselect layers 1, 2, 3 and 4, as well as 5.

10. Select the `sea-closeup` object and move to the **Textures** tab.

11. We can now delete the `surface-tension` texture that we have applied as a modifier. So, select that texture and click the **X**, by the texture name to remove it from this material.

12. Select the `wave foam` texture and using the **Move Texture** slots down arrow, move the last `wave` texture down one slot to give a gap between `wave-bump` and `wave foam` textures.

13. In that free slot, create a new texture of type **Image or Movie** and name it `foam`.

14. In the **Image** tab, **Open** the file `foam-mask-4.png`, which should be in the textures folder below where you unzipped the `large-scale-ocean-default.zip` file.

15. In the **Mapping** tab, select **Coordinates Object** and choose from the object list `camera.002`. Leave the **Projection** at the default **Flat** but change the **Offset Y** to `0.05`. Also, change the **Scale XYZ** to `0.29`.

16. Under the **Influence** tab, select **Diffuse/Intensity** `1.500` and **Color** `1.500`. Select **Shading/Emit** `0.628` and **Ray Mirror** `1.000`. Set the **Blend** type to **Add** and **RGB to Intensity** with the color changed to **RGB** `1.000`.

17. Finally, in the **Image Mapping** tab, change the **Extension** to type **Extend**.

Save your work, incrementing the filename to `large-scale-water-12.blend`.

Time to render a single frame to check the completed scene!

How it works...

Essentially, we have just used two image files to represent the foam area around the rocks. These images were created within Blender but modified in Gimp. In Chapter 8, we will explore how such images can be created and modified directly in Blender.

Mapping images, using the default mapping co-ordinates like flat, cube, sphere, and so on, creates certain problems in their application. Firstly, you can only see the image projected onto the surface if you render. There is no way of judging the position, scale without rendering each time you make a change to the settings for Loc X, Y, Z, or Size. The image was produced by using an overhead camera and just rendering the ocean as solid black and the rocks as solid white. The image was then blurred in a paint package to produce a slightly larger white on black image to represent the foam.

Trial and error was used to get the scale correct for both images. The location was somewhat easier because they were created using the `camera.002` that we mapped the foam texture to. The `surfaceT-POS` **Empty** is in exactly the same position as that camera, however, the scaling of the empty was required to get the displacement to work correctly. While it may sound sensible to use the same camera object to map to, it is not a good idea to scale a camera even though it is allowed in Blender. That is why we have used an Empty, at the same camera position but rescaled to give the correct proportions to the mapped image.

The other good thing about using the `foam` texture in this position, in the texture slots, is that it will be warped by the movement of the `wave-bump` texture. This will give some very subtle but realistic movement to the foam around the rock just like you might see around a real sea surrounded rock.

This material recipe is best appreciated if you render an animation. I would suggest you set the render size to 50% HDTV 1080 p. Render as a series of PNG files to a special sub-directory such as `animations`. On my system, 250 frames rendered over two nights.

See also

Chapter 8

> ▶ *Post processing rendered images from within Blender (ocean animation)*

Creating a non-repeating leaf material

Nature has a wonderful way of creating organisms that, whilst being similar to each other, have a uniqueness that only nature can provide. If you examine a tree in summer, it may have thousands of leaves. You can identify a particular variety of tree by examining its shape and structure. However, almost all of the leaves on any tree will be unique in one way or another. The color, structure, and shape of each leaf will subtly vary. If you wait for the season to progress, parasites will begin to attack and eat into the leaves. The sun, rain, and wind will further change each leaf until the seasonal nature of the tree may make each wither and die with varying rates. Even evergreen leaves will be different to each other in some way.

Simulating the surface of a leaf is quite a difficult task. We could use photo reference but a simulated tree comprising of identical looking leaves just won't do. In the following recipes, we will look at ways of producing uniqueness into repeated objects that share a similar material. We will examine tricks to create complex models using very simple geometry. We will do this by creating a non-repeating leaf material.

Getting ready

This recipe will rely on photo images to act as a reference for the bump/normal as well as the color and specularity. You can either scan some leaves local to your country and season or download from the following the Packtpub website: `Chapt-06/ivy-leaf.zip`.

Unzip these to your Blender textures directory.

These are scans of ivy leaves collected near to where I live. You will notice that, although they are all from the same variety of ivy, each is different.

Because Images form the main constituents of the material simulation it will be necessary to do some preliminary work, in a paint package, to extract the images we need. While Blender can do many things it is not a paint package. For serious work, you will have to use a reasonably featured paint package such as GIMP or Photoshop. Luckily, GIMP is an open source project like Blender. It's developed and maintained by hundreds of dedicated programmers across the world. Most importantly it is free.

Of course, you may already have a good paint package at hand. As long as it has features like layers, and filters such as blur, unsharp mask, and edge detection, you will be able to complete all the tasks necessary to prepare your images.

Creating image and bump maps, with alpha channels

We will use a paint package to modify a simple leaf scan, adding transparency, bump, and color variation to our leaf material.

How to do it...

The first thing we need to do is create an alpha mask that will provide the information for Blender to make the edges of the leaf appear transparent in Blender. Unfortunately, there is no single button in any paint package to do this. In the majority of cases, you will have to create a new transparent layer and draw around the edge of the leaf either with a path tool or manually painting the edges. This can be a tedious exercise but will be rewarded later when you use the alpha channel to cut the leaf out from a simple plane. Once you have created that black and white layer, you should refer to your paint package documentation to find out how to convert it to an alpha channel.

In GIMP, it's available from the **Layers** menu **Transparency**, **Color to Alpha**. If you want black to be transparent, choose that in the color selector. Once you have created an alpha channel, you need to save the image in a format that supports transparency. The following are supported in most graphics packages:

- **PNG** or Portable Network Graphics
- **TGA** or **TARGA** first developed for the Truevision Graphics Adapter
- **TIFF** or Tagged Image File Format

You will notice that the JPG file format does not support transparency.

Blender supports a vast range of other graphics file types including:

- **OpenEXR**, a high dynamic-range (HDR) image file format developed by Industrial Light & Magic
- **Jpeg2000** created by the Joint Photographic Experts Group
- **GIF** or Graphics Interchange Format developed by CompuServe.

 While all of these formats support alpha channels, GIF only supports 256 colors and not many paint packages currently can save in either OpenEXR or Jpeg2000 format.

Once you have created the image with an alpha channel, save it as `leaf-color-map.png`.

We now need to extract two more images from the `leaf-color-map.png` just created.

A leaf vein image, to provide both a bump, and a mask map, for other textures in the material we will create.

This was extracted by duplicating the layer of the colored image, then using the **Color/ Threshold** command in GIMP. This has controls to vary the amount of detail revealed. It will produce a negative image but can be inverted from the Color menu in GIMP.

I also applied a little **Gaussian Blur** from the **filters** menu in GIMP to soften the edges and remove any aliasing. Save this image with a filename of `ivy-leaf-vein-bump.png`.

The last image we need to create is one that will give a selective bump to our leaf material. This can be produced by copying the previously created threshold layer, applying a **Gaussian Blur**, and copying that layer and applying a greater **Gaussian Blur** with some levels adjustment.

A 50% gray layer was created below these two blurred layers and each blur layer set to **multiply** on the 50% gray.

Finally, the second blurred layer is screen mixed on top of the gray blurred layer to produce a reasonable bump and mask image.

Save this image as `ivy-leaf-bump.png`.

If you are not using GIMP, you will need to refer to your documentation to discover ways of producing similar results. Knowing how to use any paint package will be useful to you as a 3D materials designer. Many of the principles of mixing and filtering layers are used within Blender, so you are encouraged to practice these skills with a competent paint package.

In the next recipe, we will move over to Blender and apply these images to a leaf material.

There's more...

Below are listed websites that will aid you in creating and dealing with images. Apart from the locations for downloading some really useful open source paint programs, I have included some tutorial sites that cover many of the general principles that you should know to take full advantage of images in Blender:

- Gimp.org, the place to download the open source paint package (`http://www.gimp.org/`)

- Digital painting course using free/open source software by David Revoy, Published by the Blender Foundation, April 2010 (`http://www.blender3d.org/e-shop/product_info_n.php?products_id=122`)

Using images as the basis for a leaf material

One of the easiest Blender material techniques is to apply a photographic image to a surface. Blender has many ways of achieving this. Here, we will explore some of the easier methods.

Getting started

You should have either completed the previous recipe or you can download the following step blendfiles from the Packtpub website: `chapt-06/ivy-leaf.zip`

Just unzip the relevant step-file to your Blender directory. If you have completed the previous recipe, you should have the images files used for this recipe already in your Blender textures folder. You can unzip these separately from the `ivy-leaf.zip` textures directory to your own textures directory, if you are starting from this recipe.

You can create your own start-file following the instructions given. However, subsequent step files are included for each stage of the recipe if you want to start each recipe in the section out of order.

How to do it...

We will start by creating the simplest of meshes, to represent our leaf, then apply both a color and bump map to give it shape.

1. Create a plane mesh in the center of the view with default dimensions of 1 blender unit. Now, position your camera to obtain a reasonable view when rendered.

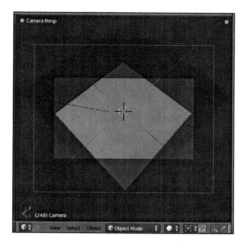

2. With the plane selected, create a new material and name it `ivy-leaf`. For the moment, we will keep all of the standard settings for **Diffuse** and **Specular**.

3. Move to the **Texture** panel and in the first slot, create a new texture of type **Image or Movie** and name it `ivy-leaf-color`.

4. In the **Image** tab, click the **Open** button and browse to where you saved the `leaf-color-map.png`.

5. Once the image has loaded, you should see a preview in the **Texture** panel, **Preview** window.

6. Ensure that under **Image Sampling/Alpha**, the **Use** checkbox is unchecked. For the moment, this will turn off any alpha channel in the image. We will cover transparency later.

Time to save your work as `ivy-leaf-01.blend` before performing a quick test render.

As you can see, the material has produced a quite realistic appearance of an ivy leaf. However, the Blender material effects are making virtually no contribution to this basically pasted image on a plane. It also pastes the whole image, including the black background, which isn't really what we want. Before removing those areas, let's use some of those other bump and mask images, created earlier, to produce some variation to our currently flat material.

7. In the next free texture slot, create a new texture of type **Image or Movie**. Open the `ivy-leaf-bump.png` created earlier and name the texture `ivy-leaf-bump`.

8. Under **Influence**, select **Geometry/Normal** and set to `1.500`. Make sure that **Diffuse/Color** is turned off.

Save your work, once more incrementing the filename to `ivy-leaf-02.blend`. Perform another test render and you should see that your leaf now has some characteristic bumps between the veins of the leaf. We can go further with this by now adding another image to represent the vein bumps.

9. In the next free texture slot, down, create a new texture of type **Image or Movie**, and open the `ivy-leaf-vein-bump.png` created earlier.

10. Under the **Influence** tab, deselect **color** and under **Geometry**, select **Normal** and the default amount as `1.000`.

If you perform a test render now, you will get a very unrealistic ivy leaf as detailed in the following image:

Bitmap images, particularly high contrast ones like the `ivy-leaf-vein-bump.png`, can be quite tricky to use as bump maps. The resolution of an image can sometimes clearly show the stepped effect of aliasing. However, Blender provides a few tricks to help with such a problem.

11. Under the **Image Sampling** tab, increase the **Filter Size** to `2.00`. This will have the effect of blurring the image within Blender. If you raise the filter size too much, the image will blur so much that the bump will not be seen. However, raising it slightly is a useful technique when using lower resolution images.

12. Under the **Influence/Geometry** tab, reduce the normal amount to `0.030`. The normal setting does not have to be large to work. Sometimes, small and subtle is best.

Save your work, incrementing the filename to `ivy-leaf-03.blend`. Another test render should produce a very nice ivy-leaf surface.

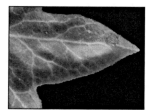

How it works.....

Applying images to a surface can be achieved quite easily in Blender. However, using such images for surface properties, such as bump, can create its own problems. A frequent error that the novice will make is applying far too much bump using badly aliased images. Even large images, when viewed close up, will produce bad results. Blender offers the ability to blur the image using the **Filter Size** option in the **Image Mapping** tab. Also, a general piece of advice, keep **Normal** settings low in most circumstances. There will be times when a larger setting might be required but these tend to be the exception rather than the rule. If you start low to begin with, you can nudge up the **Normal** setting until it appears correct. Violently swinging between whole numbers will waste a lot of time.

Our leaf has a reasonable surface but lacks the shaped edges. In the next recipe, we will use the alpha channel in the image to remove that black background.

Using alpha to create a leaf shape on a simple mesh

Blender is equipped to deal with alpha channel images, using them to produce visual holes in any surface. In order to use this image transparency, there are a few important steps to follow.

Getting started

You will need the blendfile saved at the end of the last exercise: `ivy-leaf-03.blend`. If you starting this recipe from scratch you can download and unzip the following file from the Packtpub website: `chapt-06/ivy-leaf.zip`

How to do it...

Blender provides all the tools necessary to use alpha channels. You will need to open `ivy-leaf-03.blend` to continue this recipe.

1. With the plane selected, switch to the **Materials** panel if it's not already active.

2. Select and check the **Transparency** tab. Select the **Z transparency** button and turn down **Specular** to `0.000`. Leave **Alpha** at `1.00`.

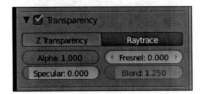

 The reason we are using **Z Transparency** rather than **Raytrace** is because it is so much faster. Raytrace rendering will increase the render times exponentially. On my system, it took six times longer to render the ivy leaf using raytrace transparency.

3. Switch to the **Textures** panel and select the first texture slot we named `ivy-leaf-color`.

4. Under the **Image** tab, check the **Premultiply** checkbox.

5. In the **Image Sampling** tab, check the **Alpha/Use** checkbox.

6. Under **Influence/Diffuse/Alpha**, select and set to `1.000` and change the **Blend** type to **Multiply**.

Save your work before performing a render, incrementing the filename to `ivy-leaf-04.blend`.

How it works....

Alpha channels have been around in images for years and 3D designers have been using the technique of creating complex shapes using transparency for almost as long. It is an extremely efficient method of cutting out a complex shape on a simple model. Blender can handle alpha channels much faster than rendering complex meshes. It is therefore a useful technique to employ in your material and model creation.

See also...

Chapter 3

▶ *Creating a burning sheet of paper*

Chapter 9

▶ *Easily add fire to a scene without complex rendering*

Adding a non-repeating bump to the leaf material

So far, we have created a leaf that looks quite good but we could hardly use this repeated a few hundred times to create an ivy covering of a tree trunk for instance. It would look very false because each leaf would be exactly the same as each other. It is possible in Blender to instance a mesh object many times without increasing the memory overhead of a render. However, as you can understand, we need to find some way to add variety to the each instanced leaf.

The scanned image of the ivy leaves shown at the beginning of this section illustrates the variety from a single cutting. You may be able to see that apart from the shape variety there is also some color differences and some leaves have been damaged by insect action.

How to do it....

Apart from the outline shape of the leaves, it is possible to simulate the other differences using textures within Blender. Use the `ivy-leaf-04.blend` saved at the end of the last recipe or download and unzip the following file from the Packtpub website: `chapt06/ivy-leaf.zip`.

1. With the leaf mesh selected, switch to the **Texture** panel and select the next free texture slot. Create a new texture of type **Clouds** and name it `leaf-curl`.

2. In the **Clouds** tab, select **Grayscale, Noise/Soft, Basis** as **Blender Original, Size** to `1.10`, and **Depth** to `6`.

3. Under **Colors/Adjust**, set the **Brightness** to 0.700, and **Contrast** to 2.100.

No other adjustments are required because we will not use this texture to affect the material. We will instead create a **Displace** modifier in the **Modifier Stack**.

Because we will not need the texture in the material, we could either delete it here, by clicking on the **X** icon by the texture name, or turn it off for the material. Even if we delete it from the material, it will still exist ready to be used in the displace modifier provided we do not save before we use it again. Un-connected textures are discarded on save if they are not used anywhere in the blendfile. You can actually force a material or texture to remain, even it is not directly used, by clicking the F button next to the material or texture name. However, we can only change any of its settings from within a texture slot. So, it's best to keep it in the material but turn it off so that it doesn't affect the material directly.

4. In the top of the **Texture** panel, you will see the list of all textures currently loaded into the material. A small checkbox exits following each texture name. To turn off the leaf-curl texture, un-check its checkbox.

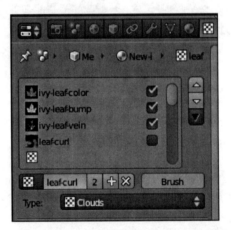

5. Switch to the **Modifiers** panel and **Add Modifier**, and from the list, choose **Deform/Displace**.

6. In the settings, select **Texture** and click on the checker icon and choose from the available textures leaf-curl. Ensure that **Direction** is set to **Normal**, and **Texture Coordinates** is set to **Global**. Below, set **Midlevel** to 0.500, and **Strength** to 2.00.

7. Add another modifier and make this a **Subdivision Surface**, the default settings are fine. If you haven't done so already ensure that the mesh is set to **Smooth** shading.

Save the file, incrementing the filename to `ivy-leaf-05.blend`. Render the scene and you should see the leaf has magically warped to give a new shape to the leaf. Move the leaf mesh around in the view and do some more renders.

 When you move the mesh in **Object** mode, you will not see the displacement change until you render.

How it works....

Mapping a texture to a coordinate system outside of the object it is being mapped to is a good way to create variety in instanced objects. Here, it was used to **displace** the shape of the leaf so no matter where the leaf is, it will have a variable shape. This can be an ideal way of altering what might at first appear to be an identical copy. It can be used directly in materials or as a modifying component to affect other textures or on its own as in this example to uniquely bend the leaf shape.

If the object has to move within an animated scene, the displacement will appear to stay still as the object moves. Although this may appear a disadvantage, it can be used with multiple leaves to look like the wind is moving through the leaves. Sometimes, so-called problems within a 3D package can be turned to an advantage.

Adding color complexity to the leaf material

We can use similar techniques to the last recipe to add color variation to the leaf material. However, we don't just want to paint some color changes all over the leaf. If you examine the original scan, you will see that the veins are less affected by leaf discoloration. We will therefore set our `ivy-leaf-vein` texture as a **stencil** to mask the veins from the effects of the discoloration texture.

How to do it....

You will need to open the blendfile, `ivy-leaf-05.blend`, saved at the end of the last recipe. If you did not complete that recipe, you can unzip it from the `ivy-leaf.zip` file available from the Packpub website as: `chapt-06/ivy-leaf.zip`.

1. With the leaf mesh selected, switch to the **Texture** panel and select the next free texture slot. Create a new texture of type **Clouds** and name it `discoloration`.

2. Under the **Clouds** tab, select **Grayscale** and **Noise/Hard**. Set the **Size** to `1.70` and the **Depth** to `4`. Leave all the other settings at default.

3. In the **Colors** tab, **Adjust/Brightness** to `1.000`, and **Contrast** to `1.40`.

4. Under **Mapping**, set **Coordinates** to **Global**.

5. Under **Influence**, set **Diffuse/Color** and set to `0.364`. Set **Blend** to type **Subtract**, and in the color select, make **R** `0.28`, **G** `0.74`, and **B** `0.27`.

It would be a good idea to re-order this texture so that it immediately follows the `ivy-leaf-vein` texture. That's easy to do in Blender by selecting the **discoloration** texture slot and clicking the **Move Texture slots up and down** buttons until it's just below the `ivy-leaf-vein` texture.

Now, we can create a stencil from the `ivy-leaf-vein` texture.

6. Select the `ivy-leaf-vein` texture slot in the **Texture** panel. In the **Influence** tab, set **Negative**, **RGB to Intensity**, and **Stencil**.

Save your work, incrementing the filename and perform a final render. You should see a darker discoloration randomly across the leaf surface but behind the veins.

How it works...

Creating random materials based on photographic images is a very important skill for 3D designers. You will constantly have to find ways of masking regularity, particularly if the image is repeated within a scene. Here, we developed several versions of an image and then applied them to alter or mask the mesh or colors.

We learnt how to extract both color and bump information so that it gave us more control compared to a single image. We also covered how Blender can help blur bit-mapped images to reduce the aliasing found with this type of image.

Alpha channel images are very useful to help create complex shapes without the necessity of large mesh objects. We learnt what controls are available to implement that transparency within Blender.

In the very last recipe, we also used an unusual mix type called **Subtract**. This is a mix method that might not seem the most appropriate to use compared with the usual types such as **Add, Screen, Multiply**. The advantage of **Subtract** in this example is that the white areas of the cloud texture use the color in the texture (a mid-green) to subtract from the image color. Black parts of the cloud texture do nothing. Occasionally, these obscure mix methods can be employed to create just what you want.

7
UV Mapping and Sub Surface Scattering

In this chapter, we will cover:

- ▸ Creating a face map from photographs
- ▸ Unwrapping a face mesh to produce a UV map
- ▸ Editing a UV map to optimize the image space
- ▸ Creating multiple UV maps for a single object
- ▸ Combining UV maps to create an enveloping UV
- ▸ Using a paint package to merge UV maps
- ▸ Extracting color, bump, and specularity maps from photographs
- ▸ Applying UVs to create an accurate skin material
- ▸ Skin shading using Sub Surface Scattering

Introduction

So far, we have explored various methods of mapping textures to models. However, eventually, we will meet complex surfaces that move or distort during an animation. In this circumstance, we require the textures to be mapped directly on the faces of the mesh rather than projected from some arbitrary point within the mesh. One area where this is extensively used is the simulation of skin, from the leathery exterior of a dinosaur to the ultimate nirvana of the human head.

Skin shading is one of the most difficult tasks for the 3D materials designer. Firstly, the models tend to be complex in shape with many varying angles that make standard texture projections such as flat, cube, sphere, and tube difficult because of distortion. Secondly, skin has a unique ability to scatter light within its surface, which is tricky to reproduce. Thirdly, when a UV map is wrapped around the object, seams will form where edges of the UV map meet.

Over the course of this chapter, we will work through several exercises that show common UV problems and their solutions in Blender. We will also explore an approach to Sub Surface Scattering that will make the Blender solutions easy to apply.

Creating a face map from photographs

Creating a model of a human head is extremely difficult to do. However, most 3D artists will need to approach this task at least once in their career. As soon as you have a well laid out mesh model of a head, you then have to devise ways of coloring and texturing the surface to stop it looking like a piece of plastic. All of these tasks will take time and a great deal of effort. However, the rewards from successfully creating a realistic head will teach you both modeling and materials creation like no other process.

Blender offers a huge range of tools to UV map an image to a mesh model. UV mapping unwraps all the mesh faces onto a flat surface. Once we have a UV map, it becomes easier to paint or apply photographs to this flat map rather than using other projection methods to apply a texture to a model. Photographs are probably the easiest method of creating the color map for a UV mapped head. However, UV maps tend to be distorted compared with a camera shot of a person's face. Fortunately, Blender contains some neat tools to make this process easy.

The photos used in this exercise are of someone who happened to be near to my camera when I was looking for a model. You are encouraged to take your own photographs, perhaps of your face, and apply these in the following recipes.

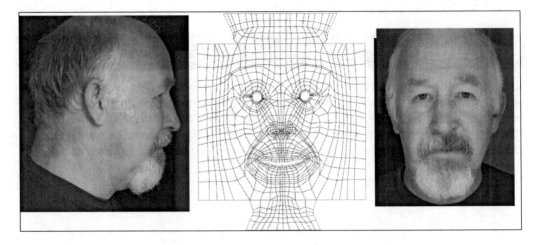

Getting ready

Taking photographs to create a full face map can be tricky mainly due to shadows and specular reflection on the face that we don't want in a 3D model. It is best to take such shots in an evenly illuminated room without using a flash gun. Mount your camera on a tripod or firm surface and use a cable release or someone else to take the actual shots if it is you in the image. For the particular example here, we are only interested in the front and side shots as the mesh model is only the front portion of a face. As we progress, you will see that the method can also be applied for a whole head model.

How to do it...

Arrange your model or yourself on a comfortable chair where they can sit upright. If you have access to an office swivel chair, the model can rotate easily while maintaining the same distance from the camera.

1. Position the model by a window that does not have direct sunlight. A cloudy day where shadows are less prominent will give better results.

2. Set up a tripod, or some other device, to hold the camera still while taking the shots. Face the camera away from the window.

3. Set the camera lens to the same height as the model's eyes.

4. If there is insufficient illumination, on one side of the model's face, use a white card to reflect the window illumination and even out the shadows.

5. If your camera has a zoom lens, set it in the middle of its zoom position or until the model's face is entirely in shot. Do not use the wide angle setting of the lens or include too much background around the model's face.

6. Ask your model to rest their features and adopt what might be called a rest position in their features. No smiles, frowns, or other exaggerated expressions.

7. Take a series of shots asking your model to rotate in their chair, pausing as each shot is taken. For this recipe, you will only require a front shot and one at 90, a profile. However, if you were doing this for a full head model, you would take 3/4 views and one of the head top and one of the front neck positions.

Hopefully, your shots will have similar exposure but be aware that camera auto exposure levels can vary the color and brightness levels that may need to be adjusted within a paint package. You do not need to worry too much about small size or rotation angles as these can be adjusted easily within Blender.

How it works...

Photographic images need to be of reasonable quality to be used as a UV map in any 3D system. If the shot you are after requires a CU (close-up), the resolution of the image needs to be as big as or higher than the resolution of the screen format envisaged. For instance, if we are producing a CU of the face on an HD resolution screen (1920 × 1080), then the image used needs to be at least this if not larger. Fortunately, modern digital cameras are now readily available with multi-megapixel resolution.

However, you may have noticed that the shots you have taken do not occupy the entire image area. Indeed, most head UV maps do not use the whole of the map for the front detailed portion of the face. So, how do you know how big a face photo needs to be?

Well, the important aspect of any face is the distance between the eyes. We, as viewers are always drawn to this visage of our fellow human beings. It is easy to measure this dimension using a paint package such as GIMP.

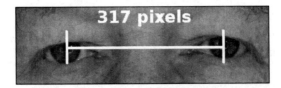

In my case, the size is 317 pixels so if it were to be used in an HD 1920 screen width, it should occupy no more than about 17% or one-sixth, of the screen. That's plenty big enough for a CU shot.

Of course, if you are working to a 4 k screen resolution, you can see that image maps would need to be enormous to cope with the resolution. However, for the majority of purposes, a six to eight megapixel camera will produce images of reasonable size for use as UV face maps.

There's more...

If you are proficient with your graphics package, you could take multiple shots of the face at closer zoom levels and manually stitch them together to produce a super resolution image. Be warned however, that this kind of image manipulation can be frustrating and time consuming. Start with an image of reasonable resolution and just do minor corrections in GIMP or Photoshop. We can employ Blender to actually bring together the side and front views to make up the entire UV map.

The following recipes will use the images just created to produce a Blender render of the face. If you want, you can use the images I have used, which are available from the Packtpub website as: `chapt-07/UV-Head.zip`

You should unzip this file into your Blender directory, which will create a textures directory, if it doesn't exit, with all the image files required to duplicate the results of the following recipes.

See also

Later recipes in this chapter:

- *Unwrapping a face mesh to produce a UV map*
- *Editing a UV map to optimize the image space*
- *Creating multiple UV maps for a single object*
- *Combining UV maps to create an enveloping UV*
- *Using a paint package to merge UV maps*
- *Extracting color, bump, and specularity maps from photographs*
- *Applying UVs to create an accurate skin material*

Unwrapping a face mesh to produce a UV map

Producing a UV map from an object in Blender entails splitting the mesh cage to accurately, and without distortion, unwrap each mesh face onto a flat map. Now, a head is a complex mesh, so working out the best method of splitting, or creating seams, can be frustrating.

In this recipe, we will learn how to choose seam points and also how to control the resultant UV map to minimize distortion. You will learn how to pin control points and manipulate the UV map. You will also discover how to maximize the available UV map to give the best resolution to the important features of the face. All these tools are available within Blender but not well covered in documentation or tutorials currently available.

Getting ready

To perform this recipe, you will need a reasonably accurate mesh model of a face to create the UV map. As this is not a Blender modeling cookbook, I do not expect you to create such a mesh from scratch, unless you want to. I provide a mesh model, and associated textures from the following location at the Packtpub website: `chapt-07/UV-head.zip`

Unzip this file to a convenient location and a blendfile, `UV-FACE-00.blend`, and an associated texture sub folder will be produced so that you can complete the recipe. You can, if you wish to, substitute the image files for those that you may have taken following the instructions in the previous recipe. The blendfile contains a reasonably proportioned male head mesh that almost any face UV map could be applied to.

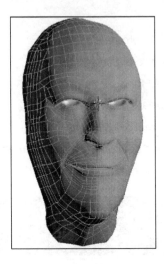

The default scene contains the head mesh and two eye meshes. The eyes have materials pre-assigned to make the recipe a little faster. You are welcome to explore this simple texture to see how an eye material can be created. I will show later numerous tutorials available that explore this material type.

As this is a complex recipe, and if this is your first attempt at creating either Blender UV maps, or a human face material, be prepared to spend a few days on the task.

How to do it...

We will use Blender's powerful UV unwrapping methods to produce a basic UV map and then edit that UV map to produce an optimized UV map for adding our photo images to.

1. Open up the blendfile `UV-FACE-00.blend` unzipped from the file downloaded at the beginning of this recipe.

2. Switch from the **Default** view to the **UV Editing** view using the **Browse ID Data** button in the main Blender header.

3. In the right window, the profile of the head mesh should be displayed. Ensure you are in mesh edit mode by pressing the *Tab* key.

4. We will mark some of the edges to create seams aiding the unwrapping process. Since we need to mark both sides of the face, we can do so more easily by switching to **WIRE** view by pressing the *Z* key.

5. We need to choose four edges that will become seams thus making the UV map as undistorted as possible. The side top of the edge and the side chin area are good candidates. So, starting with the bottom chin area, we will select five connected edges and make them a seam.

6. Using the edge selection tool, as shown in the image above, select the edges shown using the paint select mode *C* key and selecting with the mouse left click, and painting the appropriate edges. If you select the wrong edges, just press the *Alt* key while selecting the incorrect edge.

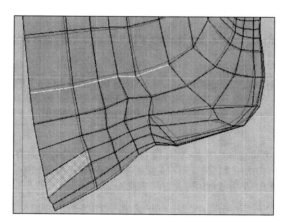

7. To turn these into a seam, select **Mark Seam** from the **Mesh Tools** pallet, or use the shortcut *Ctrl+E*, **Mark Seam**. The selected edges will change to a red color to show they are selected.

8. We will follow the same process to mark the top seams as shown in the image below.

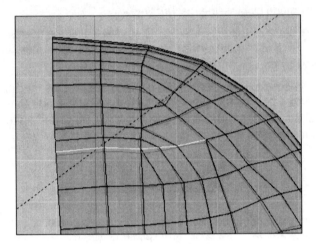

Before continuing, let us save our work, incrementing the filename to `UV-FACE-01.blend`.

We will now unwrap the face to a flat image.

9. From the **UV editor**, on the left, select **NEW** Image from the bottom header.

> You may notice that the left-hand tool box also has a NEW selector for Grease Pencil. This has nothing to do with UV, so make sure you only select the **New Image** button in the bottom header.

10. The presented dialog will allow you to create a new image with various settings. It will default to a size of 1024 x 1024 pixels. However, reset this to `1024x1273` and choose **UV Test Grid** and name it `UV-FACE`.

11. With the face object in edit mode, select all vertices or edges. Press *A* key until all are highlighted. Then, in the **UV editor**, select `UV-FACE` image by clicking the image icon to display available images.

12. Move your cursor back to the right **3D** window and press the *U* key to display the unwrap options, and choose the first choice **Unwrap**.

Blender will create a UV map based on conformal and angle-based unwrapping methods. What this means is that it will make a very good best guess to size and position the map while avoiding undue distortion. The more seams, to help flatten the map, the better the unwrapping will be.

However, we can now edit this UV map to make best use of the available space.

Save your work at this point, incrementing the filename to UV-FACE-02.blend.

13. Maximize the **UV editor** window to give a little more screen space to work, *Ctrl+up arrow*.

14. Select all of the control points by pressing the *A* key. To the right, in the toolbox, we can change the line display method to one of four types. Select **White**, which will contrast better against the gray grid background.

15. Press the *R* key to rotate all the control points about 90. You can make finer rotations by pressing the *Shift* key as you rotate. The trick here is to line the central edge along one of the background grids.

16. Press the *S* key to scale the control points to better fill the available space. You can also press the *G* key to grab the control points to the best position. If you make a mistake, you can always undo by pressing *Ctrl+Z*, or redo with *Shift+Ctrl+Z*.

17. When you are happy with the UV maps new position, save the blendfile, incrementing the filename to UV-FACE-03.blend.

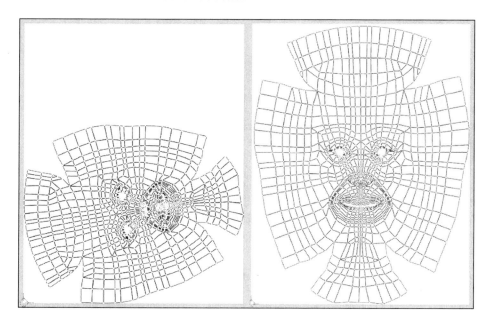

How it works...

When choosing the position of seams, you have to consider whether the seam will be prominent or can it be positioned to help hide it. When we are dealing with a face mesh, you have to recognize that the eye of the viewer will be drawn towards the eyes and therefore the front of the face. You should therefore avoid placing seams anywhere near these faces.

You may see many maps created with a central forehead seam. Although such seams can be hidden under hair, it will present problems with characters who have a receding hairline, or who are bald. Any seam can be carefully masked with judicious painting but such tasks are time consuming and should be avoided.

Likewise, too many seams will lead to complex UV maps, making it difficult to position images without a lot of tricky work. In our recipe, we select temple and chin seams that, while fairly prominent, will be partly masked by the side hair and in this case beard of the model.

You will have noticed that the editing commands, associated with UV maps, are exactly the same as mesh modeling. We can therefore use all the standard **G**rab, **R**otate, and **S**cale keyboard commands to position our UV map the way we want it. You will see later that we can perform even more subtle editing options that have a direct comparison with mesh editing.

We also observed that it is possible to display the control points in one of four ways, **Outline**, **Dash**, **Black**, and **White**. You can switch the display mode of UV lines and points to make them stand out against different backgrounds. By selecting **Smooth**, the lines will be anti-aliased making them clearer still. There are other settings here that will be explored in the next recipe.

There's more...

UV mapping has developed at a tremendous pace in the last few years. Blender is known as one of the best in the field at utilizing the most up-to-date methods of UV unwrapping and UV map editing. This development will continue, so although all of the techniques discussed in this chapter can be used for some time to come, new procedures will make the task even easier.

Blender has had a frequent update schedule with a normal upgrade version every six to nine months. The recent proactive drive of the Blender Foundation in large-scale animated shorts has ensured that the tools within Blender have developed at speed and to address the creative artist's needs. The community of artists, and coders, are extremely welcoming and as such your contribution to its future will ensure your needs are addressed.

You can keep up-to-date and contribute to this development by participating in the following news and forum sites.

BlenderNation is one of the best Blender news sites around. Here, you can catch up on recent developments both from the coder and artist viewpoint:

http://www.blendernation.com/

BlenderArtists is a forum for Blender users. Some of the threads are very informative about future developments in Blender. It's also a good place to ask questions if you are stuck with a particular Blender technique.

http://blenderartists.org/forum/

See also

Previously in this chapter:

- ▸ *Creating a face map from photographs*

Later recipes in this chapter:

- ▸ *Editing a UV map to optimize the image space*
- ▸ *Creating multiple UV maps for a single object*
- ▸ *Combining UV maps to create an enveloping UV*
- ▸ *Using a paint package to merge UV maps*
- ▸ *Extracting color, bump, and specularity maps from photographs*
- ▸ *Applying UVs to create an accurate skin material*

Editing a UV map to optimize the image space

In this recipe, we will edit the UV map so that the main point of interest occupies more room on the image. In this way, we can ensure that the front of the face has more image pixels assigned than those areas that will be either hidden, or less prominent. Optimizing a UV map in this way will ensure the maximum resolution while maintaining small image sizes.

Getting ready

This recipe picks up from the end of the last, so either open the saved blendfile `UV-FACE-03.blend`, or open the file from the downloaded zip file, `UV-Head.zip`, as discussed at the start of this chapter.

How to do it...

We will start by straightening the top, bottom, and side outside seams to use as much of the height and width of the image we can utilize.

1. With the blendfile `UV-FACE-03.blend` open, you should still be in the **UV Editing** window, with the mesh model in the right window, and the unwrapped UV map in the left. If it is not showing, ensure you are in edit mode with the face mesh selected, *Tab* key, and that all the vertices are selected, *A* key to toggle.

2. Now, expand the **UV Editor** window by having the cursor in that window and pressing *Ctrl+up arrow*. You may also wish to change the background to **Blank** from the **Image** tab in the toolbox. This will make it easier to see what you are doing.

3. Although we can move any point in a UV map, it's best to pin the points we wish to move, scale, or manipulate in relation to any other. We do this by *right* clicking to select a point and press the *P* key to pin it. Do that now for each of the outside corners. They will turn bright red when pinned.

4. To make the task even easier, check from the **UVs** menu, **Live Unwrap**, and **Constrain to Image Bounds**.

5. Press the *A* key to ensure nothing is selected. Then, press the *C* key for brush select and select all the upper forehead seam vertices and pin them by pressing the *P* key.

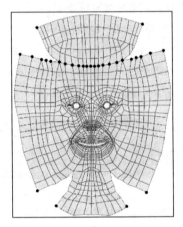

6. We will straighten these UV vertices by scaling in the Y direction. Press *S* to start scale, press *Y* to constrain to the Y axis, and press *0* (zero) to straighten the line.

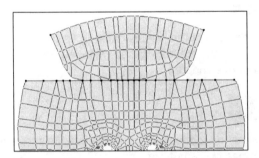

7. We will do the same with the left-hand seam so ensure nothing is selected by pressing *A* and then use the brush select *C* key to select all of the vertices of the left-hand seam and press *P* to pin them. Now, press *S* to scale, *X* to constrain to the X axis, and *0* (zero) to create a vertical straight line.

8. Do the same for the right-hand seam making sure you first deselect points using the *A* key.

9. Now that both these seams are straight lines, they are much easier to select for further modification. So, first ensuring that nothing is selected, box select the left-hand seam once more and press G, to grab, X to confine to X axis, and drag the points to the edge of the image.

10 Do the same to the right-hand seam, grabbing it to the right of the image.

11. Using the same techniques, scale and move the top and bottom seam to the top and bottom of the image.

12. Do the same with the chin seam so that the face is surrounded by a rectangle.

Time to apply an image to our UV map and make final adjustments so that the UV map accurately matches the position of the eyes, nose, and mouth.

13. Switch to the default screen, which will display the **UV** editor in the left window and the **3D** window in the right. It will also have the panel window to create materials and other tasks.

14. Switch to the **Object Data** panel and under the **UV Texture** tab, you should see a single item named UVTex, which is the default name for a UV map. Rename this to UV-Front, in the name tab.

15. Switch to the **Materials** panel and create a new material, naming it Skin. Don't worry about any of the material settings at this stage as we just need to get an image opened and assigned to the UV-Front map.

16. Switch to the **Texture** panel and in the first texture slot, create a new texture of type **Image or Movie**, and name it front-face.

17. Under the **Image** tab, open the image file front-face.png from the textures folder.

18. In the **Mapping** tab, select **Coordinates** of type **UV**, and from the **Layer** selector, select the **UV-Front** map created earlier.

19. Switch to textured view in the 3D window and you should see the image applied to the face object. We will make adjustments to the UV mapping to arrange the eyes, nose, and mouth, to the correct place on the model.

20. Select the middle face points and pin them, and then scale them up to look similar to the following image.

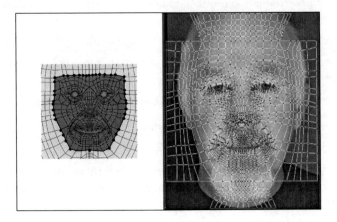

21. Zoom into the eyes, nose, and mouth and with each select points, move them to match the face image. You will find that proportional editing of connected points is already enabled and you can use the middle mouse wheel to vary the radius of proportional movement as you grab, scale, or even rotate.

 Remember, you can always undo *Ctrl+Z*, or redo *Ctrl+Shift+Z*, if you make mistakes.

If you change the **3D** view to **Solid** view, you should see the texture applied onto the model. Pressing the *TAB* key, to turn off mesh edit view, should display it clearly.

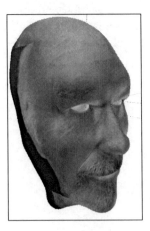

Providing you have Live Unwrap set in the **UV editor, UVs** menu, any adjustment to the UV map points will be reflected in the **3D** view. It can be used to make accurate adjustments so that the image texture is applied correctly to all of the key parts of the face.

Save your work, incrementing the filename to `UV-FACE-04.blend`. You could perform a test render here if you want. However, only the front of the face currently works as the cheeks and ears are distorted because the image didn't have that detail and are therefore distorted. The next recipe will show how you can overcome this UV projection problem.

Your new map may not look identical to mine. Don't worry, however, as minor variation may be inevitable as you make mistakes and readjust as you go on. My map above went through much iteration while writing this chapter. So, providing you are near to the approximate proportions, and the eyes, nose, and mouth match up, the resultant UV texture should look fine on our rendered model.

How it works...

Adjusting UV maps is just like editing mesh vertices. So as long as you can use these tools you should have no problem moving and manipulating a UV map. In fact, using such a technique it should be possible to match any face image onto the mesh object. You could use the photos of your own face instead of the ones used in this book even if your face is thinner or larger than the one shown. Just readjust the position of the eyes, nose and mouth to match to the face image you want to use.

You will find that using some of the time-saving mesh editing techniques such as constraining move and scaling to a single axis is very useful in UV map editing. You may need to bring in images of different dimensions as you experiment. You will find that Blender defaults to a 1024 x 1024 size, but will readjust for other proportioned images. You will therefore need to rescale frequently, and doing so constrained to the X or Y axis will save much headache. The simplest way to do so is select the transpose mode; G for **Grab**, S for **Scale**, R for **Rotate**, then press the corresponding axis X or Y key.

Don't worry too much about increasing the size of some important areas of the UV map. Too often I see lazy UV mapping where only simple rotation and moving have been used on a whole head model. As a result the parts of the UV map with most pixels are on the back of the head, which in most cases will not be what the camera will be looking at. Always think which areas need the most resolution and enlarge those to maximize the image space.

Once you have an image loaded into the UV editor you may find it useful to change the lines display method to **Outline**, **Dash**, **Black**, or **White**, so they show up against whatever your image looks like. You can further improve the display of lines by turning on Smooth in the same menu.

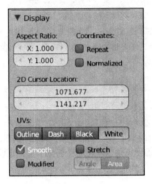

When you Unwrap a new UV map for a mesh model, the default name is **UV-Tex**. You will see in future recipes that you can create multiple UV maps for a single mesh. It is therefore vital that you rename them in the **Object Data** panel to something more meaningful. I tend to always prefix a UV map with the capital letters UV as this differentiates it from other textures and Blender items. We renamed ours to **UV-Front**, which accurately describes this UV texture.

There's more...

When you manipulate a UV map, in the way described, you will be introducing some level of distortion to the way the map is stretched or compacted to fill the available space. In our example, we wanted the front of the face to take up more pixels than the sides and edges. As a result we will have introduced some distortion. You can check how much at any time by selecting **Stretch** in the **Display** tab. This will change the view with each of the faces shown as a colored fill from Blue (meaning no distortion) to Red meaning much distortion. Providing the colors are between blue and green you should be OK.

Occasionally, you will get into a complete mess with a UV map where even _Ctrl+Z_ cannot undo enough steps to get you out of trouble. If that happens, just unwrap again, _U_ key in the **3D** edit mesh window. If you are new to these techniques, I would recommend incrementally saving after each successful edit. So, if you successfully move and scale an eye position, save at this point before moving onto the other eye.

See also

Previously, in this chapter:

- _Creating a face map from photographs_
- _Unwrapping a face mesh to produce a UV map_

Later recipes in this chapter:

- _Creating multiple UV maps for a single object_
- _Combining UV maps to create an enveloping UV_
- _Using a paint package to merge UV maps_
- _Extracting color, bump, and specularity maps from photographs_
- _Applying UVs to create an accurate skin material_

Creating multiple UV maps for a single object

When you apply a flat image, taken with a camera, onto a UV map that represents every face of a mesh model, you will end up with only the front looking right. The sides, top, and possibly bottom will have distortion as a single camera shot cannot easily photograph all sides of a face in a single shot.

Several years ago, we would have to take several shots all around the head then manually stitch them together in a paint package before finally bringing them to a 3D package to apply to an unwrapped model. Indeed, trying to match the distortion inherent in stitching flat photos to complex UV maps was very difficult.

Blender, however, allows us to create multiple UV maps, which can be mapped from different sides, and combined to create correct mapping all around a model. The human face is an excellent example of why this technique is so useful. We can use a camera to create shots of the front, sides, back, and top of a head, then map these to individual UV maps from the same direction. Then, combine each to produce a single UV map that covers all sides of the model.

In our example, we will create a new UV map of the side of the face using the image created in the first recipe of the chapter. We could take this further and create images and maps for the back and top of the head but for the sake of brevity, the idea can be shown using the front and side images as described.

Getting ready

This recipe continues from the end of the previous recipe and specifically the blendfile UV-FACE-04.blend. This file, together with all necessary images, is also available in the zip file that can be downloaded following the instructions at the beginning of this chapter.

How to do it...

Open the blendfile UV-FACE-04.blend and ensure you are on the default view, which should display the **UV editor** to the left and the **3D view** to the right. Make sure that the face object is selected in the **3D view** and that you are in **Mesh edit** mode by pressing the *Tab* key.

1. Select the **Object Data** panel, and under **UV Texture** tab, click the **+** button to create a new **UV Texture**, and name it UV-Side. Now, select that UV texture and click on the little camera icon, so it becomes highlighted.

2. In the **3D** window, switch to the side view by pressing the *1* number pad key. Ensure you are not in perspective mode by pressing the *5* number pad key until the view looks flat. You can enlarge the view if you like to see more of the model.

3. Select all of the vertices in the **3D** window by pressing the *A* key to toggle. You have to be in **Mesh** edit to achieve this.

4. With the cursor still in the **3D** window, press *U* key to unwrap the mesh and from the displayed dropdown, select **Project from View**. Do not select **Project from View (Bounds)** as this will stretch the projection to fill as much of the area as possible.

In the UV editor, you should see the UV map match the proportions of the oblique side view you have just unwrapped. However, we currently have no image in the UV editor to apply.

5. In the **UV** editor, select from the **Image** menu in the header, the **Open** command and select side-face.png from your textures folder. The image should load and the UV map should remain in proportion. If it doesn't, just unwrap again from the **3D** view as **Project from View**.

6. Select, and pin all of the control points of the UV map and move and scale and rotate until the points correspond with the following image. You may have to proportionally move some individual control points to get the eyes, nose, and mouth to line up.

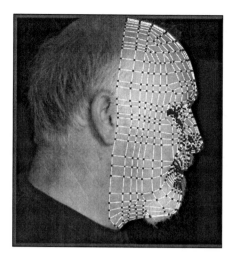

Currently, this image is not used in our material, so let us create a new texture slot so that we can render and see it in the 3D view.

7. From the **Textures** panel, select the next free slot after `front-face`, and create a new texture of type **Image or Movie** and name it `side-face`.

8. In the **Image** tab, **Open** the file `side-face.png`.

9. Under the **Mapping** tab, select **Coordinates** of type **UV**, and select the `UV-Side` **Layer** selector.

10. In the **Influence** tab, check **Diffuse/Color**, and set to `1.000`, with a **Blend** type of **Mix**. Leave all other settings at default.

If you switch the 3D window to display shaded or textured view, you should see the image mapped to the model.

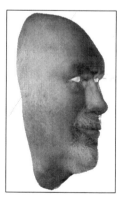

Save the blendfile, incrementing the filename to `UV-FACE-05.blend`.

The sides now have a reasonably mapped texture but the front of the face is distorted in this sideways UV-mapped object. Blender only allows you to render one UV map at a time. However, we will discover in the next recipe how to combine multiple UV maps into a single enveloping UV texture.

How it works...

Blender makes it possible to have more than one UV map associated with an object. Each of these multiple UVs can be generated using different projection points or even have seams created on different parts of the model. Take that point a little further and it is possible to create one UV map with seams and another that will mask those same seams.

In our case, we have used it to create a front view and side view of the face. At the moment, we can only render one UV at a time but as you will see, it is possible to merge UVs. However, multiple UVs are extremely useful with complex objects like the human head. Providing we have reasonably high quality images, of all sides of a head, we should be able to unwrap a UV map for each original camera position, and remap the image onto the model.

You have seen how easy it is to manipulate the control points to ensure all the relevant control points like the nose, eyes, lips, and so on correspond to the main facial features in the images. It is even possible to have live updates in the 3D window providing the texture has been added to a material and mapped using the UV Texture coordinate. You also need to have Live Update set in the UV menu of the UV editor.

With a full head model, we would normally create more than just front and side view UV maps. Possibly three-quarter views and certainly an upper head, and lower chin view could be created to cover all potential movement of head. In the last few recipes, we have concentrated on the front and side of the head for brevity. However, the principles are exactly the same for those other sections of the head should we wish to do those. Incidentally, when we UV mapped the side of the face we were actually unwrapping the mesh faces from both sides. Because the Project from View was an oblique view, the mesh faces from both the left and right sides occupy the same space, therefore, share the same image. We could have created different left and right UVs with corresponding left and right images, but you can appreciate the principle rather than have to complete an almost duplicated recipe.

To see how these multiple UV images can be combined, see the next two recipes.

See also

Previously, in this chapter:

- *Creating a face map from photographs*
- *Unwrapping a face mesh to produce a UV map*
- *Creating multiple UV maps for a single object*

Later recipes in this chapter;

- ▸ *Combining UV maps to create an enveloping UV*
- ▸ *Using a paint package to merge UV maps*
- ▸ *Extracting color, bump, and specularity maps from photographs*
- ▸ *Applying UVs to create an accurate skin material*

Combining UV maps to create an enveloping UV

Multiple UV maps are a great innovation in Blender but if you are unable to use them together in a single render, how useful can they be? Well, Blender allows us to remap UVs onto other UV maps and we can use this simple technique to create a master UV that contains the combined best features of our side and front UVs that we created in the last two recipes.

Getting ready

You will need the last saved blendfile from the previous recipe UV-FACE-05.blend. If you have not completed that recipe, you can use the file from the UV-HEAD.zip file available for download at the Packtpub website.

How to do it...

What we will do here is create two renders of each texture but applied to just one of the UV maps. The easiest way to do this is choose the front-face texture but bake the side-face textures upon it and then save this image as a new file. The original front-face image can then be layered in a paint package to create a single new UV map covering half the face in full detail.

1. Open the UV-FACE-05.blend saved from the last recipe or downloaded earlier.

2. With the face object selected, move to the **Textures** panel and ensure that the front-face texture is deselected and the side-face is selected. This sets the side texture to be the baked texture.

3. In the **Object Data** panel, and in the **UV Texture** tab, select the UV-Front map, but click and highlight the UV-Side render icon.

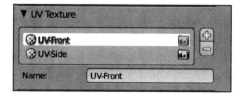

4. Move your cursor into the **3D** window and press the *Tab* key to change to mesh edit mode. Make sure all vertices are selected by pressing the *A* key until the UV map appears in the **UV** edit window on the left.

5. Switch to the Render panel.

6. Under the **Bake** tab, change the **Bake Mode** to **Textures** and click the **Bake** button. After a few moments, the **UV** editor should show that the image is being rendered and will be completed once the progress bar disappears from the top menu. The new image produced is the side UV map, remapped to the front image UV map.

7. You will notice that the **Image** menu in the header bar, at the base of the **UV editor**, has an asterisk, or star indicator, that tells us the image has changed. What has happened is that the `front-face.png` image has been overwritten with this new bake. But, only within this blendfile. We don't want to save it over the original image, therefore, we need to save it with another name.

8. With your cursor inside the **UV editor**, press the *F3* key to bring up the **Save As** option and choose a new name for this image. Name it `whole-face-sides.png` and press the **Save As** button.

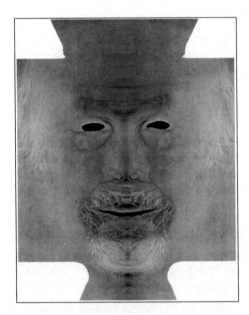

We don't have to save the blendfile because future recipes will use a new blendfile to continue our face material creation.

How it works...

Being able to bake one UV map onto another, thus creating an entirely new texture map, is a really neat trick. We have used it here with just two maps but the technique can be applied to almost any number of UV maps. However, getting the sequence right, as we have executed in the recipe, will save you much frustration so, here are the key points.

1. Have only the texture you want baked selected in the **Texture** panel of the material.

2. From the **Object Data** panel under the **UV Texture** tab, have the UV map you wish to bake to, selected, or active. This is the **DESTINATION** of the bake.

3. Have the Render icon of the UV map you want to bake from, highlighted. That is the **SOURCE** image. Select the appropriate **Bake Mode**, **Textures**, and press the **Bake** button.

4. Once baked, save the new image with a new name. **DO NOT** overwrite with the same name or you will lose the original image.

Follow these five simple steps and you will produce a perfect UV remapping every time.

See also

Previously in this chapter:

▸ *Creating a face map from photographs*

▸ *Unwrapping a face mesh to produce a UV map*

▸ *Creating multiple UV maps for a single object*

Later recipes in this chapter:

▸ *Using a paint package to merge UV maps*

▸ *Extracting color, bump, and specularity maps from photographs*

▸ *Applying UVs to create an accurate skin material*

▸ *Skin Shading using SSS and AO*

Using a paint package to merge UV maps

Blender has the capability to merge two UV bakes into a single image. However, to use this, you do require a capable graphics card that supports GLSL real-time rendering. These cards tend to be expensive and may not be installed on your computer. I therefore want to show how the same task can be achieved in a paint package such as GIMP. There are other advantages to this method in that you have more control over color correction, and image manipulation than in Blender. I will show in Chapter 8 how Blender can be used for some direct paint tasks but for this recipe, we will take the original `front-face.png` image and merge the good parts of the `whole-face-sides.png`.

Getting ready

You will need access to the `whole-face-sides.png`, and the `front-face.png` images from the last recipe. If you have not completed that recipe, the images are available from the `UV-HEAD.zip` as described at the start of this chapter.

How to do it...

We need to open the `front-face.png` image into our paint package, such as GIMP. These instructions can be replicated in Photoshop or any other reasonable paint package.

1. Open the second image `whole-face-sides.png`, **COPY** that image and switch to the `front-face.png` image and **PASTE AS A LAYER** over the top of it.

2. Using a soft edges **ERASER**, and remove the distorted middle of this second layer.

3. Use the **CLONE** tool to fill in missing areas of the layer taking particular care to avoid obvious repeats.

4. Use the **COLOR HUE-SATURATION** adjuster to color correct this top layer to match the bottom layer. In GIMP, I used just **LIGHTNESS** 15, and **SATURATION** -40, no **HUE** changes were required as the original photos were taken in similar light.

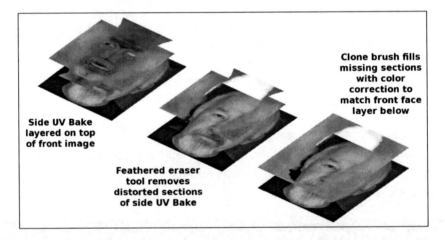

Side UV Bake layered on top of front image

Feathered eraser tool removes distorted sections of side UV Bake

Clone brush fills missing sections with color correction to match front face layer below

5. Save the adjusted image in a format that can retain layers, such as `whole-face.xcf` in GIMP, or `whole-face.psd` in Photoshop. This allows you to fine tune the image later if required.

6. Finally, save the image once more but this time as a `face-color.png` file. This will give the opportunity to flatten the visible layers making an ideal image for use in Blender.

How it works...

This is a very simple technique as layering one image above another, then using a soft eraser brush to remove unwanted sections of the layers above, can quickly combine different UV bakes into a single image. Using a paint package has many advantages over Blender because paint programs tend to have more versatile tools specific to painting tasks. This is particularly so with color correction that will inevitably be required to make the separate layers match.

Keeping a copy of the layered image in the format of the paint package is also useful so you can revisit and change the corrections made should they appear too obvious when applied in Blender. In fact, following the instructions here we have our original source images, `front-face.png`, and `whole-face-sides.png`, as well as the components of the modifications in the `whole-face.xcf`, and the finished `face-color.png` we will apply in Blender. Keep all of these images together in your textures folder so that at any time in the future, you can modify them should there be a need.

There's more...

If you are lucky enough to have access to a GLSL-enabled graphics card, you may like to explore how this can be used to display textures as you modify them in Blender. There is an excellent video tutorial by Lile Hansen, on Vimeo, which although based on previous versions of Blender, shows the steps that can be applied within Blender 2.5/6.

`http://vimeo.com/1377005?pg=embed&sec=1377005`

Another video that shows the technique being used to create a highly detailed rock has been produced by Pelle Johnsen.

`http://vimeo.com/5520712`

See also

Previously in this chapter:

- ▸ *Creating a face map from photographs*
- ▸ *Unwrapping a face mesh to produce a UV map*
- ▸ *Creating multiple UV maps for a single object*
- ▸ *Combining UV maps to create an enveloping UV*

Later recipes in this chapter:

- ▸ *Extracting color, bump, and specularity maps from photographs*
- ▸ *Applying UVs to create an accurate skin material*

Extracting color, bump, and specularity maps from photographs

The last recipe demonstrated how to create a color map that can be accurately UV-mapped around a complex model of a human head. We could just take that color map and apply it in a simple material. However, in real life, the human face has many more surface irregularities than just color. If you examine your own face, you will see that veins, hair sockets, and smile line creases add detail to show what kind of a person you are. Likewise, your skin will reflect light more on those areas of your face that are wetter than others. This natural sweat will vary across the face, not only explaining the environment or temperature, but also what you may have been doing like running or resting. Adding maps to control these material attributes will help add detail to convince the viewer they are looking at human skin rather than plastic painted as skin.

Creating bump, specular, and shading maps is not as difficult as it sounds. We can use the face color map just created and derive from that the bump, and specular maps. An Ambient Occlusion map can be generated by baking an AO pass to the image and saving that to be used with the material setup. You will almost always have to do some work on these images to get them working the way you want.

Getting ready

All you need is the `face-color.png` file saved at the end of the last recipe, *Using a paint package to merge UV maps*. It is also in the `UV-HEAD.zip` file downloaded at the beginning of this chapter. You will need access to a paint package such as GIMP or Photoshop. I will give instructions for GIMP but these can easily be transferred to Photoshop or other reasonable paint package.

How to do it...

Open up the `face-color.png` file in your paint package. We will start by creating a bump map from this image.

1. Copy the background layer to a new layer. In GIMP, you select the background layer, in the **Layer** pallet, and click on the **duplicate layer** button.

2. Select this layer, and from the **Colors** menu, select **Components**, and **Decompose**. You will be offered multiple choices; the most common between packages is **RGB** for RED, GREEN, and BLUE, components. Select this and a new image will be created with each layer having a black and white representation of each of the color components.

3. The top layer is red, and this will be a fairly flat-looking image. Deselect that layer and you will see the GREEN layer, which has a little more contrast. Deselect that layer and you will see the BLUE layer which is much higher contrast with any red spots and marks shown very clearly.

4. The best of the three candidate images for a bump is the blue layer as the contrast is slightly higher than the green layer. So, select that layer and copy it.

5. Move back to your `face-color.png` image and paste this as a new layer above the color image. Rename the layer `face-bump`.

6. With the face-bump layer selected, use either Color/Curves or Levels to increase the contrast of the image a little. Using the Curves command with a shallow S curve produces a little more detail without losing the fine graduation in the gray image. Remember, a bump map works by using the gray values in the image to apparently raise the surface where light shades are, and lower the surface where dark shades are.

7. Now would be a good time to save your work to preserve the layer format like `.xcf` in GIMP, or `.psd` in Photoshop.

Let us move onto creating a specular map.

8. Reselect the first color layer, and from the Color pallet, select Decompose.

9. This time, choose CMYK, which stands for Cyan Magenta Yellow and black. This will produce a new image with four layers.

10. Rather than discuss the merits of each layer, just select the yellow-k layer. This layer has the maximum information for producing a nice specularity map.

11. Copy that layer and move back to your `face-color.xcf` image and paste as a new layer, naming it face-specular.

12. We still need to do a little work to make it perform better as a specular map. These maps apply more specularity to light areas and less the dark areas. On the human face, the forehead, nose, cheeks, and lips are the most reflective. Therefore, we need to lighten these areas on our image just a bit.

13. Use the **Levels**, or curves command, to lighten the image somewhat. The trick is to try to retain as much of the shade variation as possible while lightening the image.

14. Finally, use the **Dodge** tool with, a soft brush at 50% opacity, to lighten those areas where we are prone to sweat more. Remember that *Ctrl+Z* is an almost universal undo key, so if it doesn't look right, undo it and try again.

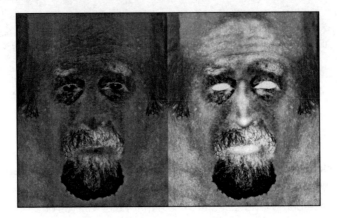

15. You will notice that both the eyes and lips have been lightened considerably.

16. To extract separate images for textures in Blender, turn off all layers apart from the one you want to save, select that layer, and save in a .png format to flatten and save the image. To save the specular layer just created, turn off all other layers by clicking on the little eye icon to the left of them, then with the specular layer selected, and visible, save the file as face-spec.png to the textures folder of your blendfile location.

17. Do the same for the bump layer, naming the saved file face-bump.png.

You should now have three images saved in your textures folder, face-color.png, face-spec.png, and face-bump.png.

How it works...

Creating specular and bump maps has been a rather mysterious dark art with very little information on how to create them. Starting from an image that will be close to what you require will speed up the process and produce better bump and specular maps. Using the technique of decomposing a colored image using one of the color component types will produce three to four alternative images, you just have to choose the one that's nearest to what you want and then fine tune it in the paint package. It is actually possible to do that in

Blender but when we only need a single image for a character, it's easier to produce it in a paint package than fiddle in Blender. Hopefully, you will try this technique on another face image, including your own. As with any creative art, practice will make perfect.

See also

Previously in this chapter:

- ▸ *Creating a face map from photographs*
- ▸ *Unwrapping a face mesh to produce a UV map*
- ▸ *Creating multiple UV maps for a single object*
- ▸ *Combining UV maps to create an enveloping UV*
- ▸ Using a paint package to merge UV maps

Later recipes in this chapter:

- ▸ *Applying UVs to create an accurate skin material*

Applying UVs to create an accurate skin material

Now, it is time to bring all of our work in this chapter into a concluding recipe that produces an accurate and realistic representation of a face.

Getting ready

If you have not completed any of the previous recipes in this chapter, it will be necessary to download the `UV-HEAD.zip` from the Packtpub website as: `chapt-07/UV-HEAD.zip`

If you unzip this file in your Blender directory, all the step files, and a texture sub-directory with the relevant textures will be created. If you have previously downloaded and unzipped `UV_HEAD.zip`, you should find the blendfile `UV-FACE-06.blend`. This is a new file, and not one created in any of the recipes preceding this one. It contains some additional objects, such as eyelashes, which will make the renders appear more lifelike. The materials used for these objects are simple painted lines created on an exported UV grid. The materials have transparency, so that it appears to be eyelashes on the four eyelids of the face object.

You will also need the three textures recently created for color, bump, and specularity.

How to do it...

We will start by creating the general settings for our skin material.

1. Open UV-FACE-06.blend, and with the face object selected, move to the **Materials** panel. You will notice that there is a material already load called skin. We don't need to change any of its settings at this stage.

2. Switch to the **Texture** panel and, in the first slot, create a new texture of type **Image or Movie**. Name this texture face-color.

3. From the **Image** tab, **Open** the file face-color.png from your textures directory.

4. Under the **Mapping** tab, choose **Coordinates** type **UV** and from the **Layer** select UV-Front. This is the same UV layout used to extract the images in previous recipes.

5. Under the **Influence** tab, select **Diffuse/Color** and set to 1.00. The **Blend** type should be **Mix** and all other settings can be left at default.

6. Finally, for this color texture, move to the **Image Sampling** tab, and under **Filter/Filter Size**, reduce the number to 0.10, which is the lowest.

Save your work at this point, incrementing the filename to UV-FACE-07.blend. You could do a test render at this point but I would recommend waiting until we have added a little bump and specularity to the material.

7. In the next free texture slot, create a new texture of type **Image or Movie** and name it face-bump.

8. From the **Image** tab, **Open** the file face-bump.png from the textures directory.

9. Under the **Mapping** tab, select **Coordinates UV**, and **Layer** UV-Front.

10. Under the **Influence** tab, deselect everything bar **Geometry/Normal** and set its value at -0.300.

11. In the next free texture slot, create a new texture of type **Image or Movie** and name it face-spec.

12. From the **Image** tab, **Open** the file face-spec.png from the textures directory.

13. In the **Influence** tab, deselect everything apart from **Specular/Intensity** and set its value to 0.150. Also, check the **RGB to Intensity**.

Save your work, incrementing the filename to `UV-FACE-08.blend`, and perform a render.

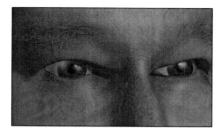

I have reduced the camera view to speed up the renders and am therefore concentrating on one area to demonstrate the bumps and specularity produced by our images. Not bad, but we can improve this image immeasurably by adding Ambient Occlusion and Sub Surface Scattering, which we will do in the last recipe.

How it works...

Mapping images by UVs is probably the simplest material type. It does not require **diffuse** colors in the material settings because the face-color texture is providing all the color required. The **Mix** blend type has applied the color from the image overriding the materials default gray color. We have also changed the default filtering size to its lowest value of 0.10 to give the highest resolution, with no smoothing, of the image.

The bump and specular maps produce a quite subtle variation across the skin because of the low settings applied here. We have also applied relatively high quality images in terms of size and sharpness.

There's more...

A frequent issue I see with those new to 3D material design is the use of small-scale images, or images with too much contrast. On the face-color texture, we changed the default image sampling down to its lowest value of 0.10. In most cases, we can leave that at the default filter level of 1.00 but with face-color maps where the viewer will be looking and examining with some detail, reducing this to the minimum means that the full resolution of the image will be mapped to object. This would not work if the image were too small as we would clearly be able to see the individual pixels of the image.

However, in the bump and specular maps, we did not lower the filter size. This is because, ideally, a bump map should be twice the resolution of a color map so that fine graduation in bump, or specularity, look smooth. Leaving the Filter at 1.00 will ensure that these images have a little blur added, thus smoothing the application to the material. This will save on image size, which in a complex scene may have many large images applied as textures thus creating very large blendfiles that require large amounts of computer memory to load and render a scene.

Although the material simulation has produced a reasonable reproduction of the surface color, bump, and specularity of the human face it lacks life and looks rather plastic in appearance. In many ways, these kinds of material simulations remind me of the old string puppet sci-fi series of the 1970s. That is OK if that is the appearance you are after, but if you want to produce live-looking skin materials, we have to employ additional properties in the material to show the scattering of light through a skin surface (Sub Surface Scattering, or **SSS**), and also the soft shadows formed when global illumination casts soft shadows across the surface (Ambient Occlusion, or **AO**).

See also

Previously in this chapter:

- *Creating a face map from photographs*
- *Unwrapping a face mesh to produce a UV map*
- *Creating multiple UV maps for a single object*
- *Combining UV maps to create an enveloping UV*
- *Using a paint package to merge UV maps*
- *Extracting color, bump, and specularity maps from photographs*

Later recipes in this chapter:

- *Skin shading using SSS and AO*

Skin shading using SSS and AO

Almost any surface will scatter light from a surface in various directions. Surfaces that possess a slight translucency will scatter some of that light below the surface, sometimes changing its color by absorption, and spreading the light further. You can see this in your own skin: if you hold up your hand in front of a strong light you will see the red almost glow on the thinnest part between your fingers. This Sub Surface Scattering is common in most real life materials to some extent, but only needs to be considered in a 3D scene for the obvious candidates such as skin (not just human), wax, or certain liquids like milk. Sub Surface Scattering in Blender will require some extensive processing and therefore will increase render times. This is particularly true when combined with other render-intensive processes such as ray transparency, reflection, and Ambient Occlusion.

Ambient Occlusion, or AO, simulates the soft shadows found on objects when illuminated by reflected bounce light. These types, a soft shadow, help define a surface by adding a greater depth between the illuminated and shadowed areas of an object. Sub Surface Scattering, and Ambient Occlusion, are comparatively recent additions to 3D suites, although Blender has had this functionality for some time. Rather than duplicate real-world physics to simulate these surface properties, Blender uses some clever internal tricks to approximate the properties.

However, the results can appear very realistic. In this recipe, we will explore how to set up both AO and SSS to the face material created in the earlier recipes of this chapter. You will also see how render-optimizing shortcuts can be applied to help save valuable render time.

Getting ready

You will need the blendfile UV-FACE-08.blend saved at the end of the last recipe. If you have not completed that recipe, a version is available in the UV-HEAD.zip file available following the instructions at the beginning of this chapter.

How to do it...

We will start by adding a little Ambient Occlusion.

1. Open the UV-FACE-08.blend in Blender. Before we add some AO, we can perform a render and save that to a render slot. Make our AO settings then render these to another slot. It then becomes easy to compare the renders with and without AO. Also, take a note of the render times for comparison as we progress.

2. In the header menu of the **UV** editor on the left, you will see a **Slot** selector.

3. Select **Slot 1** if it is not already selected and perform a render. This should only take a few minutes and when completed, change to **Slot 2**. You will notice that you have a total of eight slots available. We now have a render we can use to compare with any of our AO and SSS experiments.

4. Move to the **World** panel and in the **Ambient Occlusion** tab, check the button to select, and make sure the settings are **Factor** 1.20 and type **Multiply**.

5. When you select and check **Ambient Occlusion**, the **Gather** tab becomes active. Move to this tab and ensure the **Gather** type is set to **Raytrace**, with **Attenuation** set to a **Distance** of 10.000, with **Falloff** checked, and a **Strength** of 1.200. Also, set the **Sampling** type to **Constant jittered**, with **Samples** at 12 and **Bias** 0.050.

6. Save your work, incrementing the filename to UV-FACE-09.blend, and perform a render. Note down the render time for this AO render.

7. You can compare this AO render to that in **Slot 1** by selecting and switching between the two in the **UV editor** window.

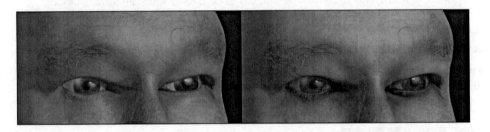

You will notice that the AO render has darkened the shadows, particularly under the eyes. In fact, it looks like the individual now has eye-shadow. We could lower the **Factor** setting to reduce this, but you will find later that SSS will reduce the appearance of any bump or AO setting you have.

How long did the render take with this AO setting? On my system, it took 3.5 times longer to render. That is a significant increase that we might want to avoid. Fortunately, Blender provides a way to employ AO without the render overhead by allowing you to bake the AO pass to a UV image and map it to the material. This is produced using the same techniques described in the fourth recipe *Creating multiple UV maps for a single object*, but substituting AO pass when you bake. To save time, I have already included that texture in the skin material within your blendfile. It just needs to be turned on.

8. Switch to the **Textures** panel and you should see another texture slot named AO. However, the checkbox is unselected. So, click that checkbox so that it has a tick against it.

9. The texture is UV mapped, using the UV-face map we created earlier. The **Influence** is just **Color**, which has a Blend type of **Multiply**.

10. Under the **World** panel, turn off **AO**. Now, only the texture AO will affect the render.

11. Select **Slot 3** from the **UV** editor, ready to receive the new render.

12. Save your work incrementing the filename to UV-FACE-10.blend, and perform a render. Note down the render time for this texture AO render.

On my computer, the render time was only a few seconds greater than the original render, yet the improvement to the image quality is clear.

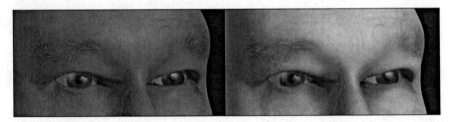

You may have to modify the AO bake to suite your own requirements. The image in the texture was lightened slightly so as not to darken the material too much. Let us now add some SSS to complete this skin material.

1. Move to the **Materials** panel and open up the **Subsurface Scattering** tab. Check the selector box and a series of settings will be presented to you.

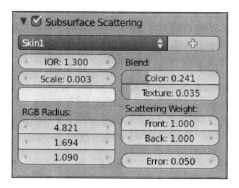

2. You should ensure that all the settings are as shown in the image above. The color swatch has been set to **R** 0.749, **G** 0.571, and **B** 0.467, a light olive pink.

3. Select **Slot 4** from the **UV editor** ready to receive a new render.

4. Save your work, incrementing the filename to UV-FACE-11.blend, and perform a render. Note down the render time for this texture AO render with SSS.

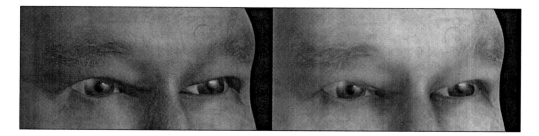

5. Now, use the texture slots to examine each render and choose the one that you feel most accurately simulates skin.

My render took about 3.5 times longer than the original render, which isn't too bad.

How it works...

Ambient Occlusion is an extremely useful technique to add depth to almost any render. However, the increased render times may require you to create an AO pass and just map this as a UV texture to the model. Doing this will give you complete control over how much of the AO you want to multiply across the surface. You only have to reduce the **Color** setting in the **Influence** tab of the texture slot to reduce the AO effect. We used **Multiply** as the blend type for this texture, which means that only the darker parts of the image are blended. That is why the AO image had been modified from the bake process to increase its contrast so that only the dark shadow areas of the image would apply to the material.

Sub Surface Scattering, on the other hand, is a little trickier to set up. The facility in Blender offers several presets and I would advise you to choose the one considered nearest the SSS type you are after, then, modify until you are happy with the result. However, it is worthwhile knowing which settings have the most impact on the final result.

The **Scale** setting has a big influence on the way SSS will interact with your material. The correct setting will depend on the size of the object based on Blender units. So, if your object were 0.492 Blender units in width, but represented an object of 160 mm in real world units, the scale is 0.492/160 = 0.0031. You can actually enter this formula directly as all Blender numerical input areas accept PYTHON math's entry. Just type into the scale setting `0.492/160` and hit *Enter*. Blender will work out the correct number.

The Color Swatch defines the overall spread color of the brightest areas of the scattering. However, it will also be affected by the **RGB radius,** with each numerical entry representing the scatter of Red, Green, and Blue. We know that with skin the main color scattered will be red so that is why this is the largest value. The preset values have been discovered by trial and error so starting from these settings will save you time. However, please experiment and save new presets by clicking the **+** sign, by the preset entry of the **Subsurface Scattering** tab.

The **Blend Color** and **Texture** settings control what influence the SSS will have on the **Diffuse** color of the material, and how much the texture will be blurred by the SSS. This is important as too much and you will lose all the bump detail if it is set too high. As with any Blender input, I would recommend keeping settings low and only raising in small increments, with test renders to observe their affect.

The other settings will have relevance to thinner materials like ears, hands, or leaves. For skin simulation, the defaults can be maintained.

There's more...

Sub Surface Scattering and Ambient Occlusion are quite render-intensive processes. You will find that many test renders will be required to fine tune your settings to obtain the effect you are after. To save time, reduce the render area by using *Shift+B* to define a smaller render area. Once you are happy that it works there, select another small area to see if it works equally in this new position before committing to a full-scale render.

See also

Previously in this chapter:

- ▸ *Creating a face map from photographs*
- ▸ *Unwrapping a face mesh to produce a UV map*
- ▸ *Creating multiple UV maps for a single object*
- ▸ *Combining UV maps to create an enveloping UV*
- ▸ *Using a paint package to merge UV maps*
- ▸ *Extracting color, bump, and specularity maps from photographs*
- ▸ *Applying UVs to create an accurate skin material*

8

Painting and Modifying Image Textures in Blender

In this chapter, we will cover:

- ► Post processing rendered images from within Blender (ocean animation)
- ► Adding more than one material to a surface
- ► Adding dirt onto a model
- ► Creating an aged photo with simple Blender materials

Introduction

If you ever use Blender in the heat of a large production, or against sometimes impossible deadlines, you will almost inevitably have to resort to other graphics systems to finish off. You may need to color correct, clean up, or even completely change the appearance of a render long after the event. Unfortunately, life is full of those little challenges for the materials designer and textures artist.

Fortunately, Blender is such a comprehensive 3D suite it provides many of the tools to aid you in that process. We will explore some of these in this chapter from the ability to alter a completed animation because of last-minute changes, or render defects that were not picked up at the time, to directly editing materials and textures in Blender. We will also explore ways to speed up renders and animations by using special painting techniques to significantly lower render times. All of these recipes could save you time as well as minimize the agony of tight timescales.

Post processing rendered images from within Blender

So, you have created the perfect material simulation for a dramatic shot in the feature. It had to render over 48 hours to obtain all of the images required for a 12-second scene. As with most rendering tasks, the rendering farm, or computer, will be unattended during this process as watching a slow render is about as enjoyable as watching grass grow. It may also be the case that when you view the scene you, or the director, will feel that it would fit better into the overall production if it had different lighting or the depth was enhanced by adding more atmosphere such as air, dust, or mist.

In Chapter 6, we created an ocean scene with a rock washed by the waves. The renders required to produce the 10-second animation took 4 minutes 11.36 seconds x 250 frames on my computer, which means a 17.5-hour total render time. Although the renders look fine, in retrospect, we could have added a little atmosphere by including a little mist. This would have two benefits. First, it would help hide the seams between the foreground and distance ocean meshes, and secondly, add the illusion of distance to the horizon. To add these elements, we could set up a Mist effect in the World settings, or create a post process Blender compositor effect to create the illusion of mist. Both of these solutions would require re-rendering the entire scene, a prospect that may not be feasible in the heat of production. It might be possible for us to rotoscope the mist to the scene but this process can be very time and labor intensive as well. Wouldn't it be great if we could take the images we have already created and automatically add the mist without re-rendering the 3D elements that are so processor intensive?

Fortunately, Blender has an advanced node-based compositor that not only allows us to add effects to our scenes but also allows sequenced images to be post processed. We will use this technique to add mist and re-render the entire 250 frames in a matter of minutes.

In this recipe, we will perform two tasks. The first is to extract the depth information from the original scene. The second is to create a new blendfile that will load each image of the original sequence, and apply both a mist and a distance defocus to create a new modified sequence of images.

Getting ready

We will be using the file `large-scale-water-10.blend` created at the end of the first recipe in Chapter 6. If you haven't completed that recipe, all the files necessary are available in a zipped format from the Packtpub website as: `chapt-08/postpro.zip`

The file contains the `large-scale-water-10.blend` file, and all the image files required for the exercise. It also contains all 250 frames, at 50% HD resolution, of the ocean sequence so that you can see the time-saving capabilities of Blender as well as create the finished 10-second animation. Just unzip the file to a suitable location on your hard drive. Your zip program will create the sub-directory containing the image files.

How to do it...

Let us first go back to the original file to extract the depth information as two image files.

1. Open the file `large-scale-water-10.blend` in Blender. This file was used to create the 250 images that make up the 10-second animated sequence. Before continuing, we will save it with a new name to ensure that the original blendfile is retained.

2. **Save** the blendfile as `LS-water-mist-masks-01.blend` to the same directory.

3. From the **Render** panel and **Post Processing** tab, check the **Compositing** checkbox.

4. From the **Layers** tab, check the **Passes Z** checkbox. This will ensure that the render contains the depth information.

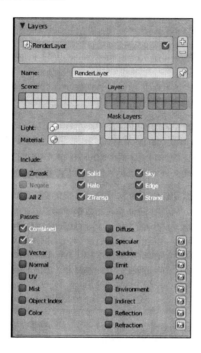

We don't need to waste time rendering the materials because we are only after the depth information within the render so we can turn these off. There is a quick way of doing this in the layer menu where it says **Material**. You can load in here a single material that will override all the materials currently associated with the objects in the scene. If you click on the material icon on its name entry, the available materials will appear. We just need to choose a simple material with no reflection or transparence. Unfortunately, we only have two textures available: sea and rock. So, let's create a simple texture to act as a substitute here.

5. Select the `rocks` object and move to the **Materials** panel.

6. Unlink the `Sea-Rock` material by clicking the **X** to the right of the material name.

7. Click the **New** button to create a new material and name it `gray`. We don't need to make any special changes to this material.

8. Move back to the **Render** panel and in the **Layers** tab, click the **Materials** selector and choose the newly created `gray` texture to override all other textures.

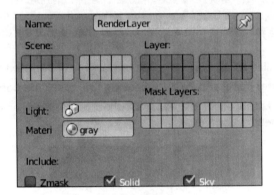

9. The **Layers** tab takes up a lot of panel space, so minimize it by clicking on the little triangle icon by the **Layers** tab name.

10. Change the view type to **Compositing** from the top menu. This will provide a **Compositor** window to the top of the screen. Select the **Use Nodes**, and also the **Backdrop** checkbox. You can find out how to create such a view in Chapter 4, *Creating an ideal Blender interface for material creation*.

Save the blendfile, incrementing the name to `LS-water-mist-masks-02.blend`. If you were to render at this point, you would just get a gray plastic-looking render. However, we are not interested in the material render, just the depth information.

The depth information cannot be viewed directly but we are able to create a Composite node tree that can obtain this information visually, so that we can use it to change the appearance of our previously rendered images.

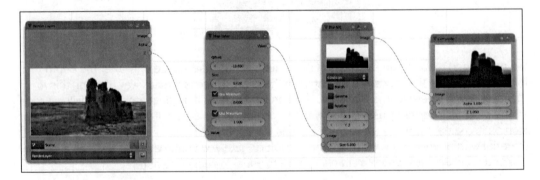

11. In the **Node** editor, there should be a **Render Layer** node linked to the **Composite** output node. We are not interested in compositing the image, just the **Z** depth information.

12. Create a new node of type **Vector/Map Value** by pressing *Shift+A*, and choosing from the selection.

13. Link the **Z** socket from the **Render layer** node to the **Value** input socket on the **Map Value** node. Link its **Value** output socket to the **Image** socket **Composite** output node.

14. In the **Map Value** node, alter the **Offset** to `-13.6000`, and the **Size** to `0.020`. Ensure the **Use Minimum** is checked and set to `0.000` as well as the **Use Maximum** at `1.000`.

If you render at this point, you will get a black and white image representing the distance of objects from the camera. However, you may also note that the edges have quite bad aliasing. We can use two methods to remove this. One is to slightly blur the image and the other is to render it at two, three, or four times the image size. We will employ both.

15. Add a **Filter Blur** node between the **Map Value** and **Composite** nodes. The **Value** output socket of the **Map Value** node to the **Image** input socket of the **Blur** node. When you do this, Blender will probably connect the direct link to the **Alpha** input of the **Composite** node. Just disconnect it by dragging the socket connector away.

16. Change the settings within the **Blur** node to **Type Gaussian**, with an **X** and **Y** value of 3; also reduce the **Size** value to `0.800`.

17. From the **Render** panel, alter the **Resolution** percentage value to `200%`. This will produce a four times larger image than the original large-scale-water renders.

Save your work once more, incrementing the filename to `LS-water-mist-masks-03.blend` and perform a render. If you examine the render, you will see that the aliasing has been considerably reduced.

Save the rendered image to your textures directory, by using the *F3* shortcut with a filename of `ocean-blur-mask.png`.

We can also create another Z depth image to add a little defocus to the horizon.

18.. With the `LS-water-mist-masks-03.blend` open, and from the **Composite** window, change the **Offset** value, in the **Map Value** node, to `-35.700`.

19. Save the blendfile to `LS-water-mist-04.blend` and perform another render, saving the image as `ocean-horizon-mask.png`, in your textures directory.

To finish this recipe, we will create a new blendfile to use those two depth mask images, in sequence, onto 250 frames of our already rendered ocean, adding mist, and a small defocus. This rendering process will not take all night to render however.

20. Create a new blendfile and switch to the **Default** view. From the header, change the window to **Node** editor.

21. From the **Render** panel, and **Dimensions** tab, set to **Render Presets HDTV 1080p**, and change the resolution to `50%`.

22. In the **Output** tab, change the output directory, and filename, to `render-output\` `waves\waves-post-`. This will ensure that the post processed images go into a sub-directory below the original images we will be post processing.

23. Save the blendfile as `waves-postpro-01.blend`.

Time to set up a simple composite node setup that will call each of the original rendered images. Use the two mask images created previously to add mist and defocus, then save the post processed image in a new directory.

24. In the **Composite** editor, ensure that the **Use Nodes**, and **Backdrop** checkboxes are selected in the header. You can delete the **Render Layer** node as we will not be rendering the default scene at all.

25. Add a new **Input** node of type **Image**. Open the first image of the sequence produced in Chapter 6, `\render-output\waves-0001.png`. This is the location you unzipped the `postpro.zip` file as described at the start of this recipe.

26. Under the **Source** selector, choose **Sequence**. Three selectors will appear enabling you to choose the number of frames in the sequence, what start frame to begin at, and also any offset you might want to employ. Set the **Frames** to `250`, **Start Frame** to `1`, and `0` **Offset**.

27. Add a new **Input** node of type **Image** and open the `ocean-blur-mask.png` from your texture directory. The default **Source** type of **File** is what is required with this image.

Remember, in the first part of this recipe, we rendered this image at 200% HD size. To use it as a mask on the waves sequence, we must rescale it down to match the size of that image.

28. Add a **Distort/Scale** node, connecting the **Image** out socket of the **Image** node to the **Image** input socket of the **Scale** node.

Rather than repeat these instructions for each socket, I will only explain where the output to input connection isn't to an image input socket. You will soon get the hang of these things with a little trial and error. Remember, Blender sometimes tries to guess where the connections should be. If that guess is wrong, just grab the wrong input socket and drag to break the false connection.

29. Change the **X** and **Y** scale values to `0.250`. The image is `200%` HD; the required size is `50%` HD, and therefore, dividing by a quarter `0.250` matches both images nicely.

We will now add a blur to defocus the horizon using `ocean-blur-mask.png`.

30. Add a **Filter/Blur** node with the **Sequenced** Image node connected to the **Image** socket, and the **Scale** node connected to the **Size** socket. Also, connect the output to the **Composite** socket to complete the node tree. Change the **Blur** type to **Gaussian**, check the **Bokeh** checkbox, and set the **X** and **Y** values to `3`.

31. The **Backdrop** behind the nodes should update to show the effect of the **Composite**. If it doesn't perform a test render, and once completed, press *Esc* to return to the **Composite** editor and it should be there. If you want to see the difference between the original image and the defocused one, add two **Output/Viewer** nodes, one connected to the output of the sequenced image, and the other connected to the output of the blur node. Selecting each **Viewer** node in turn will show the effect.

Save your work, incrementing the filename to `waves-postpro-02.blend`. Let us now use the second image mask we produced to add the horizon mist.

32. To make this much easier, we can copy some of the nodes that will use similar settings rather than create them from scratch. So, select the **Image** node and the **Scale** node just created in the previous steps. You do so by holding the *Shift* key as you click to select.

33. With both selected, press *Shift+D* to duplicate and drag the copies below to a clear part of the window.

34. From the **Image.002** node, unlink the filename by clicking on the **X** to the right of the name, and **Open** `ocean-horizon-mask.png` from the textures directory.

35. Add a new node of type **Color/Mix**. Connect the output from the **Blur** node to its top **Image** input, and connect the **Scale.001** output to the **Fac**(tor). Plug the output of the **Mix** node to the **Composite** node.

36. Change the **Mix** type to **Value** and alter the color swatch to **R, G,** and **B** `0.800`.

Save your work, incrementing the filename to `waves-postpro-03.blend`. If you now render the animation, Blender will load each of the original images in turn applying the composite defocus and mist and saving the post processed images into a new directory. You will notice that the renders only take about 1 second to render, so the whole animation will be just over 5 minutes, which is a bit better than 17.5 hours.

If you want to see the animation, select either, **Play Rendered Animation** from the **Render** menu, or press *Ctrl+F11*.

How it works...

Although it would be possible to employ a defocus, and mist, in the original blendfile, using Blender to post process after the event can save significant time. By rendering the Z depth to an image, we can use quite simple masking techniques to repaint the rendered images as though the scene had been directly rendered with these additional settings.

In a sense, it is just a cheat but such shortcuts are the mainstay of the professional industry. Frequently, renders will not turn out exactly as expected and while it may be fun to place these in the DVD/Blu-ray extras section, as bloopers, you will get more satisfaction if you are able to quickly rescue such sequences.

To use this technique, we had to extract a mask from the original file to restrict the amount of blurring, for the horizon, and lightening for the mist. We used a simple technique to render the Z depth from the original animation. Because the camera did not move during the shot, we were able to just extract single images. If the camera did move, and therefore alter the Z depth between frames, it would have been necessary to animate the entire sequence. However, because we did not require the materials and textures to be rendered, we were able to turn those off and as a result even rendering the entire 250 frames of Z depth information would have been much quicker than the 17.5 hours of the original rendered sequence.

Extracting the Z depth requires us to enable that in the **Render Layers** tab. You will see that it is possible to render all kinds of other information for manipulation later. If you were doing this, you would need to render to a format that can hold that extra information such as **OpenEXR**. In our example, we just needed a couple of masks to define those areas of the image that required mist and the other to add a defocus to the horizon.

The Z depth information, in the original blendfile, is not a visual representation of depth. To make it so, converting the nearest objects to black, to the furthest objects in white, we need to re-map the Z depth data. The two import remapping values are **Size** and **Offset**. The **Size** value should be reduced to a very small number. In the recipe, it was reduced to 0.020. At these small sizes, the Z depth will begin to be visible if you have an output **Viewer** node connected. Think of this value as being the range of the spread of depth. The **Offset** value needs to be set as a negative value. It can be used to move the division backward and forwards in the scene. Therefore, it is possible to make fine adjustments to where, and what range you want the Z depth mask to be.

Unfortunately, the Z depth information is not anti-aliased because it's not really designed to be used as an image. However, we employed two techniques to anti-alias the image, quadrupling the render size, and applying a very small three pixel blur. When the mask is used, it will be reduced to match the size of the original image and, as a result, the blur will be small enough to eliminate terminator problems that might have been present using a smaller rendered mask.

Modifying the sequence of images was a simple task requiring a node compositing setup in a new blendfile.

The Blender compositor can be used for more than just refining a 3D scene. Here, we have created a composite node tree that only modifies images. It takes the first image of the original rendered sequence, applies a blur that is controlled by the `ocean-blur-mask.png` image, and then mixes that with a white texture controlled by the second `ocean-horizon-mask.png` image to produce mist. It repeats this for each image in the sequence, automatically saving the post-processed images in a new directory.

The **Bokeh** effect, selected in the **Gaussian Blur** node, helps improve the appearance of the blur method. However, it does require a little extra processing but in our example we are not worried about this extra time as the renders for each image are short anyway.

Blender has other compositor nodes that can add a blur to distant objects. In particular, there is the very accurate **Defocus** node. This is the preferred method to defocus a render within a 3D scene. But, here we are dealing with just images that do not have inherent Z depth information so we have to employ masks to mimic depth information. However, this is a quick and effective shortcut for producing simple defocus within images.

We used a **Mix** method called **Value** to combine the defocused shot with a white color that is controlled by the second mask. This mix method is not a common method of mixing, but here it does just the job. Essentially, pixels are converted to hue, saturation, and value before being blended. The hue, and saturation, of the base image, is combined with the blended value, before being converted back to red, green, and blue. However, it produces just the right effect for mist on a sunny day.

The render time is incredibly quick because the calculations to perform these post process tasks is relatively simple compared with processing 3D information. We could have completed a similar task in a graphics package but Blender sets up such an easy and integrated solution to the problem that you will find using post processing techniques within the 3D suite is a better and quicker solution.

There's more...

The Blender compositor is constantly under development with a number of new node types being added or modified as the 3D suite is developed. Certain tasks can currently be a little frustrating, such as nodes attempting to guess where they should be connected as they are added. This can be a problem when developing both composite and material nodes because you will move back and forth between nodes, adding, and deleting as you develop your node solution. So, it is important to know how to move and disconnect nodes as you create your node-based solutions.

 Some in the Blender community are in favor of dropping automatic connection so it may not be there in future versions.

Useful node procedures

▸ Dragging a node from an input socket will delete that node connection, unless you just drag it to a correct node input socket.

▸ By holding down the *Ctrl* key while *Left* mouse dragging a selection marquee around the unwanted connector will delete it.

▸ You can use the middle mouse wheel if you have one, to zoom in and out of the node tree. Using the *Alt* key in combination with a *Left* mouse drag will move the whole node tree in the view. Individual nodes can be moved by dragging or pressing the **G** grab key when selected. You can de-clutter a node element by pressing the **+** icon in the node header where all unused sockets will be hidden. You can collapse a node to its name by clicking the triangle icon to the left of the node name.

▸ Viewer nodes are a great way to almost instantly see the effect of the node tree at various points of the composite. You don't have to keep on re-rendering to see your changes.

▸ Copying previously created nodes can save you time, particularly when it is only minor changes between the same type of node. It also makes it easy to copy multiple nodes.

▸ You can also create node groups by selecting all the nodes you want, grouping, then pressing *Ctrl+G*. Blender will collapse all nodes into a single node with a green title that can be renamed. Grouped nodes can be appended from other blendfiles just like any material or object. However, for clarity in this example, I did not suggest any grouping to keep the recipe simple.

I have found all of these to be useful when developing my own node material and compositor solutions.

See also

Chapter 1

▸ *Creating a sea rock material*
▸ *Creating a texture node to simulate seaweed at the base of a rock*

Chapter 4

▸ *Creating an ideal Blender interface for material creation*

Chapter 6

▸ *Creating realistic large-scale water in Blender 2.5*

- ▶ *Creating loopable fire and smoke sequences in Blender*
- ▶ *Easily add fire to a scene without complex rendering*

Adding more than one material to a surface

Man-made objects frequently have multiple components. Modeling all of these as separate Blender objects can present problems. To begin with, you will have to attach each component if you wish the whole object to move in an animation. You may also get problems with mesh intersection where two materials are so close together that the computer will find it difficult to work out which is in front of the other. This can lead to flashing textures that can become emphasized in an animation. Wouldn't it be great if Blender provided some way of assigning different materials to various parts of a mesh? Well, fortunately, Blender can do this and, as we will discover, it is very easy to achieve.

The faucet, created in *Chapter 5, when simulating reflections in metal materials,* is an excellent candidate for multiple materials as most bathroom taps have hot and cold labels attached to the top of the stopcock. We will attach an enamel-looking label to the top of this faucet.

Getting ready

Although this recipe picks up from the end of the faucet recipes in Chapter 5, we will use a pre-created blendfile that is available from the Packtpub website as: `chapter-05\faucet-cap-01.blend`.

The file already has some additional materials and textures installed to make the recipe easier. However, you will have to apply them using the instructions given.

How to do it...

We need to identify which part of the object will have another texture assigned to it. We do this by assigning materials to vertices.

1. Open the blendfile `faucet-cap-01.blend`. Select the faucet object and zoom up to the top of the stopcock so you can clearly see all of the vertices. Switch to **Mesh** edit mode by pressing the *Tab* key.

2. All of the vertices should be selected. Press the *A* key until they are all deselected.

3. Using one of the vertex selection methods, press *Shift+B* for box select, or *C* for brush select, and select all of the top cap vertices. You can unselect any wrongly selected vertex by using the *Alt* key in brush select. You may also find it convenient to switch to exclude hidden faces in solid view. Use *Z* to switch between wireframe and solid view, and select the exclude hidden faces icon in the header while in solid view.

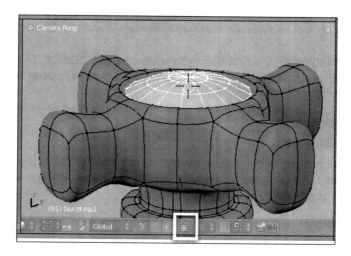

4. With the cap vertices selected, move to the **Materials** panel and you should see that the `old-copper` material is currently assigned to the whole faucet. Click the **+** button to the right of the material name to create a new, or copy a material. We don't want a copy, so just click the **X** to the right of this new material to delete this particular material from this new material slot.

5. We can now create a new material from scratch but to save time, I have included one in the blendfile. To load it, click on the material icon, to the left of the material name box, and from the displayed list, select `F cap`. Finally, to assign this material to the selected vertices, click the **Assign** button above the material name.

Save your work, incrementing the filename to `faucet-cap-02.blend`. If you render, you will see that the cap portion of the faucet has a rather nice enamel-looking hot sign that was clearly forged in the Blender bathroom works.

How it works...

It is possible to assign many materials to a mesh. You only have to select the mesh faces you want a new material to be assigned to, create a new **Material** slot, with a material of your choice, and assign that material to the selected faces.

The technique is not new as it has been part of Blender since its inception. However, it is an extremely useful tool when you want to quickly assign different surface properties to a complex mesh. The materials can be any type of Blender material, even with UV textures. It can save considerable render time because you don't have to create separate objects for each surface type and less faces means faster renders.

You do have to watch the termination between materials assigned, as they can show seams because of the abrupt change from one material to another, particularly if the two materials are a contrast. It's also a good idea to use a subsurface modifier, as in our example, so that the termination between materials does not appear too faceted.

There's more...

The `cap` material is a simple two-texture material that uses an image texture to paint the hot sign on the cap. It is mapped using an empty that has been renamed `label-location`. This allows the empty to be rotated to get the image into a good-looking position for the render. If the `label-location` empty is parented to the faucet object, we can freely move the faucet and have the empty still attached in the correct relative position, but still allow us to rotate the empty for different camera positions.

There is also an environment map assigned to this texture to give a tiny amount of reflection giving that enameled appearance.

See also

Chapter 5

  ▸ *Using environment map textures to simulate reflections*

  ▸ *Varying environment map reflections to simulate corrosion or wear*

Adding dirt onto a model

When we create materials for 3D objects in the digital world, they can tend to look too clean. Adding dirt is a common trick to add character and realism to our models. Creating dirt and grime can be a time consuming and difficult process using direct paint techniques. Blender has many tools that can be used to manually paint dirt marks onto materials. However, we will employ an ambient occlusion technique that in ordinary circumstances one would try to avoid because usually we try to steer clear of noise and artifacts in our ambient occlusion setups. Here, we will use it to create a rather nice cartoon look to a Disney-like candle stick with cartoon outlines as shown in the finished render in the following image:

Getting ready

This recipe requires that you download a pre-created blendfile with preliminary materials and textures already created. However, we will explore how to add the character of the crevice dust and grime, as well as the cartoon-like outline around the edges of the render above. The file is available from the Packtpub website as: `Chapt-08/candlestick.zip`

Unzip this file to a suitable location on your hard drive and you will see that it creates just one blendfile named `candlestick-01.blend`. There are no image textures used in this blendfile, so we don't have to worry about unzipped texture locations.

How to do it...

We will begin by exploring the `candle-stick-01.blend` setup.

1. Open the `candlestick-01.blend` in Blender and select either the handle or dish of the candlestick.

2. Switch to the **Materials** panel and you will see that this material is called `bumpy brass`. It is a simple orange yellow diffuse color, with an off white yellowish Wardiso specular shader.

3. Switch to the **Texture** panel and you will see that there is one cloud texture that influences the color, with a darker green yellow shade, and a **Geometry/Normal**, producing a quite deep, but smooth bump.

4. Select the candle and switch to the **Modifier** panel. You will see that the candle has a **Multi-resolution modifier** that has been sculpted in Blender to produce the nice candle wax drips and lines reminiscent of Victorian candlesticks popular in old Disney features.

5. Switch to the **Materials** panel and you will see that the candle material is incredibly simple. It literally has a single diffuse color change from the default, giving a light yellow white color. There are no textures associated with this material.

6. Perform a quick render to see where we will begin from.

You can see that the appearance of the materials looks somewhat plastic, which is not surprising since the default materials are based on simulation techniques designed to mimic plastic. The other thing is that it all looks terribly clean. Now, cleanliness is a very good thing in the real world but dirt and grime can add real drama to an image. In our production, the candlestick may have been languishing in a dusty corner of the puppet maker's cottage for several weeks. So, let us use Blender to add the dust and grime, not just to the surface, but more particularly into all the crevices of the candle and holder.

7. Switch to the **World** panel and in the **Ambient Occlusion** tab, select the checkbox to turn it on. Change the **Factor** to 1.85 and set the type to **Multiply**.

8. Under the **Gather** tab, select **Raytrace, Attenuation/ Distance** to 10.000, check the **Falloff** and set the **Strength** to 1.200. Under **Sampling**, change to type **Constant jittered**, with **Samples** set to 12 and **Bias** set to 0.050.

Save your work, incrementing the filename to `candlestick-02.blend` and perform a quick render.

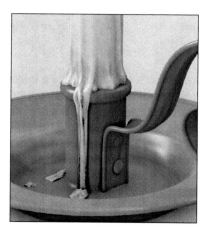

The ambient occlusion has produced some nice dark and granular shading to all the crevices of both the candle and the holder. Let us add some cartoon-like outlines to finish off this stylized material simulation.

9. From the **Render** panel, expand the **Post Processing** tab if it is not already expanded.

10. Select the **Edge** checkbox and set the **Threshold** to 180 and the color to pure black **R, G, B** 0.000.

11. From the **Dimensions** tab, change the render percentage to 100% so that we will see a full-size image when we do render.

Save your work once more, incrementing the filename to `candlestick-03.blend` and perform a final render.

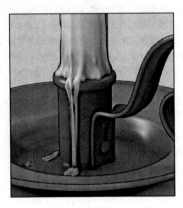

A creation that Walt would have been pleased with.

How it works...

Blender's ambient occlusion simulation is designed to help make renders more realistic. To do this, you usually have to use one of the more render-intensive algorithm types like **Adaptive**, or **Constant QMC**. One should normally up the sample rate to a high level to obtain the most accurate results. However, here, we have done the exact opposite by using the most inaccurate of the four sample types and a relatively low number of samples. Doing this has created noise in the ambient occlusion process and because AO is at its simplest designed to increase shadow contrast, the noise tends to be in the crevices, and shaded parts of the objects. So, we have taken a defect, or shortcoming of the AO system, and employed it to add dirt, grime, and drama to our render.

You can actually set the samples down lower, which would shorten the render time, but experimentation showed that at this HD resolution, 12 samples gave the best result.

We also added some post processing edge outlines, which is a very old facility within Blender. You only have two controls with Blender edge rendering, the **color** and the **Threshold**.

The color can be anything and altering this for different colored objects can help emphasize the outline. The threshold controls how much of the mesh lines making up the model will be outlined. Too high and the actual wire mesh will start appearing. Too low and you will just get a pure outline with no inside edges drawn. You will also find that altering the resolution of the render will have significant effect on the outline produced. Smaller resolution will produce thicker lines but aliasing will begin to appear. Too high a resolution and the lines will be finer and less prominent.

Although **Edge** can be a rather blunt instrument, to create edge lines, it does provide a quick and easy method of producing the cartoon-like look reminiscent of the hand drawn error of animation.

There's more...

There is currently a branch of Blender under development called Freestyle, which has been designed to offer much more control over the way edges, and indeed textures, can be applied to renders to imitate hand drawn, or freestyle images. Hopefully, this branch will eventually be fully integrated within Blender.

See also

Chapter 7

> ▸ *Skin shading using Sub Surface Scattering*

Creating an aged photo with simple Blender materials

Many recent 2D paint packages will provide some means of faking 3D to produce images that appear to have perspective. Such pseudo tools are usually inaccurate and quite tricky to use. We know that Blender has excellent 3D capabilities, so wouldn't it be great if we could bring into Blender images and photos and simply create quite complex 3D representations?

Blender can be used to automatically transform an image into something with realistic characteristics of depth, specularity, and accurate camera-based views. We will explore how we can create simple image manipulation setups that can be automatically applied to any image or across any Blendfile to produce an aged photograph.

Getting ready

This recipe is very simple to produce, so we don't have to start out with a pre-created blendfile. In the first section, we will create a simple plane, together with a special material that uses a node texture. This node texture can accept any image as an input and will output a color, and bump texture, for use in the material. However, there is one that will be necessary to create the aged photograph background, together with some other images that you can download from the Packtpub website as: `chapt-08/old-photo.zip`

Just unzip that file to your textures directory. The old photographic background image was designed by a very talented artist called Renee, who offers her marvelous collection of backgrounds via flickr.

`http://www.flickr.com/people/playingwithpsp/`

Please visit that site to explore other backgrounds that you can use in your own productions.

How to do it...

We will start by creating the basic scene ready for the material and textures to be applied.

1. Start Blender, and in the default window, **Add** a simple plane object at the center cursor position, *Shift+A*, **Mesh**, **Plane**.

2. Scale the plane by 4: *S*, *4*, *Enter*.

3. Move the camera until your camera view (*Keypad 0* in a **3D** window) matches the image below.

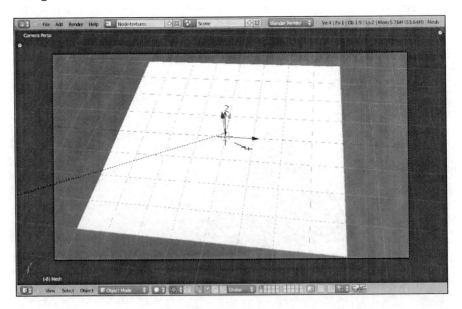

4. The scene uses the default light setup suggested in Chapter 4. That is, two lights, a **point** key light with energy set to 1.000, and a **hemi** fill light with an energy setting of **0.200**.

Before moving on to create the node texture, I suggest you switch to the node-material screen we also devised in Chapter 4. That screen will make it easier to work on our texture setup. I suggest saving your work at this point, naming the blendfile old-photo-01.blend.

5. With the **plane** selected, and from the **Materials** panel, create a new material, naming it old-photo.

6. Under the **Specular** tab, change the type to **Wardiso**, and set the **Intensity** to 0.150, and the **Slope** to 0.300.

This has created a simple material, which we now need to design a node texture to enable the magic.

7. Select the **Texture Node** button from the **Node** window and check the **Use Nodes** checkbox. Name this Node-texture.

8. Delete the **Checker** node, which connects to the **Output**, by selecting it and pressing **X** to Delete.

9. **Add** a new node of type **Input/Image**, and **Open** an image into this. You can use one of your own images if you like. However, if you wish to use the same as in the recipe, **Open** house-14.png from your textures directory.

10. **Add** a new node of type **Convertor/RGB to BW** and connect the image to its input socket.

11. **Add** a new node of type Color/RGB Curves, between the RGB to BW and the **Output** node. Alter the curve to match the image below.

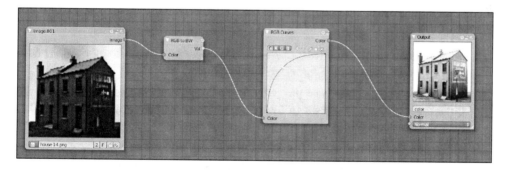

12. Connect the **RGB Curves** node to the **Output** and name the **Output** color. You should see the image has been lightened and turned to grayscale.

Let's add the magic that will mix our image with a nice old world photo.

13. Just below the **RGB to BW** node, **Add** a new node of type **Input/Image** and **Open** the included file from your texture directory named `old-photoframe.png`.

14. **Add** a new node of type **Color/Hue Saturation Value**, with the photoframe image connected to its **Color** input socket.

15. Now, **Add** a **Color/Mix** node of type **Multiply** with the **Hue Saturation Value** output connected to the **Color 2** input socket. Also, connect the **RGB Curves** node output to **Color 1** input and, finally, connect the **Mix** node to the **Output** node.

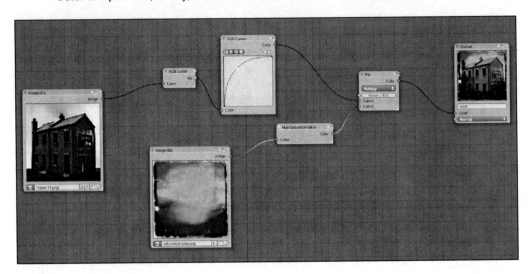

Save your work, incrementing the filename to `old-photo-02.blend`. This has created the color texture for our special old-photo material, so time to create the bump map texture from this same texture node.

16. Copy the **RGB to BW**, and **RGB Curves** nodes by selecting both of them (*Shift* click both to select), and press *Shift+D* to duplicate.

17. Move these copies down past the photoframe image and connect the **Image** to the **Color** input socket of the **RGB to BW** node, which should already be connected to the **RGB Curves** copy.

18. **Add** a new **Output** node from the **RGB Curves** copy and name it bump.

19. Finally, alter the curve shape of the **RGB Curves** copy to match the following image.

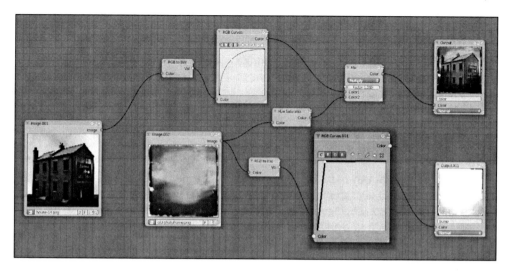

Save your work, incrementing the filename to `old-photo-03.blend`. Now, it's time to add the textures to the material creating the automatic image manipulation simulation.

20. With the **Plane** object selected, move to the **Texture** panel and you should see that the first part of our node texture has been added to the first texture slot. However, under **Output**, select `color`.

21. Under the **Influence** tab, select **Diffuse/Color** and set to `1.000`. Under the **Blend** type, select **Multiply**.

22. Select the next free texture slot and click the checker material icon next to the name and choose the same node texture as the first slot. However, under **Output**, select `bump`.

23. In the **Influence** tab, **only** select **Geometry/Normal** and set to `0.100`. The **Blend** type should be **Mix** and the **RGB to Intensity** should be selected.

Save your work, incrementing the filename to `old-photo-04.blend`. If you render at this point, you will see the colored image of the house in my case, or your image if you used that transformed into an aged photo that has faded over the years and sustained some damage due to the many decades since it was taken. However, we can now take this further to set up a repeatable node tree that performs this old photograph function to any image and across any blendfile.

24. With `old-photo-04.blend` open, move to the **Node** window and using the border select *B* key marquee, select around all of the middle nodes, excluding the first image node and the two output nodes.

25. When they are selected, press *Ctrl+G* to group them and they will contract into a single group node with one color input, for any image, and two texture outputs, the top for `color`, and the bottom for `bump`.

26. You can name that node group by clicking inside the name box, to make it easier to remember what it does. I named mine `old-photo#1`.

27. If you want, create some new **Input/Image** nodes with other images connecting each in turn to the single color input and render. If you alter the **Factor** amount below `1.00`, you can lessen the effect of the mix between your image and the photo frame background.

How it works...

Texture nodes are a great way of setting up complex image manipulations that can then be applied to materials. In this example, we can take any image and apply the aged photo node texture to produce very convincing results. Because we are rendering in a 3D suite, we can accurately apply the image to a photo-like surface and move our camera to obtain a true 3D perspective.

Creating this type of effect within a node texture enables multiple output textures to be created from a single image. Here, we created both a color, and bump map, while at the same time desaturating the image and adding a slight red/orange hue using the **Hue**, **Saturation**, **Value** texture node. Bringing all of these nodes together, into a group, makes it even easier as only the required controllers now appear. That's the input, for the image, and two outputs, for the color and bump maps. The **Factor** value can be used to lessen the mixing of the photo frame on the image without affecting the bump. This means we retain a small amount of control from the grouped texture node without having to change any of the material texture settings.

There's more...

Another advantage of grouped nodes is that they will now appear as named groups within the blendfile. You can append or link these across blendfiles just like materials or objects making an efficient method of sharing reusable material and texture solutions across many blendfiles. It is important to name grouped nodes with a meaningful name. This is important so that you will remember what it does several months down the line and still be able to apply it for future projects. It is also possible to do the same thing with Compositor node groups but that is perhaps beyond the scope of this book.

Once you have grouped several nodes, you can still edit the individual components of the group by selecting the group and pressing the *Tab* key to enter Edit mode. You can make any changes before pressing *Tab* again to exit edit mode and the nodes will shrink back to its grouped size. It is also possible to ungroup by pressing *Alt+G* while the group is selected. Once you do this, the group will become individual nodes once again.

There are many resources where you can pick up quality images for reuse in these kinds of image manipulation tasks. Search for Creative Commons images via Google or one of the image sites such as Flickr. These repositories of images are great to both explore and use providing they are cleared for use by others. In fact, when joining these repositories why not add your work so that others can both learn and use your creations?

- `http://www.flickr.com/`
- `http://googlesystem.blogspot.com/2009/06/find-creative-commons-images-in-google.html`
- `http://commons.wikimedia.org/wiki/Main_Page`
- `http://www.freephotobank.org/main.php`
- `http://creativecommons.org/image/`

9
Special Effects Materials

In this chapter, we will cover:

- ▸ Creating explosive smoke in Blender
- ▸ Igniting a flame and making things burn in Blender
- ▸ Creating loopable fire and smoke sequences
- ▸ Adding complex FX without the render overhead

Introduction

Special effects are the holy grail of the digital media revolution. Being able to create the fantastic and impossible images required from the modern screenplay has helped propel 3D creation suites like Blender to the forefront of the creative media environment. Material and texture techniques are crucial to the process of creating a stunning special effect. We, as artists, will find creating such unique and visually stimulating simulations one of the most enjoyable aspects of our craft.

In this chapter, we will be creating some of the most difficult things in any 3D suite, smoke, fire, and explosions. Once you know how to create these material simulations in Blender, you will be able to apply them to create many special effects for your own, or directors', productions. You will see how simple texture changes can radically alter the appearance of smoke and fire. You will also explore ways to reduce production and render times normally associated with such difficult recreations.

As with any digital special effect creation task, these recipes will require significant computer processing power. However, I have attempted to tailor them to a relatively low power system with a minimum amount of RAM. My system operates with a 32-bit dual core processor with 3 GB of memory. If your system is a lower specification than this, you will be able to complete the recipes but they may take longer to process or render. You will also find that some of the physical simulations such as smoke will require significant disk space for saving bakes of the physical simulation. I will point out where necessary those areas where you may have to reduce settings, or size, to produce the same effect on a lower spec computer system. However, even if you are using a really old and slow computer, you will be amazed at the special effects possible from within Blender.

Creating explosive smoke in Blender

Nothing is more challenging for the 3D artist than to create a realistic simulation of an explosion. Blender's recent upgrade to the 2.5 series of 3D suites has provided a new smoke simulation system together with a true 3D texture called **Voxel Data**. These two physically based tools combine to offer realistic explosions, flame, and all kinds of smoke to enhance your scenes. However, as with any complex 3D tool, they require some expertise to make best use of their capabilities.

Because the smoke physics facility is so closely tied to the 3D **Voxel Data** texture, it can be considered a texture-related simulation as well a physical one. In fact, smoke without a material and texture simulation is impossible. For that reason, this first recipe will show the correct way to set up a smoke simulation from the physical simulation to some default material and texture setups. Further recipes will explore how the materials and textures can be modified and refined to produce almost any kind of smoke or fire.

You will find that these recipes will test your computer system processing power, RAM, and patience. Smoke simulation requires long bake times and significant hard disk space, so, be prepared for some extended Blender sessions, and possibly crashes as you test the capabilities of your computer.

Blender employs a method of saving the processed data to RAM, or hard disk, called baking. This information, once baked, does not need to be reprocessed and can be used to view the effect quickly and repeatedly. If you make any changes to the effect settings, you will need to re-bake to see the changes.

Because this can be frustrating, the first recipe will show some key steps to protect and reduce your work as you progress. For this first recipe, follow the steps exactly as specified, and avoid experimenting with settings. Doing so will ensure you do not suffer the aggravation of lost work and will soon become a special FX Blender master.

Getting ready

Rather than supply a created smoke setup blendfile, it will be best to create all the smoke setup procedures in the first few steps. These steps can be applied to almost any physical smoke simulation in Blender. Learning by doing is one of the best ways of appreciating the power and complexity of such an extensive tool. However, since the lighting and camera setup also play a large part in the appearance of any object in Blender, I have supplied a blendfile with those set ready for us to create the smoke from scratch. You can download the file from the Packtpub website as: `\chapt-09\smoke-start.zip`

Once downloaded, unzip the file to your Blender directory and **Open** it and resave it as `smoke-test.blend`. As we work through the recipe, you will see that we have to overwrite the blendfile several times. Having a fallback file, `smoke-start.blend`, will ensure we can at least recover to the beginning of the recipe should our systems crash.

To create a smoke simulation in Blender, we need to:

- ▸ Define a domain in which the simulation will be confined
- ▸ Set up an emitter from which the smoke will flow
- ▸ Define the resolution and characteristics of the smoke flow
- ▸ Apply a special material and texture to define the smokes shape, color, and density

Out of all of these, the material and textures are the simplest and quickest part of the process to compute. However, the smoke physics requires long processing and large amounts of disk space, depending on the resolutions set. If we lose this data during our development, which is very easy to do, we would have to re-process all over again from scratch. Baking this data to disk, and then protecting it from, system freezes, and inadvertent fiddling, will save you time, money, and sanity.

How to do it...

Open up the blendfile `smoke-test.blend` saved as stated above. This has all the camera, lighting, and framing setup prepared ready for you to add the smoke simulation.

1. Ensure the cursor is in the center by pressing *Shift+S*, and selecting **Cursor to Center**.

2. Create a new cube object *Shift+A*, **Mesh**, and **Cube**. Rename the cube object `Domain`, in the **Object** panel.

3. Create a new object of type **Plane** and name this `smoke-emitter` in the **Object** panel.

4. Move it down to just above the base of the domain cube. Its position should be **X, Y** `0.000`, and **Z** `-3.686`. This will ensure that the smoke will be created from within the domain and has the maximum clear space above in which to flow.

5. Change to the **Modifier** panel and create a **Sub-division** modifier of **2** subdivisions for both **View** and **Render**. Now, **Apply** that modifier to fix those subdivisions into the mesh.

These are the only objects we need to create a smoke simulation. The cube is the domain in which the smoke will be created, and the plane is the emitter from where the smoke particles will flow.

We need to set the size of the domain to ensure it encloses the whole of the smoke generated. The smaller the domain the less disk space, and smoke processing, will be required. However, you may not know the correct size yet so I will give some reasonable settings that should work as a starting point.

6. Select the `Domain` cube and press the *N* key to bring up the **Transform** toolbox to the left of the 3D window. Under the **Scale** controller, set **X** and **Y** to `2.600`, and **Z** to `4.000`.

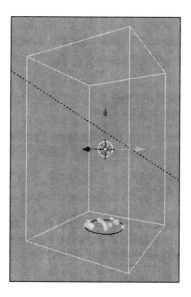

Time to save your work, only this time **Do Not** increment the filename. This is important because when we start creating smoke simulations Blender will create a sub-directory using the blend filename to store the physics calculations. If we were to create a different name each time we saved, duplicate directories would be created for each new blend filename. Potentially, these directories can be several gigabytes in size, so restricting unnecessary duplication is imperative.

Let us now set up the physical smoke simulation.

7. With the `Domain` cube selected, move to the **Physics** panel, this is the last in the editor-type panel selector.

8. Expand the **Smoke** tab by clicking on the triangle icon to its left.

9. Select **Domain** and leave all of the settings at their default.

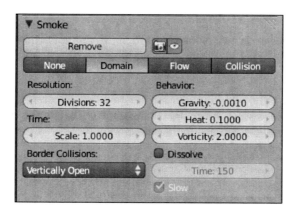

10. Select the plane object named `smoke-emitter`, and from the **Particles** panel, create a new particle system, naming it `smoke-plane`.

11. Under the **Emission** tab, set the **Amount** to `3600`, the **Start Frame** to `1`, the **End** to `250`, and **Lifetime** to `1.000`.

12. In the **Render** tab, uncheck the **Emitter**, and select the **None** button so that neither the emitter or particles will render.

13. Under the **Display** tab, select the **Point** button. This ensures we can see that particles are being emitted while we experiment with smoke settings.

Now that we have created a particle system on the emitter, we have to tell Blender that this specific particle system will form the basis for smoke emitted from the plane.

14. With the smoke-emitter plane object selected, move back to the **Physics** panel, select **Smoke**, and this time **Flow**. Ensure the **Particle System** selector displays `smoke-plane`, which we created above. All the other settings can remain at their default values.

Save your work **Without** incrementing the filename.

It is important to save the file before you start generating smoke, the physics calculations will need to reside in memory. If you later increase some of the smoke resolution settings, you could run out of memory and either Blender or your computer might crash. Saving the file will create a directory below the saved blendfile location where temporary calculation will be saved.

If you now press *Alt+A*, Blender will attempt to display the smoke generated in the viewport. Depending on the power of your computer, this may be quite slow. Blender displays a Frames Per Second (**FPS**) indicator in the top left of the 3D window. The calculations are repeated each time the frames return to the first frame. We need to lock these calculations by baking them to disk.

15. Firstly, we will create a bake of the particle system.

16. With the `smoke-emitter` plane selected, move to the **Particle** panel.

17. In the **Cache** tab, under **File Name**, enter SMP, and also check **Disk Cache**, and **Use Lib Path**.

18. Click the **Bake** button and Blender will create a new directory called `blendercache_smoke-test`, below the directory where the blendfile is saved, and bake the particle settings to that directory.

We should now do the same with the smoke settings.

19. With the `Domain` cube object selected, move to the **Physics** panel.

20. Under the **Smoke Cache** tab, select **Compression Heavy** and enter the **File Name** `lo`. Ensure that the **Use Lib Path** is checked.

21. Move to the **Smoke High Resolution** tab and ensure it is checked. The **Resolution** should be at its lowest setting of 1 **Divisions**. As soon as you select the high resolution setting, a **Smoke High Resolution Cache** will become available.

22. Under **Smoke High Resolution Cache**, select **Compression Heavy**, and enter **File Name** `hi` with **Use Lib Path** checked.

23. In the **Smoke High Resolution Cache** tab, click **Bake**.

The bake will take time to compute with an indication of its progress given by a counter appearing when you bring the cursor into the 3D view. This is a percentage counter, so however many frames are being processed, you will know how far through Blender has computed. If you computer is at least 2–3 GHz, the processing time should be relatively short at approximately two to three seconds per frame. Once the counter reaches 100, you should be able to play the animation with *Alt+A* and see a representation of the smoke in the 3D window.

So far, we have set up the physical properties of the smoke; next, we need to create a material to be able to render the smoke.

24. Select the `Domain` cube object and move to the **Materials** panel.

25. Create a new material, of type **Volume**, and name it `thick-smoke`.

26. In the **Density** tab, reduce the **Density** slider to `0.000` and increase the **Density Scale** to `8.398`.

27. Under the **Shading** tab, change the **Scattering** slider to `2.800`. All the other settings in this tab should be left at their default values.

28. In the **Transparency** tab, select **Z Transparency**.

29. Move to the **Textures** panel and create a new texture of type **Voxel Data**, naming it `smoke`.

30. Under the **Voxel Data** tab, choose **File Format** type **Smoke** and choose from the selector `Domain`, and **Source Density**.

31. In the **Influence** tab, check **Density** and set to `2.000` and also check **Emission Color** at `1.000`. The **Blend** type should be **Mix**.

32. Move to the **Colors** tab and check **Ramp**. Create a ramp with the following three color stop settings.

    Stop 0 – **Pos** 0.000, **R G B** 1.000, **Alpha** 0.00

    Stop 1 – **Pos** 0.500, **R G B** 0.500, **Alpha** 0.50

    Stop 2 – **Pos** 1.000, **R G B** 0.000, **Alpha** 1.00

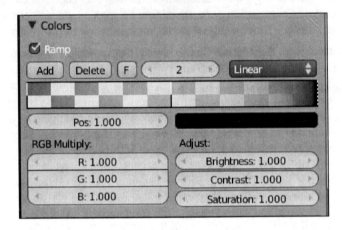

Save your work once more, remembering **Not** to increment the filename. If you were to render a frame, the smoke would look rather unrealistic as we currently only have the lowest resolution set for the smoke simulation. We will next increase this resolution together with some other settings to produce a more realistic smoke. Be aware that as we increase resolution, we may hit the limits of your computer system so try the indicated settings and if these do not work, reduce the resolution until it computes the smoke calculations without using up all of your ram or disk space.

33. With the Domain cube object selected, move to the **Physics** panel.

34. Under the **Smoke** tab, observe that the **Resolution Divisions** is set to 32 and the **Border Collisions** is set to **Vertically Open**. This means the resolution is quite small and the top of the domain will allow smoke to disappear out of the top without being confined and filling the domain with smoke. Changing any of these settings will radically alter the simulation so leave them as they are.

35. We can add detail to our smoke by using a special **Resolution** setting in the **Smoke High Resolution** tab. However, we should always free any bakes and ensure that the data held on disk is deleted before we try new settings.

36. In the **Smoke High Resolution Cache**, click the **Free All Bakes** button. This will clear from memory and smoke data. However, the disk cache will remain.

37. To clear the disk cache, move to the **Smoke** tab, and increase and then decrease the **Resolution** by 1. As soon as you do this, the cache will be erased from the disk.

This is an irrevocable selection and there is no way of recovering the cache without re-running the bake with identical settings.

Before increasing and re-baking the simulation, we can reduce the number of frames for the simulation. As the smoke seemed to reach the top of the domain, at about 157 frames, alter the **Start** Frame to 2 and the **End** frame to 200.

38. Under the **Smoke High Resolution Cache** tab, alter the **Start** and **End** frames there to 1 to 200. You should also do the same to the **Smoke Cache** settings.

39. Now, under the **Smoke High Resolution** tab, increase the **Resolution Divisions** to 3.

Before we bake these new settings, confirm you have at least 12 GB free on your hard drive. Any less and your operating system will start misbehaving anyway. Also, be prepared for the baking to take several hours, even on a relatively fast computer. If Blender crashes on your computer during this process, restart Blender and reduce the Resolution Divisions to 2 in Step 39 above. Don't worry, your computer will not blow up.

Save your work remembering **Not** to increment the filename.

40. With the `Domain` cube selected, and in the **Physics** panel, click any of the **Bake All Dynamics** selector buttons in the caches, and wait.

If the bake is successful, the 3D view should show a much better approximation of smoke. Before we render this, save your work once more with **No** increment. We will finally lock that simulation so we do not inadvertently wipe it from disk.

41. With the Domain cube selected, move to the **Physics** panel and under the **Smoke Cache** tab, check the **External** checkbox, and under the **File Path**, use the folder locator to select the directory that holds the cache data. It should be `blender_ smoke-test`.

42. Move down to the **Smoke High Resolution Cache** and check the **External** checkbox there, and choose the `blendcache_smoke-test` directory as above. Immediately, the baking controls will disappear making it impossible to free the cache.

Save your work one last time and then render an animation of the large explosion.

How it works...

Blender's smoke generator can produce some spectacular results but as with any complex system, small changes can produce large differences in appearance. We may have become used to fiddling with settings to tease out the best look for an animation. However, with smoke physics, you need to be much more organized or you will waste a lot of time and disk space. In this recipe, I have applied some tips to control the potential pain of long bakes as well as ways of protecting your work once baked. If you follow the key points used in this recipe, you will produce fantastic smoke simulations.

There's more...

So, here are my top tips for securing a perfect smoke simulation in the shortest time.

Creating the perfect domain

Never make the domain cube too large. On my system, that's about four Blender units maximum. You can alter the size of the domain after the first low resolution bake until only the smoke is enclosed in the domain. That is how I worked out the size of the domain for the recipe. Starting with a four Blender unit cube, I baked the lowest resolution and then scaled the sides of the domain until they just enclosed the smoke generated. You will probably find that initial puff of smoke at the beginning of the simulation is the largest smoke area. Of course, it is possible to have forces applied to smoke like wind, which would alter the shape of the smoke, so check it throughout the range of the animation to ensure smoke does not hit the side of the domain. The top of the domain was set to **Vertically Open** so that although the smoke will not be visible outside of the domain, it continues to travel upward without being deflected.

Only use the high resolution simulation

The Smoke simulator has two modes of operation, basically, low resolution and high resolution. If you design in one, you cannot switch to the other and expect the same result. As a consequence, I would recommend only working in the high resolution cache. However, still set the standard cache to ensure it's held in the simulation.

I would also recommend that you use the **Heavy Compression** choice in both the cache settings. This will reduce the size of the physics cache files saved to disk. However, they can still be large; on my system, the cache for this recipe was over 1.5 GB.

Low settings to start with

Start with low settings to obtain the correct acting performance from the smoke before increasing resolution. Having the **Resolution** at 32 **Divisions**, and the **Smoke High Resolution Cache** at 1 **Divisions**, will ensure you can bake relatively quickly.

Increasing the **Resolution Divisions** above 32 will alter the simulation because you will be increasing the domain resolution in which the same number of particles have to travel. You would need to increase the number of particles exponentially each time you double the **Resolution Divisions**. These changes will not only produce higher quality, but also enormous disk caches, and very long bake periods. I would, therefore, recommend no more than 64 **Divisions** on a 32-bit system and no higher than 3 **Smoke High Resolution Cache Divisions** if you have less than 3 GB of RAM.

Clear bakes before re-baking

When you are sure you need to re-bake a simulation, always free bakes and clear the cache by incrementing and decrementing the **Smoke** tab **Resolution Divisions**. This will automatically remove any of the cache files in the cache directory. This is important because if you have any redundant cache data remaining, it may mess with your simulation. It's easy to bake the whole animation then reduce the number of frames and bake again. If you later decide you wish to increase the number of rendered frames, the smoke will be reading different smoke cache data during the animation. So, delete it if you are sure you want to re-bake.

 If you would like to be ultra safe, you could always copy the cache directory to another location before clearing and re-baking. However, remember the size of a cache can be huge.

Once happy with the simulation, protect your cache

There is nothing worse than working long hours to complete a complex smoke project and inadvertently clearing the cache. Once you are satisfied with the flow of the smoke, **lock the cache** by selecting the **External** checkbox in both caches. You can then select the correct cache directory and experiment with materials and textures to create the perfect type of smoke you are after. It also means you can share smoke simulations between blendfiles by using the **Append** command and pointing to the correct **External** cache directory.

Simple materials make great smoke

You will have noticed that the smoke material for this recipe was very simple. When we create a smoke material, we are creating it for the whole of the domain. However, by using a **Voxel Data** texture, which has real 3D qualities, we can apply transparency to simulate the density of smoke particles within the domain. That is why we reduced the overall density of the thick-smoke material to 0.000 using the **Voxel** texture, controlled by the smoke generator, to give a variable density that flows like real smoke. The **Density Scale** was also increased to provide a thick and dense smoke that might be associated with a large explosion.

In the **Shading** tab, we increased the **Scattering** to 2.800, which ensured that the default colors for **Emission, Transmission**, and **Reflection** are spread throughout the smoke.

The **Voxel Data** texture is assigned to the **Domain** object in the **Voxel Data** tab and if it isn't, it will shade the entire domain as a smoky cube. If you see this, it is a clear sign that you may have missed this important setting.

The **Color Ramp** represents the density, and color, of the smoke. Here, we only used a simple gray gradient evenly varying the transparency from opaque to clear. This gives fine wispy smoke edges that are accurate for the type of explosion we have created. Because the caches are baked and protected at this stage you can experiment with different color ramp setups without affecting the bakes.

Because the **Voxel Data** texture is a true 3D shader, we can employ lighting to illuminate the inside of the smoke. Depending on the density of the smoke, sphere lights can cast color or brightness levels to represent burning or the flash of the initial explosion. It's also possible to animate the density of the smoke to vary the light scattering as time progresses. You can see a demonstration animation at the following location:

http://vimeo.com/17290731

See also

There are many introductory Blender smoke tutorials on the Internet. Many of them only cover the basics of smoke production but have useful tips on certain smoke and flame generation techniques. I recommend those by Gottfried Hofmann from cgtuts+:

http://cg.tutsplus.com/tutorials/blender/introduction-to-smoke-simulation-in-blender-2-5-day-1/

These are five well-prepared 30-minute videos that helped me discover this complex Blender tool.

Igniting a flame and making things burn in Blender

There is never smoke without flame and Blender provides the tools to magically ignite a smoke simulation to simulate fire. Fire like smoke is a difficult physical simulation in Blender and will require significant processing to bake the flames just as we experienced with the first recipe in this chapter. However, our task in this flame recipe is to understand the material and texture changes to produce bright self-illuminating flames that as they rise and cool, produce wispy smoke.

There are changes necessary to the smoke settings to create the flow of flame-like tendrils in our simulation. These will be covered but the main purpose of this recipe is to show how easy it is to create a realistic-looking flame that appears to be burning at its base and gradually cooling as its rises, eventually dissipating as a dirty smoke. We will use the renders from this recipe in later recipes to create a loopable flaming torch scene that renders incredibly quickly.

Getting ready

This recipe scene is very processor intensive, I have provided a start blendfile but you will need to bake the smoke cache before you can add the materials and textures to turn it into flames. This will take a few hours and will occupy at least 1.78 GB of disk space.

Download the `smoky-fire-start.blend` from the Packtpub website:

`chapt09/smoky-fire-start.blend`

How to do it...

We start by creating the smoke cache and saving it so that the material and texture creation can proceed.

1. Open the `smoky-fire-start.blend` and immediately resave it as `smoky-fire.blend`. This will ensure we retain a fallback blendfile should things mess up.

2. Move to the **Physics** panel and from the **Smoke Cache**, and **Smoke High Resolution Cache** tabs, uncheck the **External** checkbox and **Save** the blendfile once more.

3. In the **Smoke High Resolution Cache** tab, click **Free All Bakes**.

4. In the main **Smoke** tab, increment, and then decrement the **Resolution Divisions** number. You will see that this is set at `64`, which is twice the resolution of the first recipe.

5. Finally, in the **Smoke High Resolution Cache** tab, click **Bake All Dynamics**.

This bake will take several hours so it may be best to start this before going to bed or on a day you do not need access to your computer for other purposes. However, once completed, we need to lock the cache.

6. With the `smoky-fire.blend` file open and the `Domain` object selected, move to the **Physics** panel and under the **Smoke Cache**, and **Smoke High Resolution Cache**, check the **External** checkboxes and from the **File Path**, choose the directory `blendcache_smoky-fire`.

 The number of **Divisions** is twice that of the first smoke recipe in this chapter. As a result, you may find your computer cannot process this level of detail. Should Blender crash while baking the smoke, you could reduce the **Divisions** to 32. However, be aware that the flame appearance will behave quite differently from what is shown in this recipe. You should just about be able to bake this with a 32-bit operating system of 2–3 GHz and 2–3 GB of RAM.

7. If you haven't done so already, ensure the blendfile for this recipe is renamed as `smoky-fire.blend`.

8. With the `Domain` object selected, move to the **Materials** panel and create a new material, of type **Volume**, and name it `flame`.

9. Under the **Density** tab, reduce **Density** to `0.000`, and increase the **Density Scale** to `2.350`.

10. In the **Shading** tab, change the **Scattering** to `2.820`, and the **Emission** to `5.000`. Leave all of the other settings in this tab as default.

11. Under the **Transparency** tab, select **Z Transparency**.

Save your work at this point and this time you can increment the filename to `smoky-fire-01.blend`, because the smoke simulation is reading the cache from an external directory.

Let us now add the textures for smoke and flame to the material.

12. With the `Domain` object selected, move to the **Textures** panel and create a new texture of the type **Voxel Data** and name it **Smoke**.

13. Under the **Voxel Data** tab, select the **File Format** to type **Smoke** and in the **Domain Object**, select **Domain**.

14. In the **Colors** tab, check the **Ramp** checkbox and set three color stops as follows:

    Stop 0 – **Pos** `0.000`, **R G B** `0.000`, **Alpha** `0.00`

    Stop 1 – **Pos** `0.067`, **R G B** `0.250`, **Alpha** `0.80`

    Stop 2 – **Pos** `1.000`, **R G B** `1.000`, **Alpha** `1.00`

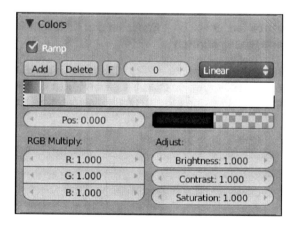

15. In the **Influence** tab, check the **Density** selector and set to `1.000`. Also, ensure that the **Blend** type is **Mix**.

Save your work once more, incrementing the filename to `smoky-fire-02.blend`. You can perform a test render at this stage and see what your work looks like so far.

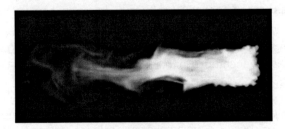

As you can see, it is quite a dense smoke with an almost self-illuminating quality to the particles. However, we need to ignite the smoke to make flame as well as smoke.

16. With the `Domain` object selected, move over to the **Textures** panel and in the next available texture slot, create a new texture of type **Voxel Data**, and name it `Fire`.

17. In the **Voxel Data** tab, select **File Format** of type **Smoke** and **Domain Object** `Domain`.

18. In the **Colors** tab, check the **Ramp** checkbox and set four color stops as follows:

    Stop 0 – **Pos** `0.000`, **R G B** `0.000`, **Alpha** `0.00`

    Stop 1 – **Pos** `0.167`, **R** `0.500` **G** `0.010` **B** `0.000`, **Alpha** `0.65`

    Stop 2 – **Pos** `0.364`, **R** `0.565` **G** `0.264` **B** `0.000`, **Alpha** `1.00`

    Stop 3 – **Pos** `1.000`, **R** `1.000` **G** `0.850` **B** `0.440`, **Alpha** `1.00`

19. Under the **Influence** tab, check both **Emission** and **Emission Col**, and set to `1.000`. Change the **Blend** type to **Multiply**.

Save you work incrementing the filename to `smoky-fire-03.blend`. If you perform a render, you will see that the smoke now looks as if it is burning at its base, cooling to a red color as its spreads from the base of the fire and finally dissipates as smoke.

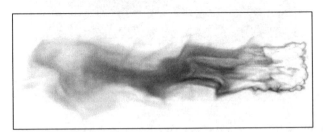

If you render out an animation, I would suggest that you render at 25% resolution in the **Render** panel to avoid long render times. However, the result is a reasonable representation of a torch-like fire. Of course, the render is currently orientated in landscape, which may not be the way we will use this simulation in a real scene. Nevertheless, we will use this setup to generate a series of sequenced images maximizing the quality in an HD TV screen size. You will see how we can apply these rendered sequential images as a loopable sequence to easily add fire to other blendfiles and re-orientate the sequence so it looks as if the fire is rising vertically rather than horizontally.

How it works...

The smoke physics simulation used in this recipe has several changes from the first recipe of the chapter. When you are creating fire, or flame, the flow of the smoke simulation needs to be faster and have wispy tendrils rather than the dense smoke created in the first recipe. One of the key settings that produce this flame-like movement is controlled by using a different **Noise** method as set in the **Smoke High Resolution** tab of the **Smoke** physics simulation. Here, we employed **FFT** (Fast Fourier Transform), rather than **Wavelet**. The **FFT** noise method is better at generating flames, particularly when we are simulating flames close up rather than at a distance. By varying the **Strength** settings below the noise method you can also control the effect as applied to the volume. Here, we reduce the effect to 0.75 again producing a closer-looking flame.

In the main **Smoke** tab, we have also changed three important settings apart from the overall increase in resolution.

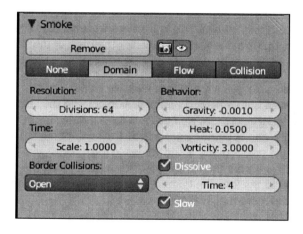

Under the **Behavior** settings, we have added a very small amount of **Heat**, which in combination with the particles setup will make the flames expand quickly as though the base of the flame is hotter than the top. We have also increased the **Vorticity** to 3.000, which will add more turbulence, and spin to the simulation, just like real flames.

We also enabled a **Slow Dissolve** of 4 seconds to the simulation to produce the effect of a flame dying out as all combustible components of the smoke are consumed. Only change the **Dissolve** amount after other settings are confirmed for the flow of flame or smoke as changing any other smoke setting will alter the timing of the simulation dramatically.

If you now examine the particle settings for the emitter, you will see that we have used 20,000 particles for this simulation. That is because we are dealing with quite a large domain area with its largest dimension of 4.7 Blender units. We are also using a high smoke resolution of 64 divisions which, as was explained in the first recipe of this chapter, requires an exponential increase in the number of particles used. Unfortunately, we are only able to use real particles in a smoke simulation as child particles are ignored. One other setting that is important in the **Particles** panel is in the **Velocity** tab. Here, we have increased the Normal to 8.000; this is eight times higher than the default thus pushing the smoke out at a quicker speed just like a hot flame would do. Indeed, if you now switch to the **Smoke Flow** settings for the emitter, you will see that **Initial Velocity** has been checked, meaning the flow will now be affected by the velocity of the particles.

The material and textures used in this recipe are the key features that make the flame look real. The material settings set reasonably standard **Density Scale** and **Scattering**. However, the **Emission** amount has been increased to 5.000, which will give the material in combination with the textures, a self-illuminated characteristic. Of course, there is no real light in the flame and if we were using this in a real scene, we would need to create additional lamps to synthesize the effect of the flame illuminating other surfaces and objects.

The two **Voxel Data** textures used in this simulation, although similar to the smoke one created for the first recipe, have been modified to help with the flame's illumination, color, and density. The smoke texture has a ramp shader, but the alpha values of the color stops are much higher than with ordinary smoke. This is because we want the texture to be more visible as a flame would be. As this is influencing the density, the base of the smoke will be opaque whereas the tip will be semi-transparent.

If you examine the fire texture, you will see that we have employed color as well as alpha variations. These influence both emission and emission col with the voxel data being multiplied onto the Material colors. So, we have a texture that moves from bright opaque yellow at its base through cooler straw color towards the center and, finally, red transparent near its tip. By varying the position and alpha values in this texture, you can create all kinds of flame. For instance, if you want the flame to stretch further along the smoke, you can move the stop one red marker to the left. The flame will then appear to be consuming more of the smoke as though there is more fuel available.

There's more...

Smoke simulation uses vast computer resources. This simulation is only 75 frames long yet consumes 1.7 GB to store the cache. You can recognize that adding additional scene elements can quickly grind even a powerful computer to a crawl. For this reason, it is worth finding ways in which we can use the power of the smoke simulator without the processing overhead in our scenes. The next two recipes show how you can create reusable FX shots quickly and easily in any Blender scene.

If you have jumped straight into this recipe before any of the others, I would recommend at least reading the *How it works* section of the recipe at the beginning of this chapter. It offers some really useful tips on how to protect your smoke data, which because of extended processing and enormous storage requirements may save you heartache as you explore this exciting addition to the Blender 3D suite.

Creating loopable fire and smoke sequences

The previous recipe created 75 frames of the flame, starting then burning for a few seconds, before abruptly stopping. At no point in the animation does the flame repeat as it is based on a real physics algorithm that randomly generates the flow of a flame. That means if we want a blazing torch in a scene that is longer than three seconds we would either have to have a huge bake taking days to compute or take those images rendered and turn them into a loopable sequence. Fortunately, Blender, being an entire 3D suite, has a facility to edit video where we can place a series of images and by cross mixing produce a repeating sequence.

Getting ready

Unless you have rendered the sequence of images in the last recipe, you will need to download a zipped file that contains pre-rendered images ready for you to create the loopable sequence. The file is available from the Packtpub website as:

```
chapt-09/smokey-fire-images.zip
```

Unzip the file to your blendfile directory. It will create a subdirectory structure called `\\render-output/smokey-fire`. If you already have a render-output directory, it will prompt to overwrite, which you may confirm.

However, if you have completed the previous recipe you should already have the image files rendered to that location.

You do not require a blend start file as full instructions are given. However, if you are feeling particularly lazy, you can download the completed blendfile, although you will still need to render to obtain the loopable result:

```
chapt-09/smokey-fire-seq.blend
```

How to do it...

We will use the Blender **Video editor** to create the loopable sequence. To use this very capable video editor, we first need to specify the output resolution. Because the rendered images from the last recipe will be used in this sequence, it is desirable to set the render output to the same resolution. In the completed file and the pre-rendered zip file, the images are all 50% HDTV 1080 p. If you rendered at 25% HDTV 1080 p, you will need to adjust your render output values in the next steps.

1. From Blender, create a new scene and in the **Render** panel, select **Render presets HDTV 1080 p**, and set the percentage down to 50% (or 25% if you rendered the smaller size in the previous recipe).

2. In the **Post Processing** tab, check only the **Sequence** checkbox.

3. In the **Output** tab, create a path to render the sequence to. In my case, I selected `//render-output\smokey-fire\sequence\SF-`. Also, enable `.png` output and **RGBA** to preserve the alpha channel.

4. In the top menu, select the icon to the left of the **Default** window and choose the **Video Editing** setup.

The new screen will be divided up with the familiar timeline at the bottom, a render preview window to the top right, a graph editor to the top left, and a video strip window in the center. We can place videos or images to these strips and then perform common video editing tasks like cross fade to produce a dissolve from one strip to the other. Save your newly created blendfile as `smokey-fire-seq-01.blend`.

We select the best sequence of images rendered in the last recipe. Looking on my system, I see that frame 17 is the first shot where the initial fireball has dissipated and the flame is steadily burning.

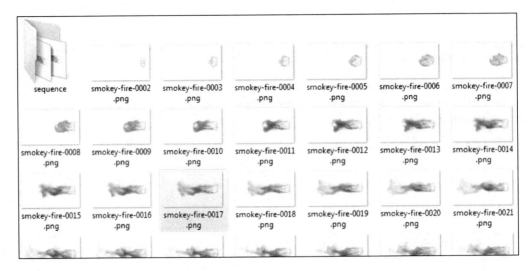

We only rendered 75 images, therefore, we have 59 frames to load into one of the video strips.

5. With your cursor in the **Video Sequence Editor** view, press *Shift+A* to bring up the **Add** menu, and choose **Image**.

6. A directory list will be displayed. Navigate to the directory where your images are stored. On my system, that is, \render-output\smokey-fire\.

7. Select image smokey-fire-0017.png by clicking on it. It will be highlighted with an orange background. We need to choose the remainder of the images, so to do this, press the left mouse button and drag a marquee around all the remaining images. Once all the image files from 17 to 75 are selected and highlighted with the orange background, click the **Add Image Strip** button on the top right of the window.

8. Blender will display a strip representing all of those images in sequence. *Right* click the strip to select it. It will be highlighted with a white border.

9. Use the right-hand mouse button to drag the strip to the first frame in the bottom row. If you move the cursor and click anywhere inside the timeline or video editing window, the preview will update.

We know that this sequence currently does not repeat. However, it's easy to create that effect in the sequence editor.

10. With the strip selected, press *Shift+D* to duplicate the strip and move it to the end of the current strip. We should now have two identical strips, the second repeating immediately after the first ends.

11. Selecting either of these strips create another duplicate. *Shift+D* and drag this above both of the other copies. Move it so it starts on frame 31.

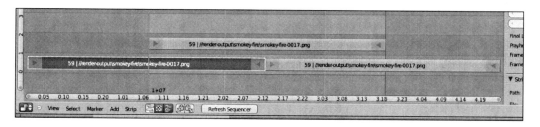

12. We now need to cross fade between strip 1 and the one above it and do the same for the second half of the upper strip back down to the copy at the end of the sequence. So, *Right* click select the bottom first strip, hold the *Shift* key, and *Right* click the strip above it.

13. Press *Shift+A* to bring up the **Add** menu and choose **Effects Strip/Cross**. This will create a new strip above which indicates that strip 1 will cross fade with strip 2.

14. *Right* click to select the middle image strip copy (strip 2), and holding the *Shift* key *Right* click to also select the copy to the right on strip 1. Press *Shift+A* and choose **Effects Strip/Cross**. A second effects strip will appear indicating that the upper strip 2 will cross fade down to the second copy on strip 1.

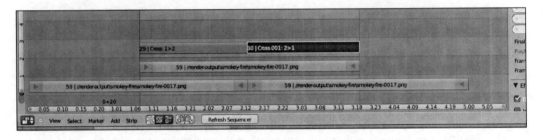

The only repeatable portion of this sequence is between frame 31 and frame 90, so we can set these as the start and end frames in the sequence.

15. In the bottom of the **Timeline** window, change the **Start** frame to `31`, and also change the **End** frame to `90`.

Save your work, incrementing the filename to `smokey-fire-seq-02.blend`. We can now render the animation.

16. Press *Ctrl+F12* and the sequence will be rendered. You can replay this render sequence by pressing *Ctrl+F11* and check how all the flames now repeat as the animation playback loops around.

How it works...

The sequence editor in Blender can edit almost any video. It has good audio capabilities as well as a pedigree of professional productions produced on it, including Elephants Dream, Big Buck Bunny, and Sintel. However, the editor is also useful for simpler tasks as we have used here. It is an excellent tool for making a non-repeatable sequence loopable. It can be used for instance to create repeating sequences of the procedural textures, which in normal use never repeat.

You will have also noticed that the screen refresh and render rates were extremely fast. So, you can review your work before quickly rendering the results. Here, we have taken the best of our previous flame sequence and created an entirely new loopable sequence, which we could use as a billboard animated texture very quickly in another scene. Creating special FX shots like this has been used in movies since the early days. When a director wants an explosion or fire in a scene, they can either be supplied with careful physical FX, or pre-filmed and applied to the movie, as a post pro effect.

Because smoke physics can be a processor and resource-intensive endeavor, it makes sense to create individual stock FX that can be easily used in more complex scenes. Even if you are creating unique smoke FX, consider creating it separate from the main scene to avoid huge render times and potential computer crashes.

Adding complex FX without the render overhead

We have seen how processor-intensive producing special effects shots in Blender can be. However, it is possible to add the result from such tasks as a simple billboard render or animation. We saw in Chapter 3 how textures and movies can be applied as a sequenced texture when we created the television recipe and the red alert box. Pasting images to flat surfaces to represent something much more complex is known as billboard rendering. When you are creating a complex environment for your animated characters, it can be more effective to texture a simple plane with a background object rather than have to have many complex models to represent the background. In the old days, backgrounds in 2D animation were more frequently painted by very good matt artists.

With the advent of 3D animation systems, users began to discover that because you can apply an animated image to a plane, or another simple model, why not create animated billboard backgrounds. The *billboard* term obviously springs from the idea of a poster applied to a billboard in the real environment.

We will use this technique to create two flaming torches as might be seen on the castle wall illuminating a medieval banquet.

Getting ready

You will need to download the blend start file as we only need to concentrate on the material and texture to create this effect. If you have not completed the previous recipe, you will also need to download the loopable image sequence. Both files are available from the Packtpub website as:

```
chapt-09/torch-start.zip
```

```
chapt-09/smokey-fire-sequence.zip
```

Unzip these to your blendfile directory. The `smokey-fire-sequence.zip` will create subdirectories automatically.

To make the use of the sequenced images easier, I have renamed the rendered sequence files as `SF-0001.png` to `SF-0060.png`. If you are using your own rendered sequence, you should rename likewise.

How to do it...

We will begin by briefly exploring the scene to see what has been prepared for you and what you have to do to complete the recipe.

1. Open the blendfile `torch-start.blend` and immediately resave it as `torch-01.blend`.

2. Select either of the two torch holders and switch to the **Materials** panel. You will notice a simple metal material has been created that looks like dented and rusted cast iron.

3. Switch to the **Textures** panel and you will see that two procedural textures are used to create this material. The first texture slot is a **Clouds** texture with an **Influence** on the **Normal** producing bump. The second is a **Musgrave** texture that supplies the rust and color to the surface.

4. There are two sphere lights in each of the orbits of the torches. These are lights that are animated to give the impression the flame is actually flickering as it illuminates the surrounding scene. The movement and energy levels have been animated using a noise modifier in the **Fcurve** editor. Please explore these settings later after completing the recipe.

5. Select either plane above each torch. This is a flat plane oriented to the camera but with its **Z** axis parallel to the **Global Z** axis. We will apply the fire sequence to these planes and because they are flat, we always want their **Z** axis straight up.

6. The size of each plane has been defined to avoid distortion to the images applied. The X and Y axis were simply scaled to the pixel dimensions of the image sequence.

We will create a new material for the nearest torch plane.

7. Select the nearest plane and move to the **Materials** panel. Create a new material and name it billB-flame.

8. Under the **Shading** tab, check **Shadeless**.

9. In the **Options** tab, uncheck **Traceable**. This will ensure that shadows and lights will not be blocked by the flame.

10. Also, under the **Shadows** tab, uncheck all of the shadow checkboxes.

11. Switch to the **Textures** panel and create a new texture, of type **Image** or **Movie**, naming it seq-fire.

12. Under the **Image** tab, **Open** the first image in the sequence SF-0001.png and select **Source Sequence**. Check the **Premultiply** checkbox, and also the **Cyclic** checkbox. The number of frames should show 60, with the **Start** as 1 and the **Offset** as 0.

13. Under the **Image Sampling** tab, make sure **Alpha Use** is checked.

14. Under the **Influence** tab, check **Diffuse/Color** at 1.000 and also **Alpha** 1.000.

15. Under the **Preview** tab, check **Show Alpha** and the preview should show the alpha of the image. If you just have a black background, you did not render with alpha in the last recipe. No problem, just download the pre-rendered zip file and use those images instead.

Save your work, incrementing the filename to torch-02.blend. You could render an animation at this point but let us add the fire to the other torch.

16. Select the background torch plane and in the **Materials** panel, click the material icon and choose the same material billB-flame.

The material will immediately be applied and a counter will appear to the right of the material name to show it is shared by two objects. If we rendered an animation at this stage, it would be obvious that the flame textures are just copies because they will move in unison. We need to change the second material and texture to alter the timing of the repeats.

17. With the background plane selected and in the **Materials** panel, click the **2** button to the right of the material name and the material will be made unique to this object. It will append a number to the new material billB-flame.001.

18. Move to the **Texture** panel and make that texture unique by clicking the **2** to the right of the texture name. This texture will also have a number following it, seq-fire.001.

19. Under the **Image** tab, for this texture, change the **Offset** to 14.

Save your work, incrementing the filename to torch-03.blend. You can now render an animation of this blendfile reducing the render size if you wish to save time. However, the resultant animation will show two apparently unique flames looping throughout the animation with none of the resource-hungry physics calculations that would be necessary if we used smoke physics on each flame.

How it works...

Mapping a sequence of images to a plane is as simple as mapping a single image. Here, the material was set as shadeless because a flame cannot really have specularity or shadows. A flame can't actually cast shadows either because it is meant to be a light source. For that reason, we also turned off all shadow choices in the material.

Setting up a sequence of images was explored in Chapter 3, *Creating Animated Materials*. There, we used only a few images but as you can see, it is possible to use large sequences of images, which in this case, is better than first converting to a movie format. This way, we maintain maximum resolution with no degradation due to movie conversion codecs. The sequence input expects a sequential numbered series of images. This should start at 1 or Blender may get confused about the correct frame number to start from. If you have thousands of images that all need renumbering, I would suggest using one of the many bulk renaming programs or methods for various platforms. I use the Bulk Rename Utility in Windows.

When we copied the material to the other plane, it produced an exact copy and thus would have looked very false when animated as both flames would move exactly in unison. Rather than just alter the offset in the copy, we first made the material and texture unique. The reason for doing so was any changes we make to a shared material, or texture, will be duplicated into all copies. We have to make one of the copies unique to make individual changes. Blender is very clever in the way it stores data so that although we have two different materials, they both share similar characteristics. The system only needs to record the few differences rather than every variable in each material. Here, both textures share the same sequence of image data and, as a result, Blender does not have to load two copies of the sequence into memory to process the data.

Because physics processing is so intensive in Blender, I would recommend creating some stock smoke, flame, and explosion sequences. By changing the camera angle, you will be able to create a new sequence quite easily without having to reprocess long and complex simulations. You can then apply them using the billboard technique within your scenes and save considerable time. Although we used a repeating sequence in this recipe, explosions and FX like that tend to be one time only. We can still apply the billboard technique to place such short and single events.

There's more...

For those of you requiring an easy way to rename multiple files, you can explore the following sites:

For MS Windows:

http://www.bulkrenameutility.co.uk/Main_Intro.php

For Mac OSX try:

`http://lifehacker.com/034704/rename-files-in-bulk-the-mac-edition`

For Linux users, there are plenty of Bash scripts and terminal entry methods as discussed here:

`http://tips.webdesign10.com/how-to-bulk-rename-files-in-linux-in-the-terminal`

See also

Previously in this chapter:

- *Creating explosive smoke in Blender*
- *Igniting a flame and making things burn in Blender*
- *Creating loopable fire and smoke sequences*

Chapter 3

- *How to change textures during an animation*
- *How to texture with movies*

Index

U

UV mapping 208
UV maps
  about 200
  applying, for skin material creation 227-229
  combining 219-221
  creating 203-207
  editing, for image space optimization 209
  enabling, for image space optimization 210-214
  merging, paint package used 222, 223

V

Voxel Data texture 264, 274

W

wake around objects
  creating, in water 180-183
Wardiso specular setting 12, 54
Warp settings 58
water
  wake around objects, creating 180-183
wave surface
  creating, textures used 172-175
weathering surface attributes
  adding 58-60

Z

Z depth
  rendering, from original animation 245

Thank you for buying
Blender 2.5 Materials and Textures Cookbook

About Packt Publishing

Packt, pronounced 'packed', published its first book "*Mastering phpMyAdmin for Effective MySQL Management*" in April 2004 and subsequently continued to specialize in publishing highly focused books on specific technologies and solutions.

Our books and publications share the experiences of your fellow IT professionals in adapting and customizing today's systems, applications, and frameworks. Our solution based books give you the knowledge and power to customize the software and technologies you're using to get the job done. Packt books are more specific and less general than the IT books you have seen in the past. Our unique business model allows us to bring you more focused information, giving you more of what you need to know, and less of what you don't.

Packt is a modern, yet unique publishing company, which focuses on producing quality, cutting-edge books for communities of developers, administrators, and newbies alike. For more information, please visit our website: www.packtpub.com.

About Packt Open Source

In 2010, Packt launched two new brands, Packt Open Source and Packt Enterprise, in order to continue its focus on specialization. This book is part of the Packt Open Source brand, home to books published on software built around Open Source licences, and offering information to anybody from advanced developers to budding web designers. The Open Source brand also runs Packt's Open Source Royalty Scheme, by which Packt gives a royalty to each Open Source project about whose software a book is sold.

Writing for Packt

We welcome all inquiries from people who are interested in authoring. Book proposals should be sent to author@packtpub.com. If your book idea is still at an early stage and you would like to discuss it first before writing a formal book proposal, contact us; one of our commissioning editors will get in touch with you.

We're not just looking for published authors; if you have strong technical skills but no writing experience, our experienced editors can help you develop a writing career, or simply get some additional reward for your expertise.

open source *
community experience distilled

Blender 3D Architecture, Buildings, and Scenery

ISBN: 978-1-847193-67-4   Paperback: 332 pages

Create photorealistic 3D architectural visualizations of buildings, interiors, and environmental scenery

1. Turn your architectural plans into a model

2. Study modeling, materials, textures, and light basics in Blender

3. Create photo-realistic images in detail

4. Create realistic virtual tours of buildings and scenes

Blender 2.49 Scripting

ISBN: 978-1-849510-40-0   Paperback: 292 pages

Extend the power and flexibility of Blender with the help of the high-level, easy-to-learn scripting language, Python

1. Gain control of all aspects of Blender using the powerful Python language

2. Create complex meshes programmatically and apply materials and textures

3. Automate the rendering process and extend Blender's image manipulation capabilities

4. Extend Blender's built-in editor

5. Interact with version control systems and store render results on a FTP server

Please check **www.PacktPub.com** for information on our titles